NINETEENTH-CENTURY RHETORIC

GARLAND REFERENCE LIBRARY
OF THE HUMANITIES
(VOL. 787)

NINETEENTH-CENTURY RHETORIC
An Enumerative Bibliography

Forrest Houlette

GARLAND PUBLISHING, INC. • NEW YORK & LONDON
1989

© 1989 Forrest Houlette
All rights reserved

Library of Congress Cataloging-in-Publication Data

Houlette, Forrest, 1954–
   Nineteenth-century rhetoric: an enumerative bibliography / Forrest Houlette.
      p. cm. — (Garland reference library of the humanities; vol. 787)
   Includes index.
   ISBN 0-8240-6645-6 (alk. paper)
   1. English language—Rhetoric—Bibliography. 2. English language—Composition and exercises—Bibliography. 3. English language—Grammar—1800–1869—Bibliography. 4. English language—Grammar—1870–1949—Bibliography. 5. Rhetoric—History—19th century—Bibliography. 6. English language—Study and teaching—History—19th century—Bibliography. I. Title. II. Series.
Z2015.R5H68   1989
[PE1403]
016.808'042—dc19   88-21765
                                                                                    CIP

Printed on acid-free, 250-year-life paper
Manufactured in the United States of America

To Judy and Alexandra, who have lived with this work as much as I have.

Table of Contents

Preface ix
Acknowledgments xv
Articles in Books 3
Articles in Periodicals 19
Books 117
Subject Index 297

Preface

The volume you hold represents the culmination of the first stage of the nineteenth century rhetoric bibliography project, which I began two years ago. While I hate to begin the preface by stating the limitations of the work, I am obliged to point out that this is not yet a definitive bibliography. It is a beginning, and it serves more to point out the enormity of the bibliographic problem facing scholars of nineteenth century rhetoric than it does to answer those problems.

The first problem discovered was that of defining what constituted rhetoric during the nineteenth century. After Blair, Campbell, Whately, Adams, and Channing, it could be said that scholarly rhetoric attempted to go underground for a century. The items cataloged under the heading <u>rhetoric</u> in catalogs published during the period tend to be composition textbooks. (It is worth pointing out that two bibliographies printed during the period appear in the "Articles in Periodicals" section of this bibliography.) Scholarship outlining the history of rhetoric during the period focuses on topics ranging from the Boylston professorship to teaching methods in the classrooms at Aberdeen. For the purposes of this bibliography, therefore, <u>rhetoric</u> was defined as loosely as possible in order to reflect the values of those publishing in the field at the time and those studying the history of the field in contemporary time.

As a result, this work is an enumerative bibliography of works published in rhetoric, composition, grammar, and the teaching of English between 1800 and 1920. Both primary and secondary materials published during the period have been included. The list was developed by searching any index or library catalog covering the time period and organized according to subjects. In each catalog, the contributing bibliographers searched the following topics:

Argumentation
Composition
Description
English Language
Essays
Exposition
Grammar
History of Education
Oratory
Paragraphs
Persuasion
Preaching
Rhetoric
Speech
Style

Whenever possible, the pages of the source index or catalog were photocopied and these photocopied items were pasted onto cards. When the items from the source had to be hand copied onto cards, great care was taken in proofreading at the point of copying. Each item was then entered into a data base designed under Bank Street Filer. The database itself was proofread three times by independent readers. Next, the files were converted for printing under Bank Street Writer, at which time they were proofread three times, again by independent readers. The word processor files were then printed as camera ready copy. This enumerative list, therefore, represents the items discovered in the source catalogs and indices accurately.

An attempt was made to verify each item by inspection. That attempt, in general, failed. At the time of this failure, the group which produced this bibliography discovered further bibliographic problems facing scholars of nineteenth century rhetoric. Of the items located for inspection, very few were in the first edition. The majority of those located with the publication date listed by the U. S. Catalog, for instance, were in later editions than the first, indicating a publishing history that had not been evidenced by either the U. S. Catalog or indices covering the period. After it became clear that verification of these items would take years of painstaking leg work, I made the decision to bring the project to publication first as an enumeration of what was found in subject indices and catalogs, and to continue the amplification and verification of the items in preparation of a second edition.

As a result, in this edition, each item is encoded to indicate the source where it was found. The codes pair with their parent sources as follows:

AC	American Catalog
AK	Kitzhaber's Bibliography of Rhetoric in American Colleges, 1850-1900
BMI	British Museum Index
CC	Classified Catalog of the Carnegie Library
CLPI	Catalog of the Library of the Peabody Institute
CSIGP	Contents-Subject Index to General and Periodical Literature
EGL	Essay and General Literature Index
HEW	Subject Catalog of the Department Library, U.S. Department of Health, Education, and Welfare
HR	Horner's Historical Rhetoric
II	International Index to Periodicals
LC	Catalog of the London Library
LLC	Catalog of the Lamont Library, Harvard College
PI	Poole's Index to Periodical Literature
PS	Horner's Present State of Scholarship in Historical and Contemporary Rhetoric
RG	Reader's Guide or 19th Century Reader's Guide
SIBP	Subject Index of Books Published Up to and Including 1880
USC	U. S. Catalog

These codes are provided to help interested scholars locate items for which source catalogs and indices provided incomplete publication data. They are also provided, in the case of library catalogs, as pointers to possible locations for finding the items on library shelves.

Items were selected for inclusion in this volume according to four criteria. First, they had to appear listed in an index or catalog under the subjects searched. Second, they had to represent works known to be relevant to rhetoric, the teaching of writing, or the teaching of English. This criterion excluded only a few scholarly grammars well indexed elsewhere. Where relevance could not be determined, the item was included. Third, items included had to be written in English. This criterion eliminated only three items. Fourth, items had to bear a publication date within the inclusive interval 1800-1920. The upward date within the inclusive interval 1800-1920. The upward bound of 1920 was chosen since the founding of the National Council of Teachers of English (NCTE) and the resulting discussions seem to represent the end of the debates about how to teach writing evident in the 1890's. The decade of NCTE's founding was therefore included. However, items dated later than this have been included when the sources consulted indicated they were clearly relevant to the topic and time period. Such items include modern editions of items published during the period or anthologies containing works published during the period.

Items are presented in this volume in three sections representing the type of publication: articles in books, articles in periodicals, and books. Within these divisions, items are listed alphabetically by author and title. Most items with the same author and title are listed in date order; however, the sort algorithm for Bank Street Filer occasionally failed to sort in strict date order. There are very few items affected by this limitation, though. Items are presented in Modern Language Association format, with as much publication data provided as was available. Immediately following the MLA entry for each item is a subject descriptor, if one could be assigned based on the title. Each item is assigned only one subject descriptor. An index to items by subjects is provided to help scholars begin assembling stronger concepts of the topics which preoccupied nineteenth-century teachers of rhetoric, composition, and English. Books referenced in the "Articles in Books" section appear as full citations in the "Books" section. If such a book was omitted by oversight, it is readily available in the parent source for such items, the Essay and General Literature Index.

In the final print, there was one curious computer error. Occasionally Bank Street Writer would insert an extra line. The reason was never fully ascertained. (Another surprise occurred during the print of the final copy. Bank Street Writer can number up to 255 pages only. Page 256 is numbered as page 0, and the count begins again.) Those contemplating using this software for projects similar to this one should be aware of these limitations.

One of my colleagues recently asked why such a bibliography is important. The answer is that scholarship in nineteenth century rhetoric has become a reasonably popular pursuit. It has had to proceed in the absence of a complete bibliographic tool. The largest bibliography to date, Albert Kitzhaber's, listed 328 items. At the close of its first stage, this bibliography lists 3,929 items. At the end of its next stage, it will probably list 6,000-7,000 items. Knowing what was published on this topic will certainly lead to stronger historical scholarship. The importance of this version of the bibliography is that it provides an interim tool to facilitate the work of scholars actively studying the nineteenth century.

None of these remarks are intended to denigrate the excellent overviews of the period provided by James Berlin (Writing Instruction in Nineteenth-Century American Colleges [Carbondale: Southern Illinois Univ. Press, 1984]) and Donald Stewart (see his chapter in Winifred Horner's The Present State of Scholarship in Historical and Contemporary Rhetoric [Columbia: Univ. of Missouri Press, 1983], 134-66). But five years hence, I will likely have to cite more comprehensive historical resources in the second edition. The goal of this project is to facilitate the detailed historical investigation that the period deserves.

That the period deserves investigation should not need defense, but I have been asked the question. I see it as an important period because, through my work with the Indiana Writing Project, I often meet teachers who are dissatisfied with the teaching they are doing. Yet they feel trapped in the methods they use because they believe teaching has always been that way. They have no sense of the history of their profession or their methods. The history of rhetoric in the nineteenth century is the history of the development of the writing curriculum. Those who teach writing ought to know their immediate history. The knowledge confers the power to reject methods largely produced as historical accidents and to discover methods that have been hidden by contemporary fads. It also liberates by demystifying traditions. It gives teachers roots that they need. I see no need to question the validity of studying this period in rhetoric.

The second stage for this endeavor involves a change in technology. The limitations of the Apple II Bank Street software have proven too restricting. The project will therefore be converting to the IBM family of hardware with Nota Bene as the central software. After the conversion, the search for less obvious items will continue. At this stage, the search becomes more tedious, involving looking up each author identified in the National Union Catalog, for instance, in pursuit of additional titles and information about the total number of editions published for each title. After this search, each item will be verified, and a location for each extant edition found will be provided.

Obviously, this second edition will require some time to prepare.

The next edition will also include a review of research in the field as it has developed since the recent reviews by James Berlin and Donald Stewart cited above. But these are promises. It is time to return to work so that they might come true.

--Forrest Houlette
Ball State University

Acknowledgments

The following students share authorship with me as contributing bibliographers:

Bassam A. Abuzeid
Sandra J. Clark
Linda J. Coe
William R. Hunter
Bonnie K. Landis
Alice A. New
Heidi Podlasli
Susan L. Winger

This group traced subject headings through several indices and library catalogs as a class project for a graduate seminar in composition. Neither they nor I anticipated the wealth of information we would uncover or the enormity of the problem we would begin to solve.
    Two editors at Garland deserve thanks, Phyllis Korper and Paula Ladenburg. They have suffered my delays in the production of the final manuscript with a great deal of patience. They have also known how to leave me the freedom to get the work done. They have been an excellent team to work with.
    Bruce Kirkham, the Melancholy Lobster, deserves many thanks for helping to trace down several works in the flesh. He was also known for finding books not cataloged in any of the resources consulted during the development of this bibliography.
    Any number of others deserve to be mentioned. Linda Meeker provided consistent moral support, and has helped to point out many of the search strategies necessary to stage two of this work. The Graduate Composition Area at Ball State provided the occasion which led to the inception of this work. The Language and Linguistics Area gave encouragement I could not have found elsewhere. Steve, Audrey, Lisa, and Carla were indefatigable student assistants. And Alice New was a graduate student who originally worked on the project foolish enough to return to

help complete the project in its last stages. Larry Davis provided consistent support as department chair. And Max Morenberg, Dennis Hall, and Joe Comprone started me on this path in the first place.

There are three whose motivation must remain unmentioned, but they know who they are and what they have contributed. To those whom I have overlooked, my thanks indeed.

Articles in Books

Articles in Books

1. Allen, F. L. "Goon and His Style." In Bachelor, J. M. and Henry, R. L. ed., <u>Challenging Essays in Modern Thought</u>, p. 186-89. Style. EGL.

2. Auerbach, J. S. "English Style." In <u>Essays and Miscellanies</u>, v. 1, p. 160-93. Style. EGL.

3. Aydelotte, F. "Correlation of Literature and Composition." In <u>Oxford Stamp</u>, p. 135-48. Literature and Composition. EGL.

4. Aydelotte, F. "Experiment with the Freshman Course." In <u>Oxford Stamp</u>, p. 86-134. Freshman Writing. EGL.

5. Bailey, J. C. "Grand Style: An Attempt at a Definition." In <u>Continuity of Letters</u>, p. 21-51. English Association, London. <u>Essays and Studies</u>, v. 2, p. 104-33. Style. EGL.

6. Barclay, J. "Outline of English Grammar." In his <u>Complete Dictionary of English Language</u>, v. 1, n. d., p. 953; 1813, p. xi. Grammar. CLPI.

7. Belloc, H. "On Certain Terms." In <u>A Conversation with an Angel, and Other Essays</u>, p. 263-70. Style. EGL.

8. Belloc, H. "On Lucidity. " In <u>A Conversation with an Angel, and Other Essays</u>, p. 180-91. Style. EGL.

9. Bennett, A. "Question of Style." In Aydelotte, F. ed., <u>English and Engineering</u>, p. 4-14. Mallory, H. S. ed., <u>Backgrounds of Book Reviewing</u>, p. 432-39. Taylor, W. comp., <u>Representative English Essays</u>, p. 249-58. Style. EGL.

10. Bennett, A. "Style." In <u>Things That Have Interested Me</u>, 1st Ser., p. 102. Style. EGL.

11. Benson, A. C. "Art and Life." In *Along the Road*, p. 162-71. EGL.

12. Benson, A. C. "Literary Finish." In *At Large*, p. 290-312. Style. EGL.

13. Bentham, J. "Fragments on Universal Grammar." In *Works*, v. 8, p. 339. Grammar. CLPI.

14. Birkenhead, F. E. S. "Eloquence." In *Law, Life and Letters*, v. 2, p. 98-160. Style. EGL.

15. Booth, D. "New Grammar." In his *Analytical Dictionary of the English Language*, p. 1. Grammar. CLPI.

16. Bostwick, A. E. "Appropriateness of Style." In *Earmarks of Literature*, p. 32-39. Style. EGL.

17. Bostwick, A. E. "Character in Style." In *Earmarks of Literature*, p. 40-46. Style. EGL.

18. Bostwick, A. E. "Clearness of Style." In *Earmarks of Literature*, p. 21-31. Style. EGL.

19. Bostwick, A. E. "Style--Its Grammatical Form." In *Earmarks of Literature*, p. 10-20. Style. EGL.

20. Brownell, W. C. "Style." In American Academy of Arts and Letters, *Academy Papers*, p. 213-52. Style. EGL.

21. Brunetiere, F. "Apology for Rhetoric." In Pritchard, F. H. ed., *From Confucius to Mencken*, p. 407-17. Rhetoric. EGL.

22. Buchan, J. "Style and Journalism." In *Homilies and Recreations*, p. 233-58. Style. EGL.

23. Buffon, G. L. L. "Style is the Man Himself." In Kaufman, P. comp., *Points of View for College Students*, p. 92-101. Style. EGL.

24. Buffon, G. L. L. "On Style." In Fulcher, P. M. ed., *Foundations of English Style*, p. 47-49. Style. EGL.

25. Burroughs, J. "Bits of Criticism." In Pritchard, F. H. ed., From Confucius to Mencken, p. 907-909. Criticism. EGL.

26. Burroughs, J. "Poetry and Eloquence." In Literary Values, p. 177-84. Style. EGL.

27. Burroughs, J. "Style and the Man." In Literary Values, p. 59-88. Style. EGL.

28. Burroughs, J. "Suggestiveness." In Literary Values, p. 229-40. Style. EGL.

29. Burton, R. "Literature as Craft." In Forces in Fiction, p. 150-67. Style. EGL.

30. Canby, H. S. "Good English." In American Estimates, p. 155-57. Style. EGL.

31. Canby, H. S. "Heaven's First Law." In American Estimates, p. 160-67. Style. EGL.

32. Canby, H. S. "Importance of Style." In If I Could Preach Just Once, by various authors, p. 139-58. Style. EGL.

33. Canby, H. S. "Letter of Style." In Taylor, W. ed., Types and Times in the Essay, p. 309-11. Style. EGL.

34. Canby, H. S. "Pure English." In American Estimates, p. 152-54. Style. EGL.

35. Canby, H. S. "Writing English." In College Sons and College Fathers, p. 184-209. Writing Process. EGL.

36. Canby, H. S. "Writing of English." In American Estimates, p. 157-59. Writing Process. EGL.

37. Cardozo, B. N. "Law and Literature." In Law and Literature, and Other Essays and Addresses, p. 3-40. Literature. EGL.

38. Chapman, R. W. "Decay of Syntax." In Portraits of a Scholar, p. 109-27. Morley, C. D. comp., Modern Essays, 2nd Ser., p. 154-72. Smith, C. A. ed., Essays on Current Themes, p. 223-35. Style. EGL.

39. Chesterton, G. K. "On Maltreating Words." In
    Generally Speaking, p. 158-64. MacLean, M. S. and
    Holmes, E. K. Comps., *Men and Books*, p. 41-45.
    Error. EGL.

40. Coleridge, S. T. "Accuracy." Fulcher, P. M. ed.,
    Foundations of English Style, p. 96-97. Style.
    EGL.

41. Cooper, L. "Correction of Papers." In *Two Views of
    Education*, p. 88-104. Evaluating Writing. EGL.

42. Cooper, L. "Good Usage." In *Two Views of Education*,
    p. 47-71. Usage. EGL.

43. Cooper, L. "Teaching of Written Composition." In
    Two Views of Education, p. 72-87. Teaching Methods.
    EGL.

44. Croce, B. "Impenetrability of Consciousness." In
    Conduct of Life, p. 302-12. EGL.

45. Cromer, E. B. "Eloquence as a Fine Art." In
    Political and Literary Essays, 2nd Ser., p. 318-25.
    Style. EGL.

46. Davis, E. O. "The Teaching of English in the Primary
    Grades of the Cleveland Public Schools." In
    *National Society for the Scientific Study of
    Education, 5th yearbook*, Pt. 1, 1906, 66-75.
    Teaching Methods. HEW.

47. Day, H. N. "Elements of the English Language." In
    his *Introduction to the Study of English Literature*,
    p. 428. Style. CLPI.

48. De Quincey, T. "English Language." In *Collected
    Writings*, v. 14, p. 146. Style. CLPI.

49. De Quincey, T. "How to Write English." In
    Uncollected Writings, v. 2, p. 55. Style. CLPI.

50. De Quincey, T. "On Language." In McLaughlin, E. T.
    ed., *Literary Criticism for Students*, p. 118-21.
    Style. EGL.

51. De Quincey, T. "Style and Matter." In Fulcher, P. M. ed., Foundations of English Style, p. 42-43. Style. EGL.

52. Dunsany, E. J. M. D. P. "Letter On Style." In Taylor, W. ed., Types and Times in the Essay, p. 312-13. Style. EGL.

53. Eaton, W. P. "Confession in Prose." In Atlantic Monthly. Atlantic Classic, 1st Ser., p. 225-42. Johnson, B. ed., Essaying the Essay, p. 291-305. EGL.

54. Eliot, T. S. "'Rhetoric' and Poetic Drama." Sacred Wood, p. 71-77. Selected Essays, 1917-1932, p. 25-30. Rhetoric. EGL.

55. Fisher, D. F. C. "Theme Writing." In Heydrick, B. A. ed., Familiar Essays of To-day, p. 135-42. Teaching Methods. EGL.

56. Frye, P. H. "Structure and Style." In Romance and Tragedy, p. 312-41. Style. EGL.

57. Fulcher, P. M. "Seven Lamps of Style." In Fulcher, P. M. ed., Foundations in English Style, p. 3-17. Style. EGL.

58. Fulcher, P. M. "These But the Trappings." In Fulcher, P. M., ed., Foundations in English Style, p. 189-206. Style. EGL.

59. Gales, R. L. "On the Vulgar Tongue." In Gay, R. M. ed., Fact, Fancy and Opinion, p. 147-54. Error. EGL.

60. Gales, R. L. "On Victorian English." In Studies in Arcady, 1st Ser., p. 309-15. Style. EGL.

61. Gales, R. L. "Some Old-fashioned Phrases." In Studies in Arcady, 1st ser., p. 294-308. Style. EGL.

62. Gales, R. L. "Whitewashing of English." Studies in Arcady, 1st Ser., p. 316-23. Style. EGL.

63. Gardiner, A. G. "Letter on Styles." In Taylor, W. ed., Types and Times of the Essay, p. 314-17.

Style. EGL.

64. Gerould, K. F. "Letter on Style." In Taylor, W. ed., <u>Types and Times of the Essay</u>, p. 318-23. Style. EGL.

65. Gourmont, R. "Form and Substance." In Fulcher, P. M. ed., <u>Foundations of English Style</u>, p. 44-46. Lewisohn, L. ed., <u>Modern Book of Criticism</u>, p. 35-37. Style. EGL.

66. Gourmont, R. "Vision and Emotion." In Lewisohn, L. ed., <u>Modern Book of Criticism</u>, p. 31-35. EGL.

67. Grierson, F. "Style and Personality." In <u>Celtic Temperament</u>, p. 41-47. Style. EGL.

68. Harrison, F. "On English Prose." In <u>Tennyson, Ruskin, Mill and Other Literary Estimates</u>, p. 149-65. Aydelotte, F. ed., <u>English and Engineering</u>, p. 15-27. Style. EGL.

69. Harrison, F. "Practical Hints." In Fulcher, P. M. ed., <u>Foundations of English Style</u>, p. 174-79. Style. EGL.

70. Hazlitt, W. "On Familiar Style." In Kaufman, P. comp., <u>Points of View For College Students</u>, p. 105-14. Moore, J. R. ed., <u>Representative Essays, English and American</u>, p. 183-91. Peacock, W. and Wheeler, C. B. ed., <u>Selected English Essays</u>, p. 274-82. Roe, F. W. ed., <u>Nineteenth Century English Prose: Early Essayists.</u>, p. 191-97. Wann, L. ed., <u>Century Readings in the English Essay</u>, p. 242-45. Style. EGL.

71. Hewlett, M. H. "Analogy From the Tailor's." In <u>Extemporary Essays</u>, p. 67-71. EGL.

72. Hobbes, T. "Art of Rhetoric." In <u>English Works</u>, v. 6, p. 419. Bohn, H. G. ed., <u>Aristotle's Treatise on Rhetoric</u> (Classical Library), p. 273. Rhetoric. CLPI.

73. Hughes, J. "Of Style." In Durham, W. H. ed., <u>Critical Essays of the Eighteenth Century, 1700-1725</u>, p. 79-85. Style. EGL.

74. Hume, D. "Of Simplicity and Refinement in Writing." In Peacock, W. and Wheeler, C. B. ed., Selected English Essays, p. 152-56. Style. EGL.

75. Jackson, H. "Purple Patches and Fine Phrases." In Eighteen Nineties, p. 135-46. Style. EGL.

76. Johnson, S. "Grammar of the English Tongue." In his Dictionary of English Language, v. 1, 1755; 1828, p. 31. Grammar. CLPI.

77. Jones, F. W. "Of Argument." In Unscientific Essays, p. 198-208. Modes. EGL.

78. Kenrick, W. "Rhetorical Grammar of the English Language." With his New Dictionary, p. 1. Grammar. CLPI.

79. Keyser, C. J. "Description and Definition." In Mole Philosophy and Other Essays, p. 130-34. Modes. EGL.

80. Keyser, C. J. "Style." In Mole Philosophy and Other Essays, p. 170-72. Style. EGL.

81. Kirkland, W. M. "Print and Pulpit." In View Vertical, p. 260-64. EGL.

82. Learned, L. H. S. "Defense of Purism in Speech." In Thomas, W. H. and Morgan, S. ed., Essays in Liberal Thought, p. 145-53. Style. EGL.

83. Lee, G. S. "Letter on Style." In Taylor, W. ed., Types and Times in the Essay, p. 324-31. Style. EGL.

84. Leonard, W. E. "Letter On Style." In Taylor, W. ed., Types and Times in the Essay, p. 332-36. Style. EGL.

85. Lewes, G. H. "Principle of Beauty." In Taylor, W. comp., Essays of the Past and Present, p. 363-67. Style. EGL.

86. Lewes, G. H. "Simplicity." In Fulcher, P. M. ed., Foundations of English Style, p. 108-11. Style. EGL.

87. Lewes, G. H. "Sincerity." In Fulcher, P. M. ed., Foundations of English Style, p. 64-95. Style. EGL.

88. Lewes, G. H. "Variety." In Fulcher, P. M. ed., Foundations of English Style, p. 148-51. Style. EGL.

89. Lewis, S. "Letter On Style." In Taylor, W. ed., Types and Times in the Essay, p. 337-38. Style. EGL.

90. Lewisohn, L. "Letter On Style." In Taylor, W. ed., Types and Times in the Essay, p. 339-41. Style. EGL.

91. Lipsky, A. "Rhythm of Prose." In Law, F. H. ed., Modern Essays and Stories, p. 225-28. Style. EGL.

92. Littell, P. "Acts of Composition." In Books and Things, p. 257-63. EGL.

93. Livingston, A. "Myth of Good English." In Shepard, O. ed., Essays of 1925, p. 128-40. Error. EGL.

94. Lounsbury, T. R. "On the Hostility to Certain Words." In Harper's Monthly Magazine, Harper Essays, p. 299-314. Error. EGL.

95. Lucas, E. V. "Broken English." In Adventures and Enthusiasms, p. 126-35. Phantom Journal, p. 193-99. Error. EGL.

96. Lucas, E. V. "Letter On Style." In Taylor, W. ed., Types and Times in the Essay, p. 342-44. Style. EGL.

97. Martin, E. S. "How can Preaching Come Alive?" In What's Ahead and Meanwhile, p. 47-56. Style. EGL.

98. Massingham, H. J. "Pseudo-Picturesque." In Letters to X, p. 70-78. EGL.

99. Matthews, B. "Duty of Imitation." In Gateways to Literature, p. 77-90. Style. EGL.

100. Matthews, B. "French Poets and English Readers." In <u>Gateways to Literature</u>, p. 189-221. Literature. EGL.

101. Matthews, B. "In Behalf of the General Reader." In <u>Gateways to Literature</u>, p. 59-74. EGL.

102. Matthews, B. "Questions of Usage." In <u>Parts of Speech</u>, p. 217-38. Usage. EGL.

103. Matthews, B. "What Is Pure English?" In <u>Essays on English</u>, p. 31-57. Thomas, W. H. and Morgan, S. S. ed., <u>Essays in Liberal Thought</u>, p. 135-44. Style. EGL.

104. Matthews, B. "Style from Several Angles." In <u>Essays on English</u>, p. 223-39. Style. EGL.

105. Maunder, S. "Compendious English Grammar." In <u>Treasury of Knowledge</u>, pt. 1, p. 1. Grammar. CLPI.

106. McFee, W. "Letter On Style." In Taylor, W. ed., <u>Types and Times in the Essay</u>, p. 345-52. Style. EGL.

107. Mencken, H. L. "Literature and the Schoolma'am." In <u>Prejudices</u>, 5th Ser., p. 196-202. EGL.

108. Mencken, H. L. "What Is Style?" In American Mercury, <u>Readings from the American Mercury</u>, p. 127-29. Style. EGL.

109. Michels, A. W. "New Prose Styles for Old?" In Williams, B. C. ed., <u>Book of Essays</u>, p. 34-40. Style. EGL.

110. Morley, C. D. "Benedictine Style." In <u>Romany Stain</u>, p. 40-45. Style. EGL.

111. Murry, J. M. "Central Problem of Style." In Fulcher, P. M. ed., <u>Foundations of English Style</u>, p. 122-47. Style. EGL.

112. Murry, J. M. "What Is Style?" In <u>Pencillings</u>, p. 99-108. Style. EGL.

113. Newman, J. H. "Literature." In <u>The Idea of a</u>

<u>University</u>, p. 268-94. Literature. AK.

114. Norris, F. "Simplicity In Art." In Fulcher, P. M. ed., <u>Foundations of English Style</u>, p. 112-18. Taylor, W. comp., <u>Essays of the Past and Present</u>, p. 383-87. Style. EGL.

115. Orage, A. R. "English Style." In <u>Readers and Writers</u>, p. 74-76. Style. EGL.

116. Pater, W. H. "Style." In McLaughlin, E. T. ed., <u>Literary Criticism for Students</u>, p. 204-10. Wann, L. ed., <u>Century Readings in the English Essay</u>, p. 342-52. Style. EGL.

117. Pater, W. H. "Truth." In Fulcher, P. M. ed., <u>Foundations of English Style</u>, p. 58-63. EGL.

118. Pater, Walter. "Style." In <u>Appreciations, with an Essay on Style</u>. (New York: Macmillan, 1889), p. 1-36. Style. HR, AK.

119. Perry, W. "Grammar of the English Language." In his <u>Synonymous English Dictionary</u>, p. II. Grammar. CLPI.

120. Phillpotts, E. "Style." In <u>Essays in Little</u>, p. 49-57. Style. EGL.

121. Poe, E. A. "Philosophy of Composition." In <u>Works</u>, ed. by E. C. Stedman and G. E. Woodberry, v. 6, p. 31. Composition. CLPI.

122. Powys, L. "Letter on Style." In Taylor, W. ed., <u>Types and Times in the Essay</u>, p. 353-55. Style. EGL.

123. Priestley, J. "Rudiments of English Grammar." In <u>Works</u>, v. 23. Grammar. CLPI.

124. Quiller-Couch, A. T. "On Jargon." In <u>On the Art of Writing</u>, p. 100-26. Bowman, J. C. ed., <u>Essays for College English</u>, 2d Ser., p. 347-63. Fulcher, P. M. ed., <u>Foundations of English Style</u>, p. 155-73. Hale, C. B. and Tobin, J. E. ed., <u>Contrast and Comparison</u>, p. 199-208. McCullough, B. W. and Burgum, E. B. ed., <u>Book of Modern Essays</u>, p. 267-83. Style. EGL.

125. Quiller-Couch, A. T. "On Style." In <u>On the Art of Writing</u>, p. 278-97. Style. EGL.

126. Quiller-Couch, A. T. "Practice of Writing." In <u>On the Art of Writing</u>, p. 26-51. Composition. EGL.

127. Quiller-Couch, A. T. "Some Principles Reaffirmed." In <u>On the Art of Writing</u>, p. 153-75. Style. EGL.

128. Raleigh, W. A. "On Writing and Composition." In <u>On Writing and Writers</u>, p. 13-34. Composition. EGL.

129. Raymond, G. L. "Art as the Source of Logical Form in Oratory and Poetry." In <u>Fundamentals in Education, Art, and Civics</u>, p. 218-29. Modes. EGL.

130. Raymond, G. L. "Principles of Successful Writing and Speaking Fundamentally the Same." In <u>Fundamentals in Education, Art, and Civics</u>, p. 180-87. Composition. EGL.

131. Rogers, H. "Structure of the English Language." In <u>Essays</u>, v. 1, p. 368. Grammar. CLPI.

132. Russell, G. W. E. "Style." In Pritchard, F. H. ed., <u>Essays of Today</u>, p. 238-48. Style. EGL.

133. Sampson, G. "On Playing the Sedulous Ape." In English Association, London, <u>Essays and Studies</u>, v 6, p. 67-87. EGL.

134. Sarton, G. "Science and Style." In Robinson, K. A. and Others, comp., <u>Essays Toward Truth</u>, p. 324-35. Style. EGL.

135. Sherman, S. P. "American Style." In <u>Points of View</u>, p. 151-70. Style. EGL.

136. Spencer, H. "Economy." In Fulcher, P. M. ed., <u>Foundations of English Style</u>, p. 98-103. Style. EGL.

137. Spencer, H. "Style." In <u>Facts and Comments</u>, p. 97-111. Style. EGL.

138. Sprat, T. "Simple and an Ornate Style." In Fulcher,

P. M. ed., <u>Foundations of English Style</u>, p. 104-07. Style. EGL.

139. Squire, J. C. "Natural Writing." In <u>Life and Letters</u>, p. 66-73. Style. EGL.

140. Squire, J. C. "Stock Phrases." In <u>Books Reviewed</u>, p. 223-29. Style. EGL.

141. Steele, R. "False Refinements in Style." In Bryan, W. F. and Crane, R. S. ed., <u>The English Familiar Essay</u>, p. 93-96. Wann, L. ed., <u>Century Readings in the English Essay</u>, p. 141-43. Style. EGL.

142. Stevenson, R. L. "On Some Technical Elements of Style in Literature." In Taylor, W. comp., <u>Essays of the Past and Present</u>, p. 318-35. Taylor, W. comp., <u>Representative English Essays</u>, p. 311-31. AK lists this essay in Turner, <u>Essays and Criticisms</u>, 1903. Style. EGL, AK.

143. Stoddart, J. "Philosophy of Language: Comprehending Universal Grammar." 1854. <u>Encyclopedia Metropolitan</u>. Grammar. CLPI.

144. Strunsky, S. "Rhetoric 21." In Cockayne, C. A. ed., <u>Modern Essays of Various Types</u>, p. 31-35. Taylor, W. comp., <u>Essays of the Past and Present</u>, p. 419-21. Rhetoric. EGL.

145. Swinnerton, F. A. "Letter on Style." In Taylor, W. ed., <u>Types and Times in the Essay</u>, p. 356-59. Style. EGL.

146. Symonds, J. A. "Art of Style." In Taylor, W. comp., <u>Essays of The Past And Present</u>, p. 336-441. Style. EGL.

147. Symonds, J. A. "Beauty, Composition, Expression, and Characterisation." In <u>Essays, Speculative and Suggestive</u>, v. 1, p. 212. Style. CLPI.

148. Symonds, J. A. "Notes on Styles." In <u>Essays, Speculative and Suggestive</u>, v. 1, p. 256; v. 2, p. 1. Style. CLPI.

149. Symonds, J. A. "Personal Style." In Makower, S. V.

and Blackwell, B. H. comp., Book of English Essays (1600-1900), p. 388-95. Newbolt, H. J. ed., Essays and Essayists, p. 160-66. Taylor, W. comp., Essays of the Past and Present, p. 342-47. Style. EGL.

150. Symons, A. "Letter on Style." In Taylor, W. ed., Types and Times in the Essay, p. 360-64. Style. EGL.

151. Taylor, J. R. "Description." In Michigan University, Department of Rhetoric and Journalism, Adventures in Essay Reading, p. 336-51. Modes. EGL.

152. Thoreau, H. D. "On Style in Writing." In Michigan University, Department of Rhetoric and Journalism, Adventures in Essay Reading, p. 113-17. Style. EGL.

153. Thoreau, H. D. "Sinews of Style." In Fulcher, P. M. ed., Foundations of English Style, p. 50-57. Style. EGL.

154. Thorpe, C. D. "The Department of Rhetoric." In The University of Michigan, an Encyclopedic Survey, Part 3, pp. 558-69. Educational Institutions. AK.

155. Torrey, B. "Grace of Obscurity." In Friends on the Shelf, p. 309-18. EGL.

156. Torrey, B. "Quotability." In Friends on the Shelf, p. 289-308. EGL.

157. Tucker, G. "On Style." In Essays, p. 157. Style. CLPI.

158. Van Dyke, J. C. "Suggestion in Art." In Fulcher, P. M. ed., Foundations of English Style, p. 119-21. Style. EGL.

159. Walkley, A. B. "Catch Words." In Still More Prejudice, p. 63-67. Style. EGL.

160. Watts, L. "Art of Reading and Writing English." In Works, v. 6, p. 43. CLPI.

161. Wesley, J. "Short English Grammar." In Works, v. 14, p. 1. CLPI.

Articles in Periodicals

Articles in Periodicals

162. Abbott, A. "Aims of High-School English." <u>English Journal</u> 1 (October 1912): 509-11. II. Curriculum.

163. Abbott, A. "Course of Study in English for a Metropolitan Academic High School." <u>Teachers College Record</u> 16 (May 1915): 217-35. II. Curriculum.

164. Abbott, A. "English in Secondary Schools." <u>School Review</u> 9 (June 1901): 388-402. II. Curriculum.

165. Abbott, A. "Entrance English from the Boy's Point of View." <u>Education</u> 22 (October 1901): 78-88. RG. Curriculum.

166. Abbott, A. "Experiment in High School English." <u>School Review</u> 12 (September 1904): 550-8. RG. Curriculum.

167. Abbott, A. "To Beginners in English Teaching." <u>English Journal</u> 1 (September 1912): 419-24. II. Teaching Methods.

168. Abbott, L. "Aids to Preaching." <u>London Quarterly Review</u> 62 (1884): 287. CLPI. Sermons.

169. Aiton, G. B. "Purpose of English Language." <u>School Review</u> (1897): 148. PI. Curriculum.

170. Albert, C. S. "Changed Conditions of Education." <u>Lutheran Quarterly</u> (1901): 559. PI.

171. Alden, H. M. "Notes on Style." <u>Current Literature</u> 31 (July 1901): 53-4. RG. Style.

172. Aldrich, F. D. "Function of Grammar in the Teaching of Modern Language." <u>National Education Association</u> (1904): 525-8. RG. Grammar.

173. Alexander, G. "English Composition as a Means of Acquiring Power." Elementary School Teacher 6 (September 1905): 20-7. RG. Composition.

174. Alexander, G. "Study of English Composition as a Means of Acquiring Power." National Education Association (1905): 407-13. RG. Composition.

175. Allen, E. A. "Idiom vs. Grammar." Nation 91 (September 1910): 289. RG. Grammar.

176. Allen, T. J. "Shall Bad English Be Abolished?" Education 20 (June 1906): 38-40. RG. Error.

177. Allen, W. H. "Can Your Children Write Stories Like These?" Delineator 85 (October 1914): 21. RG. Literature and Composition.

178. Alton, M. "Individual Work in Composition Writing." Education 24 (January 1904): 306-8. RG. Teaching Methods.

179. Alton, M. "Mental Value of the Study of English Grammar." Education 34 (October 1913): 78-80. RG. Grammar.

180. Alton, M. "Third Year English in Secondary Schools." Education 32 (April 1912): 505-8. RG. Curriculum.

181. "America and the English Language." Living Age (1898): 514. PI. Dialect.

182. Anderson, J. M. "The Old and the New in Education." Education (1892): 164. PI. Curriculum.

183. Andrews, E. F. "Grammatical Stumbling Blocks." Chautauquan (1896): 339. PI. Grammar.

184. Apgar, G. "Definite Aim in Composition." School Review 14 (January 1906): 34-41. RG, PI. Curriculum.

185. Arnold, F. R. "Humanizing English Teachers." Education 36 (March 1916): 459-61. RG. Teacher Training.

186. "Art of Rhetoric." Westminster Review 148 (1897). CSIGP. Rhetoric.

187. "Association of High School Teachers of English of New York City." English Journal 2 (October 1913): 530-3. II.

188. "Association of High-School Teachers of English of New York City." School Review 23 (December 1915): 722-4. RG.

189. "Attainment in English at the End of the Sixth School Year." English Journal 3 (December 1914): 663-5. II. Curriculum.

190. Aydelotte, F. "Correlation of English Literature and Composition in the College Course." English Journal 3 (November 1914): 568-74. II. Literature and Composition.

191. "'Ayres' Verbalist English Grammar." Literacy World (1882): 56. PI. Grammar.

192. Backus, B. "Solving the Problem of the Failure in English." English Journal 9 (December 1920): 579-83. II. Teaching Methods.

193. Bacon, G. F. "Language; Grade VII." Teachers College Record 8 (September 1907): 256-62. II. Curriculum.

194. Bacon, L. "Teaching of Writing in Secondary Schools." School Review 11 (October 1903): 623-35. RG. Teaching Methods.

195. Bacorn, L. "Assignment of Essay Subjects." School Review 9 (May 1901): 298-309. RG. Teaching Methods.

196. "Bad Language." Spectator 121 (September 1918): 297-8. II. Error.

197. Bailey, F. C. "Fossilization Among Teachers of English." School Review 13 (November 1905): 712-16. RG.

198. "Bain on English Language." *Spectator* (1887): 741. PI. Rhetoric.

199. Bair, F. H. "New Type of Class Book Individualizing the Teaching of English in Secondary Schools." *English Journal* 7 (September 1918): 433-8. II. Curriculum.

200. Baker, F. T. "Teacher of English." *English Journal* 2 (June 1913): 335-43. II. Teacher Training.

201. Baker, H. L. "Teaching of Thought and Expression." *Nation* 86 (April 1908): 397. RG. Teaching Methods.

202. Balch, S. W. "Rhetoric for Science." *Education* (1896): 223. PI. Rhetoric.

203. Baldwin, C. S. "College Teaching of Rhetoric." *Educational Review* 48 (June 1914): 1-20. RG. Rhetoric.

204. Baldwin, C. S. "Freshman English." *Educational Review* 32 (December 1906): 385-94. RG,AK. Curriculum.

205. Barbour, F. A. "English Composition in the High School." *School Review* 6 (September 1898): 500-13. RG. Curriculum.

206. Barbour, F. A. "History of English Grammar Teaching." *Educational Review* 12 (1896): 487-507. PI, AK. Grammar.

207. Barbour, F. A. "Psychology of the Diagram." *School Review* 5 (April 1897): 240-2. RG,AK. Grammar.

208. Barnes, E. "Spoken English as a Factor in Americanization." *National Education Association* (1918): 171-3. RG. Dialect.

209. Barnes, N. W. "Ways in Which Our Teaching of College Composition is Ineffective." *English Journal* 5 (March 1916): 208-9. II. Teaching Methods.

210. Barnes, W. "Reign of Red Ink." *English Journal* 2 (March 1913): 158-65. II. Teaching Methods.

211. Barnes, W. "Suggestions for the English Course in the Junior High School." School Review 27 (September 1919): 523-32. RG. Curriculum.

212. Barr, R. "Shall and Will." Bookman 2 (December 1895): 287-8 . RG. Grammar.

213. Bascom, L. "English Lessons for Naval Recruits." English Journal 9 (April 1920): 224-6. II. Curriculum.

214. Baylor, A. S. "English in the Elementary Schools." National Education Association (1910): 430-6. RG. Curriculum.

215. Bean, C. H. "How English Grammar Has Been Taught in America." Education 34 (January 1914): 301-11. RG. Grammar.

216. Beardsley, G. "English Literature at the College and Universities." Educational Review 16 (1898): 185-91. AK. Literature.

217. Beasley, E. G. "Reorganization of English in the Elementary School." Elementary School Journal 16 (June 1916): 565-70. RG. Curriculum.

218. Beecher, W. J. "Pith in Exposition." Presbyterian Quarterly (1874): 619. PI. Modes.

219. Beers, H. A. "Entrance Requirements in English at Yale." Educational Review 3 (1892): 427-43. AK. Curriculum.

220. Behar, N. "English for Use." Survey 44 (September 1920): 708-9. RG. Usage.

221. "Ben Jonson's Grammar." All the Year Round (1882): 397. PI. Grammar.

222. Benedick, W. R. "Outlines from History of Education." Popular Science Monthly (1887): 51, 212. PI. History of Education.

223. Benedict, G. W. "Theme Writing." Education 14 (June 1914): 608-14. RG. Composition.

224. Benedict, W. R. "Outlines from History of Education." Popular Science Monthly (1886): 626. PI. History of Education.

225. Bentley, I. M. "The Psychology of Grammar of Science." Philosophical Review (1897): 521. PI. Grammar.

226. Betz, A. and Marshall, E. "Grammar Based in Errors." English Journal 5 (September 1916): 491-500. II. Grammar.

227. Beverley, C. "Self-Measurement by Elementary-School Pupils." English Journal 9 (June 1920): 331-7. II. Evaluation.

228. Beyer, T. P. "Anent Compulsory Composition in Colleges." Educational Review 44 (June 1912): 77-86. RG, AK. Curriculum.

229. Bicknell, P. F. "Conversational English Language." Dial (1896): 107. PI. Dialect.

230. Bidwell, A. "English Service System." English Journal 8 (January 1919): 35-8. II.

231. Bird, F. M. "Paralyzers of Style." Lippincott's Magazine (1896): 280. PI. Style.

232. Bird, W. O. "Have All of Our Methods of Teaching English Composition Failed?" School and Society 13 (March 1921): 385-7. RG. Teaching Methods.

233. Black, J. E. "Literary Expression in the Third Grade." Elementary School Teacher 8 (June 1908): 592-6. RG. Curriculum.

234. Black, W. W. "Report of the Joint Committee on Grammatical Nomenclature." Journal of Education 80 (October 1914): 375, 410-1. II. Grammar.

235. "Blackboard for Backward Pupils in Composition." English Journal 4 (June 1915): 418-20. II. Teaching Methods.

236. Blaisdell, H. E. "Clipping Files and Promotive English." English Journal 8 (September 1919):

433-4. II.

237. Blaisdell, T. C. "Letter and Its Reply." Journal of Education 83 (April 6, 1916): 382-3. II.

238. Blaisdell, T. C. "Teaching Composition." Education 29 (March 1909):422-31. RG. Teaching Methods.

239. Blake, C. E. "Some Backgrounds of English." Outlook 78 (October 1904): 528-33. RG.

240. Blount, A. "Normal School Training for the Teaching of English in Elementary Schools." English Journal 2 (April 1913): 215-20. II. Teacher Training.

241. Bobbitt, J. F. "Literature in the Elementary Curriculum." Elementary School Teacher 14 (December 1913): 158-66. RG. Literature.

242. Bolenius, E. M. "Oral Composition." Education 31 (March 1911): 449-55. RG. Speech.

243. Bouton, E. "High School English." Education 25 (September 1904): 36-44. RG. Curriculum.

244. Bouton, E. "Study of English Language." Education (1885): 91. PI. Curriculum.

245. Bowles, R. N. "Investigation into English Requirements." School Review 12 (May 1904): 331-9. RG. Curriculum.

246. Bowman, J. C. "Marking of English Themes." English Journal 9 (May 1920): 245-54. II. Evaluating Writing.

247. Bowman, J. C. "Use of the Magazine in English." English Journal 5 (May 1916):332-4. II. Teaching Methods.

248. Boynton, P. H. "Sorting College Freshmen." English Journal 2 (February 1913): 73-8. II.

249. Boynton, P. H. "Sorting College Freshmen." Univ. Chic. M. 5 (April 1913): 199-205. II.

250. Brackett, A. C. "Can We Speak English?" Harper's Monthly 51 (1875): 59. CLPI.

251. Bradley, C. B. "The Classification of Rhetorical Figures." Modern Language Notes 1 (1886): 140-42. AK. Rhetoric.

252. Brandt, H. C. G. "Derivation of English Language." Academy (1888): 257. PI.

253. Breck, E. J. "New Task for the English Teacher." English Journal 1 (February 1912): 65-71. II.

254. Breck, E. J. "Present Possibilities of Oral English in High Schools." English Journal 3 (January 1914): 28-37. II. Curriculum.

255. Bredvold, L. I. "Suggestions for Reconstruction in High School English." Education 33 (April 1913): 492-8. RG. Curriculum.

256. Breed, F. S. and Frostic, F. W. "A Scale for Measuring the General Merit of English Composition in the Sixth Grade." Elementary School Journal 17 (1917): 307-325. HEW, RG. Evaluating Writing.

257. Brewer, W. F. "English at College." Nation 63 (1896): 327. AK.

258. "Brief Summary of the Forthcoming Report of the National Joint Committee on the Reorganization of High-School English." English Journal 5 (June 1916): 411-19. II. Curriculum.

259. Briggs, L. R. "The Correction of Bad English as a Requirement for Admission to Harvard College." Academy 5 (1890): 302-12. AK. Curriculum.

260. Briggs, T. H. "Co-operation in English." English Journal 5 (March 1916): 157-63. II.

261. Briggs, T. H. "Formal English Grammar as a Discipline." Teachers College Record 14 (September 1913): 251-343. II. Grammar.

262. Broadus, E. K. "Case of John Smith." English Journal 4 (November 1915): 555-65. II.

263. Broadus, E. K. "Developments in the Teaching of English." Education 23 (April 1903): 502-5. RG, PI. Teaching Methods.

264. Broadus, J. A. "Three Methods of Preaching." Baptist Quarterly Review (1870): 91. PI. Sermons.

265. Brock, A. C. "Language and Thought." Living Age 241 (May 1904): 497-9. RG.

266. Bronson, W. C. "English Literature in the Secondary Schools." Academy 4 (1889): 384-95. AK. Literature.

267. Brooks, A. M. "College English Teaching." School and Society 5 (June 1917): 653-4. RG. Teaching Methods.

268. Brown, G. "Grammar." American Institute of Instruction (1831): 137. PI. Grammar.

269. Brown, H. G. "What Kind of Grammar in Upper Grades?" Journal of Education 77 (June 1913): 629+. II. Grammar.

270. Brown, L. R. "Needed Readjustments in the Teaching of English Grammar." English Journal 2 (February 1913): 81-92. II. Grammar.

271. Brown, M. D. and Haggerty, M. E. "Measurement of Improvement in English Composition." English Journal 6 (October 1917): 515-27. II. Evaluating Writing.

272. Brownell, B. "Test of the Ballou Scale of English Composition." School and Society 4 (December 1916): 938-42. RG. Evaluating Writing

273. Brownell, H. M. "Nine Relationships." English Journal 6 (May 1917): 344-7. II.

274. "Brown's Institutes of English Grammar." Literary World (1882): 323. PI. Grammar.

275. Brubacher, A. R. "Co-operation of Departments to Secure Good Speech and Writing." English Journal 3 (June 1914): 331-44. II. Curriculum.

276. Brumm, J. L. "In Memoriam, Fred Newton Scott." Michigan Alumnus (June 1931): 655. AK.

277. Bruneti'ere, F. "French Mastery of Style." Atlantic Monthly (1897): 442. PI. Style.

278. Buck, G. "Make-Believe Grammar." School Review 17 (1909): 21-33. AK. Grammar.

279. Buck, G. "Preliminary Considerations in Planning the Revision of Grammatical Terminology." English Journal 2 (June 1913): 11-7. II. Grammar.

280. Buck, G. "Psychological Significance of the Parts of Speech." Education 18 (January 1898): 269-72. RG, PI, AK. Grammar.

281. Buck, G. "Recent Tendencies in the Teaching of English Composition." Education 22 (November 1913): 71-82. RG, AK. Teaching Methods.

282. Buck, G. "(Reply) Psychology of the Diagram." School Review 5 (September 1897): 470-2. RG, AK. Grammar.

283. Buck, G. "The Present Status of Rhetorical Theory." Modern Language Notes 15 (1901): 67-74. AK. Rhetoric.

284. Buck, G. "The Psychology of the Diagram." School Review 5 (1897): 470-72. AK. Grammar.

285. Buck, G. "The Sentence-Diagram." Educational Review 13 (1897): 250-60. AK. Grammar.

286. Buck, G. "What Does Rhetoric Mean?" Educational Review 22 (September 1911): 197-200. RG, AK. Rhetoric.

287. Buck, P. M. "Aims of English Teaching." National Education Association (1905): 454-8. RG. Curriculum.

288. Buck, P. M. "Classical Tradition and the Study of English." Classical Journal 9 (April 1914): 284-91.

II. Curriculum.

289. Buck, P. M. "Laboratory Method in English Composition." <u>National Education Association</u> (1904): 506-10. RG. Teaching Methods

290. Buck, W. J. "Style in English." <u>Writer</u> (1898): 113. PI. Style.

291. Buck, W. J. "Style in English." <u>Writer</u> (1898): 130. PI. Style.

292. Buck, W. J. "Style in English." <u>Living Age</u> (1898): 230. PI. Style.

293. Buck, W. J. "Teaching of Grammar by the Sentence-Diagram." <u>Educational Review</u> (1897): 250. PI. Grammar.

294. Burgess, I. B. "Translation from the Greek and Latin Classics as a Training in the Use of English." <u>National Education Association Proceedings</u> 35 (1896): 563-8. RG. Teaching Methods.

295. Burnside, M. "Good-English Drive." <u>English Journal</u> 7 (December 1918): 655-8. II. Error.

296. Burroughs, J. "Style and 'The Stylist.'" <u>Critic</u> (1898): 464. PI. Style.

297. Burton, F. R. "Descriptive Writing." <u>Writer</u> (1886): 81. PI. Modes.

298. Burton, R. "(Reply) Shall and Will." <u>Bookman</u> 2 (February 1896): 503-4. RG. Grammar.

299. Butterfield, E. W. "Latin Method." <u>Journal of Education</u> 83 (April 1916): 402. II. Teaching Methods.

300. "By Means of Letters." <u>English Journal</u> 6 (March 1917): 156-69. II.

301. Cady, F. W. "Freshman Course in English." <u>English Journal</u> 3 (December 1914): 676-7. II. Curriculum.

302. Calder, A. "Socialization of the Composition."

English Journal 9 (December 1920): 593-6. II. Composition.

303. Camp, F. S. "Correlation of English and Content Subjects." School Review 26 (January 1918): 55-7. RG. Curriculum.

304. Campbell, H. "Beginning of Liberation in Education." Arena (1899): 350. PI.

305. Canby, H. S. "What is English?" English Journal 9 (September 1920): 367-73. II.

306. Canby, H. S. "Writing English." Harper's Monthly 128 (April 1914): 778-84. RG.

307. Carleton, N. "Her Grammar Dream." Journal of Education 81 (January 1915): 21. II. Grammar.

308. Carpenter, G. R. "English Composition in Colleges." Educational Review (1892): 438. PI, AK. Curriculum.

309. Carpenter, W. B.; Farrar, F. W.; and Hughes, H. P. "Science of Preaching." New Review (1891): 481. PI. Sermons.

310. Carpenter, W. B.; Farrar, F. W.; and Hughes, H. P. "Science of Preaching." Eclectic Magazine (1891): 226. PI. Sermons.

311. "Certain Corruptions of English Language." Knowledge (1885): 525. PI. Error.

312. "Chaignet's History of Rhetoric." Athenaeum 2 (1889): 248. PI. Rhetoric.

313. Chancelor, W. E. "Composition Subjects." Journal of Education 72 (October - November 1910): 403-4. II. Composition.

314. Channing, E. T. "On Models in Literature." North American Review 3 (July 1816): 202-209. HR. Literature.

315. Chapel, R. E. "High School Problems." Quarterly

Journal of Speech Education 7 (April 1921): 116-19. RG. Curriculum.

316. "Charting Errors in English." English Journal 8 (April 1919): 225-33. II. Error.

317. Chiles, E. E. "Oral Composition a Basis for Written." English Journal 3 (June 1914): 354-61. II. Speech.

318. Chiles, E. E. "Oral Exposition for Colleges and High Schools." English Journal 4 (September 1915): 458-64. II. Speech.

319. Chislett, W. "Materials for American Composition." English Journal 3 (April 1914): 245-7. II. Composition.

320. Chubb, P.; Long, D. J.; Cooley, F. W. "Avenues of Language-Expression in the Elementary School." National Education Association (1904): 452-68. RG. Curriculum.

321. Chugg, P. "Menace of Pedantry in the Teaching of English." School Review 20 (January 1912): 34-45. RG.

322. Church, H. V. "Experiment in Co-operation in English." School Review 23 (December 1915): 670-8. RG. Curriculum.

323. Clancy, G. C. "Absorption Process in English Composition." Educational Review 43 (February 1912): 204-6. RG. Composition.

324. Clancy, G. C. "Weak Student in Freshman English Composition." English Journal 2 (April 1913): 235-40. II. Composition.

325. Clapp, J. M. "Hamilton Summer School." English Journal 5 (December 1916): 705-6. II.

326. Clapp, J. M. "Language as a Business Asset." English Journal 7 (May 1918): 339-40. II. Business English.

327. Clapp, J. M. "Methods of Amelioration." Nat'l Educ.

Assn. of the United States Journal of Proceedings and Addresses (1912): 751-54. HEW.

328. Clapp, J. M. "Oral English in the College Course." English Journal 2 (January 1913): 18-33. II. Speech.

329. Clark, K. U. "Difficulties of the English Language." Outlook 52 (September 1895): 467. RG.

330. Clark, M. C. "Ethical and Practical Points in Teaching English." Educational Review 21 (May 1901): 485-96. RG. Teaching Methods.

331. Clay, M. E. "Grammar for the Grammarless." English Journal 7 (May 1918): 334-7. II. Grammar.

332. Clemens, S. L. "English Language as She is Taught." Century (1887): 932. PI.

333. Cobb, E. "Oral Composition." Education 34 (June 1914): 615-8. RG. Speech.

334. Cobb, E. "Plan for the Relief of English Teachers." Journal of Education 79 (February 1914): 160. II.

335. Cobb, J. S. "English Grammar." New Era (1875): 341-549. PI. Grammar.

336. Coburn, F. W. "Composition as the Basis of Art Instruction." Education (1906): 80. PI. Teaching Methods.

337. Cody, S. "Ideal Course in English for Vocational Students." English Journal 3 (May-June 1914): 263-81; 371-80. II. Curriculum.

338. Cody, S. "Organizing Drill on Fundamentals Like a Football Game." English Journal 6 (June 1917): 412-19. II. Grammar.

339. Cody, S. "Scientific Principles in the Teaching of Composition." English Journal 1 (March 1912): 161-72. II. Composition.

340. Collamore, E. A. "Language Training, Formative and Corrective." Kindergarten and First Grade 5

(November 1920): 359-62. II. Error.

341. "College English." *Independent* 56 (January 1904): 217-8. RG. Curriculum.

342. "Committee on English of the N. E. A." *U. S. Bureau of Education Bulletin* 41 (1913): 9-16. RG.

343. "Composition and Rhetoric at Harvard." *Critic* 27 (ns 24) (October 1895): 243-4. RG. Curriculum.

344. "Composition and Thought." *Science* ns 40 (September 1914): 344-6. RG. Composition.

345. "Composition in Correlation with Other Subjects." *School Review* 25 (September 1917): 513-14. RG. Composition.

346. "Composition of English Language." *Chambers's Edinburgh Journal* (1855): 275. PI.

347. "Conditions of 'The Grand Style.'" *Spectator* (1883): 319. PI. Style.

348. Condon, A. A. "Series of Motivated Language Lessons Introducing Description as a New Form of Composition." *Elementary School Journal* 18 (June 1918): 782-94. RG. Curriculum.

349. Conrad, F. W. "Elements of Success in Preaching." *Lutheran Quarterly Review* (1887): 157. PI. Sermons.

350. Cook, A. S. "Teaching of the English Language." *Atlantic* 87 (May 1901): 710-22. RG. Teaching Methods.

351. Cook, A. S. "Teaching of the English Language." *Current Literature* 36 (June 1904): 657-8. RG. Teaching Methods.

352. Cook, L. B. "Business English or English in Business?" *English Journal* 9 (February 1920): 80-7. II. Business English.

353. Cooke, F. J. "Minimum Grade Requirements in English and Mathematics in the Francis W. Parker School."

Elementary School Teacher 12 (February 1912): 245-53. RG. Curriculum.

354. Cooke, J. D. "Community English: A Means of Motivation for Oral and Written Composition." *English Journal* 9 (January 1920): 20-4. II. Teaching Methods.

355. Cooley, A. W. "How to Teach Language." *Education* 28 (June 1908): 613-22. RG. Teaching Methods.

356. Cooper, J. A. "Writing English Language." *Canadiana Magazine* (1897): 80. PI. Composition.

357. Cooper, L. "Correction of Papers." *English Journal* 3 (May 1914): 290-8. II. Evaluating Writing.

358. Cooper, L. "Note on Paraphrasing." *English Journal* 3 (June 1914): 381-2. II. Teaching Methods.

359. Cooper, L. "Teaching of Written Composition." *Education* 30 (March 1910): 421-30. RG, AK. Teaching Methods.

360. "Corruption of English Language." *Gentleman's Magazine* ns (1892): 429. PI. Error.

361. Coulter, J. M. "Proper Use of Science in Preaching." *American Journal of Theology* (1899): 641. PI. Sermons.

362. Coulter, V. C. "Financial Support of English Teaching." *English Journal* 1 (January 1912): 24-9. II. Educational Institutions.

363. "Course of Study in English, Its Character and Construction." *School Review* 15 (October 1907): 559-75. RG. Curriculum.

364. "Course of Study in the Elementary School." *Elementary School Teacher* 8 (May 1908): 524-33. RG. Curriculum.

365. Courtenay, M. E. "Attempt to Make Oral Composition Effective." *National Education Association* (1912): 721-5. RG. Speech.

366. Courtenay, M. E. "Attempt to Make Oral Composition Effective." *English Journal* 1 (November 1912): 562-5. II. Speech.

367. Courthope, W. J. "Study of English Language and Literature as Part of a Liberal Education." *Living Age* 198 (August 1893): 478-88. RG. Curriculum.

368. Courtis, S. A. "Standard Tests in English." *Elementary School Teacher* 14 (April 1914): 374-92. RG. Testing.

369. Cowan, H. E. "Suicide English." *English Journal* 6 (November 1917): 621-2. II.

370. Cox, S. H. "Plea for a More Direct Method in Teaching English." *English Journal* 4 (May 1919): 304-10. II. Teaching Methods.

371. Cox, T. C. "Causes of Bad English in the United States." *English Journal* 2 (February 1913): 124-6. II. Error.

372. Craven, B. "Importance of Word Study." *Journal of Education* 68 (November 1908): 511. II. Curriculum.

373. Crawford, M. "Laboratory Equipment of the Teacher of English." *English Journal* 4 (March 1915): 145-51. II. Teaching Methods.

374. Cross, A. "Staples of Grammar and Composition." *Elementary School Journal* 18 (December 1917): 253-63. RG. Grammar.

375. Cross, A. "Weighing the Scales." *English Journal* 6 (March 1917): 183-91. II.

376. Cross, E. A. "Experimental Course in English." *Education* 33 (March 1913): 410-6. RG. Curriculum.

377. Cross, E. A. "Functional Teaching of English Grammar." *English Journal* 4 (December 1915): 653-9. II. Grammar.

378. Cross, W. L. "English in the Schools." *Education* 28 (May 1908): 537-51. RG, AK. Curriculum.

379. Cross, W. L. "The Act of Composition." <u>Atlantic Monthly</u> (1906): 704. PI. Composition.

380. Crumpton, C. E. "Better Speech Week at Montevallo." <u>English Journal</u> 5 (October 1916): 569-70. II. Error.

381. Crumpton, C. E. "Speech Betterment in Alabama." <u>English Journal</u> 6 (February 1917): 96-102. II. Error.

382. Cunliffe, J. W. "College English Composition." <u>English Journal</u> 1 (December 1912): 591-600. II. Curriculum.

383. "Curriculum of the Horace Mann Elementary School." <u>Teachers College Record</u> 14 (May 1913): 143-66. II. Curriculum.

384. Cutler, F. W. "More Uses of the Conference." <u>English Journal</u> 5 (November 1916): 633-4. II. Teaching Methods.

385. "Daily Theme Eye." <u>Atlantic</u> 99 (March 1907): 427-9. RG. Teaching Methods.

386. Darling, G. "Lax Use in Speech." <u>Education</u> (1899): 555. PI. Error.

387. Darling, G. "Standards in English." <u>Education</u> 17 (February 1897): 331-7. RG, PI. Error.

388. Davenport, H. J. "Scope and Method of Grammar." <u>Education</u> (1903): 161, 208. PI. Grammar.

389. Davis, J. B. "Vocational and Moral Guidance Through English Composition." <u>English Journal</u> 1 (October 1912): 457-65. II. Composition.

390. Davis, J. B. "Vocational and Moral Guidance Thru English Composition in the High School." <u>National Education Association</u> (1912): 713-8. RG. Composition.

391. Davis, W. H. "Teaching of English Composition: Its Present Status." <u>English Journal</u> 6 (May 1917): 285-94. II. Teaching Methods.

392. Davis, W. R. "Survey of the Teaching of Composition in the Northwest." English Journal 4 (December 1915): 639-46. II. Curriculum.

393. Dawson, C. A. "Two Experiments in Experience." English Journal 2 (September 1913): 437-44. II. Curriculum.

394. Day, H. N. "Criticism of Rhetoric." American Biblical Repository 3: 589. PI. Rhetoric.

395. Dean, M. W. "Word of Protest." School Review 14 (November 1906): 686-9. RG.

396. "Decay of Rhetoric." Spectator 68 (May 1892): 672-3. RG, PI. Rhetoric.

397. DeLong, W. "Use of the Conference Hour." English Journal 4 (March 1915): 186-90. II. Teaching Methods.

398. DeMorgan, A. "On the Use of the Verbs Shall and Will." Philological Society London Proceedings 4 (1850): 185. CLPI. Grammar.

399. Denig, E. S. "Classification of the Pronoun and Adjective Function on the Basis of the Law of Association." Journal of Education 75 (June 1912): 632-3. II. Grammar.

400. Denney, J. V. "Preparation of College Teachers of English." English Journal 7 (May 1918): 322-6. II. Teacher Training.

401. Denney, J. V. "Value of the Classics to Students of English." Classical Journal 9 (December 1913): 94-101. II. Curriculum.

402. Denton, G. B. "Herbert Spencer and the Rhetoricians." Publications of the Modern Language Association 34 (ns 27) (March 1919): 89-111. AG, AK. Rhetoric.

403. DeQuincey, T. "Elements of Rhetoric." Blackwood's Magazine 34 (December 1828): 885-908. HR. Rhetoric.

404. DeQuincey, T. "English Language: How to Write." <u>Hogg's Instructor</u> (1853): 79. PI.

405. DeQuincey, T. "'Language' in Works of Thomas DeQuincey." <u>Works of Thomas DeQuincey</u> 2 (1876): 373-93. HR. Literature.

406. DeQuincey, T. "Style." <u>Blackwood's Magazine</u> (1839): 1, 214, 387, 508. PI. Style.

407. DeQuincey, T. "Style." <u>Blackwood's Magazine</u> 49, no. 304 (February 1841): 219-28. HR. Style.

408. DeQuincey, T. "Style." <u>Blackwood's Magazine</u> 48, no. 300 (October 1840): 508-21. HR. Style.

409. DeQuincey, T. "Style." <u>Blackwood's Magazine</u> 48, no. 297 (July 1840): 1-17. HR. Style.

410. DeQuincey, T. "Style." <u>Blackwood's Magazine</u> 48, no. 299 (September 1840): 387-98. HR. Style.

411. Dewe, J. A. "Thought and Speech." <u>Education</u> (1906): 168. PI.

412. Dickinson, R. W. "Popular Style of Preaching." <u>Christian Disciple</u> (1825): 427. PI. Sermons.

413. Dickinson, R. W. "Popular Style of Preaching." <u>Literary and Theological Review</u> (1838): 235. PI. Sermons.

414. Diebel, A. and Sears, I. "Study of the Common Mistakes in Pupils' Written English." <u>Elementary School Journal</u> 18 (November 1917): 172-85. RG. Error.

415. "Differentiating Instruction in Ninth-Grade English." <u>School Review</u> 27 (December 1919): 772-88. RG. Curriculum.

416. Dillard, J. H. "Grammar and Arithmetic in Our Secondary Schools." <u>Nation</u> 71 (August 1900): 92. RG. Grammar.

417. Dithridge, R. L. "Speech Improvement Week at Eastern

District High School." English Journal 4 (September 1915): 465-6. II. Error.

418. Ditty, A. F. "Ballad-Writing in the High School." English Journal 3 (June 1914): 382-6. II. Literature.

419. Dolch, E. W. "Selling English." Education 38 (February 1918): 447-9. RG.

420. Dole, C. A. "Use of the Model in English Composition." Education 24 (March 1904): 426-38. RG. Teaching Methods.

421. Donagh, M. "In the Throes of Composition." Cornhill Magazine (1904): 67. PI.

422. Donagh, M. "In the Throes of Composition." Eclectic Magazine (1905): 252. PI.

423. Doolittle, C. S. "Tompkin's Science of Discourse." School Review (1898): 548. PI. Rhetoric.

424. Dorey, J. M. "English Teacher and the Philistines." English Journal 6 (September 1917): 454-62. II.

425. Dorey, J. M. "Experiment in Senior English." English Journal 1 (May 1912): 302-5. II. Curriculum.

426. Douglas, A. "Suggestive Language Subjects." Journal of Education 71 (February-March 1910): 209, 238, 264-5. II. Teaching Methods.

427. Douglas, C. H. J. "Scientific Basis of Composition." Science 22 (September 1893): 149-50. RG, PI. Composition.

428. Dowd, M. H. "Composition and English Literature." Journal of Education 69 (April 1909): 377-9, 405-6, 434-5. II. Literature and Composition.

429. Driggs, H. R. "Is There Need for a New Type of Text in High School English?" National Education Association (1920): 395-6. RG. Curriculum.

430. Driggs, H. R. "Making Language a Real Part of the

Curriculum in Synopsis." Nat'l Education Assn. of the United States Address and Proceedings (1920): 205-07. HEW. Curriculum.

431. Drury, M. R. "The Speech of People: A Story." Munsey's Magazine (1903): 735. PI.

432. DuBreuil, A. J. "Written Composition in the High School." English Journal 1 (November 1912): 537-46. II. Curriculum.

433. Duddy, A. E. "New Synthesis: An Approach thru the Study of English." Educational Review 59 (April 1923): 15-24. RG.

434. Dukes, E. M. "Is the Teaching of English in the High School Functioning Effectively?" National Education Association (1920): 213-15. RG. Curriculum.

435. Duncan, C. S. "Content of Composition Courses." Education 35 (November 1914): 167-73. RG. Curriculum.

436. Duncan, C. S. "Rebellious Word on English Composition." English Journal 3 (March 1914): 154-9. II. Composition.

437. Dunn, B. "English for the Working Boy." Industrial Arts Magazine 10 (May 1921): 187. RG. Business English.

438. Durand, G. H. "Teaching of English in the Secondary Schools." Education 28 (September 1907): 15-22. RG. Curriculum.

439. Dye, C. "Proposed Four Years' Course in English for Secondary Schools." National Education Association Proceedings 37 (1898): 678-81. RG. Curriculum.

440. Earhart, G. and Small, J. "English in the Elementary School." Elementary School Journal 16 (September 1915): 32-48. RG. Curriculum.

441. Earle, J. "Study of English." Forum 13 (March 1892): 75-84. RG, PI. Curriculum.

442. Earle, S. C. "English Courses in the Small College."

English Journal 3 (September 1914): 422-6. II. Curriculum.

443. Earle, S. C. "Examinations in English." English Journal 3 (December 1914): 612-9. II. Testing.

444. Earle, S. C. "Organization of Instruction in English Composition." English Journal 2 (October 1913): 477-87. II. Curriculum.

445. Easton, M. W. "Comparative Grammar." Academy (1890): 489. PI. Grammar.

446. Eaton, H. A. "English Problems After the War." English Journal 8 (May 1919): 308-12. II.

447. Edgerton, F. W. "Experience Day." English Journal 1 (October 1912): 493-6. II.

448. Edgerton, F. W. "Recent Experiment with Magazine Literature." English Journal 1 (May 1912): 278-83. II. Literature.

449. Effinger-Raymond, F. "If I Were a Teacher of English." National Education Association (1913): 621-6. RG, HEW.

450. Elliott, G. R. "Compulsory Composition." Nation 93 (November 1911): 518. RG. Curriculum.

451. Ellis, H. "Learning to Write." Atlantic 102 (November 1908): 626-33. RG. Composition.

452. Ellwanger, W. D. "Religious Helps to Forming Style." Critic (1903): 406. PI. Style.

453. Emerson, E. "English Language." Mercersburg Review (1860): 216. PI.

454. Emerson, O. F. "English in the Secondary Schools." Academy 4 (1889): 233-44. AK. Curriculum.

455. Emerson, O. F. "Sweet's Primer of Historical Grammar of English Language." School Review (1896): 236. PI. Grammar.

456. Emerson, O. F. "Teaching of English Grammar."

School Review 5 (March 1897): 129-38. RG, PI, AK. Grammar.

457. "English and Other Teaching." Nation 86 (March 1908): 253-4. RG.

458. "English Composition." Atlantic Monthly 59 (1892): 129. CLPI. Composition.

459. "English Composition in Preparatory Schools." Nation (1892): 388. PI. Curriculum.

460. "English Equipment." English Journal 2 (March 1913): 178-84. II.

461. "English in College." Nation 101 (July 1915): 14-15. RG. Curriculum.

462. "English in Newspapers and Novels." Scribner's Magazine 2 (1887). CSIGP. Style.

463. "English in Schools." Macmillan's Magazine 17 (1867-8). CSIGP. Curriculum.

464. "English in the Country Schools: Report of Committee." English Journal 4 (January 1915): 41-6. II. Curriculum.

465. "English in the Universities." Nation 71 (December 1900): 504-5. RG. Curriculum.

466. "English Language." DeBow's Review (1860): 323. PI.

467. "English Language." Galaxy (1867): 62. PI.

468. Errington, D. "Fashionable English Language." Gentleman's Magazine (ns) (1883): 576. PI. Style.

469. Erskine, J. "English in the College Course." Educational Review 40 (November 1910): 340-7. RG. Curriculum.

470. Erskine, J. "The Scholar Whom We Knew." Amherst Graduates Quarterly 9 (1920): 71-77. AK.

471. "Essay and Oratorical Style." Christian Monthly

Spectator (1822): 356. PI. Style.

472. Examiners in the University of Chicago. "The Prepatory Course in English." School Review 5 (1897): 445-55. AK. Curriculum.

473. "Excess of Style." Academy (1900): 15. PI. Style.

474. "Expressiveness of Speech." Fortnightly Review 64 (1895). CSIGP. Style.

475. Faunce, W. H. P. "Expository Preaching." Biblical World (1898): 320. PI. Sermons.

476. Faunce, W. H. P. "Expository Preaching." Biblical World (1898): 81, 317. PI. Sermons.

477. Faunce, W. H. P. "Humanizing of Study." School Review 16 (October 1903): 492-6. RG.

478. Faust, W. G. "Effort to Standardize Descriptive Theme-writing for the Senior Year of the High School." English Journal 5 (April 1916): 257-71. II. Curriculum.

479. Fee, M. H. "Teaching English to Fillipinos." English Journal 2 (November 1913): 539-45. II. TESOL.

480. Fernald, J. C. "Simplicity of English." Harper's Monthly 119 (September 1909): 618-23. RG.

481. Fickett, M. G. "Composition in the Grammar Grades." Education 70 (July 1909): 104. II. Curriculum.

482. Fields, C. L. "English at the Bay Section of the California State Teachers Association." English Journal 2 (March 1913): 195-200. II. Curriculum.

483. Fillers, H. D. "Oral and Written Errors in Grammar." Educational Review 54 (December 1917): 458-70. RG. Error.

484. Findlater, J. H. "Art of Narration." Living Age 224 (February 1900): 496-500. RG. Modes.

485. Fish, S. A. "What Should Pupils Know in English When

They Enter the High School?" English Journal 3 (March 1914): 166-75. II. Curriculum.

486. Fisher, G. E. "Time-Saving Devices in English Work." English Journal 9 (December 1920): 597-9. II. Teaching Methods.

487. Fleagle, B. E. "Oral English in the High School." English Journal 1 (December 1912): 611-18. II. Speech.

488. Foerster, N. "Idea Course for Freshmen." English Journal 5 (September 1916): 458-66. II. Curriculum.

489. "Folly of Taught Grammar." Atlantic 101 (February 1908): 281-3. RG. Grammar.

490. Fontaine, M. B. "Articulation of English Teaching in the Elementary and High Schools." English Journal 3 (September 1914): 416-21. II. Curriculum.

491. "For The Love of It." Outlook 90 (November 1908): 565-6. RG.

492. Fore, H. F. "Harvard English Plan." Nation 101 (July 1915): 146-7. RG. Curriculum.

493. Fowler, H. E. "English in a Normal School." English Journal 4 (April 1915): 244-7. II. Curriculum.

494. Frank, T. "Semantics of Modal Constructions." Classical Philology 2 (April-January 1908): 163-86. RG. Grammar.

495. Frazer, N. L. "Oral Expression as a Preparation for Written Composition." Educational Review 48 (November 1914): 393-8. RG. Teaching Methods.

496. French, C. W. "Conference on English Language." School Review (1897): 343. PI.

497. Frink, H. A. "Rhetoric and Public Speaking in the American College." National Education Association Proceedings 31 (1892): 383-93. RG, PI, AK. Rhetoric.

498. Frink, H. A. "Rhetoric and Public Speaking in the American College." National Education Association Proceedings 13 (November 1892): 129-41. RG, PI, AK. Rhetoric.

499. Froehlich, H. B. "New Basis for the Study of English." Industrial Arts Magazine 8 (November 1919: 436-8. RG. Business English.

500. Fry, O. A. "In Defence of the Paragraph." National Review (1893): 38. PI. Paragraphs.

501. Fulton, E. "Infant Criticism Once More." Nation 86 (April 1908): 396-7. RG. Criticism.

502. Fulton, M. G. "Defence of the Special Teacher of Composition." Nation 86 (May 1908): 463-4. RG. Curriculum.

503. "Future of English Language." Chamber's Journal (1894): 294. PI.

504. Gales, R. L. "Christian Tradition and Popular Speech." National Review (1906): 117. PI.

505. Gammans, H. W. "Pupil Who Fails in Secondary English: How to Teach Him." Journal of Education 81 (June 1915): 601. II. Teaching Methods.

506. Gammans, H. W. "Pupil Who Fails in Secondary School English; How to Teach Him." Education 35 (February-May 1915): 565-84. RG. Teaching Methods.

507. Gardiner, J. H. "English in Relation to Other Studies." Nation 86 (June 1904): 509. RG. Curriculum.

508. Gardiner, J. H. "Our Infant Critics." Nation 86 (February 1908): 188. RG. Criticism.

509. Gardiner, J. H. "Our Infant Critics." Nation 86 (March 1908): 267-8. RG. Criticism.

510. Gardiner, J. H. "Teaching English in the School." Outlook 94 (March 1910): 626-31. RG. Curriculum.

511. Gardiner, J. H. "Training in Illiteracy." School

Review 17 (November 1909): 622-30. RG, AK.

512. Gardner, G. E. "Should Power to Create or Capacity to Appreciate Be the Aim in the Study of English?" Education 15 (November-December 1894): 133-40, 221-9. RG. Curriculum.

513. Garrison, W. P. "English at Harvard and Elsewhere." Nation 55 (October 1892): 299-300. RG, PI, AK. Curriculum.

514. Gaston, C. R. "Discovering Human Interests." English Journal 2 (February 1913): 122-4. II.

515. Gaston, C. R. "Notebook as an Aid to Efficiency in English Classes." English Journal 4 (April 1915): 215-25. II. Teaching Methods.

516. Gaw, A. "Collegiate Training of the Teacher of High School English." English Journal 5 (May 1916): 320-31. II. Teacher Training.

517. "(General) Coleridge's Miscellanies, 1885." Macmillan's Magazine 37 (1877-8). CSIGP.

518. "Gentle Art of Teaching English." Contemporary Review 105 (February 1914): 281-3. RG.

519. "Gentle Art of Teaching English." Living Age 281 (April 1914): 48-9. RG.

520. Genung, J. F. "Teacher's Outfit in Rhetoric." School Review 3 (September 1895): 405-22. RG, PI. Rhetoric.

521. Gerhard, E. S. "Philistines Among the Teachers of English." Education 40 (April 1920): 484-92. RG.

522. Gerrish, C. M. "Relation of Moving Pictures to English Composition." English Journal 4 (April 1915): 226-30. II. Film.

523. Gerrish, C. M. "Secondary School Composition." Education Review 49 (February 1915): 126-35. RG. Composition

524. Gerrish, C. M. "Work of the Committee on Standards

in English." Education 36 (October 1915): 95-101. RG. Error.

525. Gildersleeve, B. L. "Aesthetics in Grammar." Princeton Review (ns) (1883): 290. PI. Grammar.

526. "The Glittering Style." Living Age (1901): 458. PI. Style.

527. "The Glittering Style." Academy (1901): 243. PI. Style.

528. Goddard, C. B. "Most Valuable Phase of My High School Training." English Journal 2 (June 1913): 380-6. II.

529. Godkin, E. L. "College English." Nation 61 (September 1895): 219. RG. Curriculum.

530. Godkin, E. L. "College English." Nation 65 (November 1897): 351-2. RG. Curriculum.

531. Godkin, E. L. "Growing Illiteracy of American Boys." Nation 63 (October 1896): 284-5. RG, AK. Error.

532. Godkin, E. L. "Rhetorical Training." Nation (1875): 145, 171. PI. Rhetoric.

533. Godkin, E. L. "Spoken English Language." Nation (1892): 332. PI.

534. Goldwasser, I. E. "Method and Methods in the Teaching of English (Review)." English Journal 3 (April 1914): 256-9. II. Teaching Methods.

535. Goodale, D. R. "Composition Problem." Journal of Education 72 (December 1910): 607+. II. Composition.

536. Goodell, T. D. "Mode or Mood?" Classical Journal 4 (March 1909): 218-9. RG. Grammar.

537. Goodwin, W. W. "School English." Nation 61 (October 1895): 291-3. RG.

538. Goodwin, W. W. "The Root of the Evil." Harvard Graduates' Magazine 1 (1893): 189-93. AK.

539. Gordon, M. "Experiment in Teaching First-Year Composition." School Review 14 (November 1906): 671-5. RG, PI. Curriculum.

540. Gosling, T. W. "Some Social Factors in the Problem of Teaching English." School and Society 10 (December 1919): 756-61. RG. Curriculum.

541. "Grammar and Imperialism." Independent 52 (November 1900): 2703-4. RG. Grammar.

542. "Grammar and Language." London Quarterly Review (1859): 387. PI. Grammar.

543. "The Grammar of the Great." Scribner's Magazine (1900): 633. PI. Grammar.

544. "Grammarians in a Riot Over the Inverted Passive." Journal of Education 82 (September 1915): 272. II. Grammar.

545. "Grammars of English Language." London Quarterly Review (1874): 147. PI. Grammar.

546. Gray, R. P. "Correlation of English with Other Subjects." English Journal 3 (May 1914): 299-302. II. Curriculum.

547. Gray, R. P. "English and the Foreign Languages." Education Review 41 (March 1911): 306-13. RG.

548. Greene, J. "Mastery of English." School Review 1 (November 1893): 546-57. RG, PI.

549. Greenlaw, E. "English in Modern Education: Aims and Method." School and Society 5 (April 1917): 451-9. RG. Curriculum.

550. Greenough, C. N. "Experiment in English A at Harvard." Harvard Graduates' Magazine 23 (December 1914): 252-4. II. Curriculum.

551. Greenough, C. N. "Experiment in the Training of Teachers of Composition for Work with College Freshmen; with Discussion." English Journal 2 (February 1913): 109-21. II. Teacher Training.

552. Greenough, J. J. "Basis of Our Educational System." Atlantic Monthly (1895): 528. PI.

553. Greenough, J. J. "English Question." Atlantic 71 (May 1893): 656-62. RG, PI, AK.

554. Greenough, J. J. "English Question (Abstract)." School Review 1 (June 1893): 387. RG.

555. Greenwood, J. M. "English Composition." Education 22 (March 1902): 426-8. RG. Composition.

556. Greenwood, J. M. "Language Teaching." Educational Review 34 (June 1907): 26-36. RG.

557. Gregory, D. S. "Review of Philological Works by Prof. Francis A. March of Lafayette College." The Presbyterian Quarterly and Princeton Review ns 3 (1874): 745-51. AK.

558. Groce, B. "Emphasis in Teaching of English Language." Academy (nd): 529. PI. Curriculum.

559. "Growth of the English Language." Outlook 104 (August 1913): 789. RG.

560. Guild, T. H. "Going Forth to the Philistines: College Course in Composition." English Journal 1 (September 1912): 412-18. II. Curriculum.

561. Gummere, F. B. "Metaphor and Poetry." Modern Language Notes 1 (1886): 83-84. AK. Literature.

562. Gummere, F. B. "Overdone Instruction in English." Nation 35 (September 1907): 252. RG. Teaching Methods.

563. Hadley, M. E. "English Studies." Education 22 (April 1902): 500-2. RG.

564. Hale, E. E. "Bates on Writing English Language." Dial (1896): 221. PI. Composition.

565. Hale, E. E. "Ideas on Rhetoric in the Sixteenth Century." Publications of the Modern Language Association ns 18 (July 1934): 24-44. RG.

Rhetoric.

566. Hale, R. "Daily Themes and College Debating." <u>Nation</u> 101 (December 1915): 10-11. RG. Teaching Methods.

567. Hale, R. "Evils of Themes and Debating." <u>Journal of Education</u> 83 (March 1916): 319-20. II. Teaching Methods.

568. Hale, W. G. "Classification of Sentences and Clauses." <u>School Review</u> 21 (June 1913): 388-97. RG. Grammar.

569. Hale, W. G. "Work of the Joint Committee of Fifteen on Grammatical Terminology." <u>School Review</u> 20 (January 1912): 46-52. RG. Grammar.

570. Hall, F. "Antiquated English Language." <u>Nation</u> (1891): 243. PI.

571. Hall, F. "Shall We Say 'Is Being Built'?" <u>Scribner's Monthly</u> 3 (1872): 700. CLPI. Grammar.

572. Hall, F. "Some Points on Usage in English Language." <u>American Journal of Philology</u> (1882): 422. PI. Usage.

573. Hall, G. S. "Educational Reforms, 1891." <u>Pedagogical Seminary</u> (1891): 1. PI. History of Education.

574. Haney, J. L. "Correct Speaking and Writing." <u>Ladies' Home Journal</u> (April 1, 1911): 28,50. RG. Error.

575. Haney, J. L. "Correct Speaking and Writing." <u>Ladies' Home Journal</u> (May 1, 1911): 44. RG. Error.

576. Haney, J. L. "Correct Speaking and Writing." <u>Ladies' Home Journal</u> (June 1911): 50. RG. Error.

577. Haney, J. L. "Correct Speaking and Writing." <u>Ladies' Home Journal</u> (September 1911): 58. RG. Error.

578. Haney, J. L. "Correct Speaking and Writing."

Ladies' Home Journal (October 1911): 58. RG. Error.

579. Haney, J. L. "Correct Speaking and Writing." Ladies' Home Journal (November 1911): 58. RG. Error.

580. Haney, J. L. "Correct Speaking and Writing." Ladies' Home Journal (March 1912): 29,52. RG. Error.

581. Haney, J. L. "Correct Speaking and Writing." Ladies' Home Journal (April 1912): 54. RG. Error.

582. Haney, J. L. "Correct Speaking and Writing." Ladies' Home Journal (May 1912): 58. RG. Error.

583. Hanna, J. C. "English the Core of a Secondary Course." National Education Association Proceedings 37 (1898): 665-71. RG. Curriculum.

584. Hannigan, D. F. "Evolution of Education." Westminster Review (1898): 246. PI. History of Education.

585. Harbarger, S. A. "Theme Subjects for Engineering Students." English Journal 5 (November 1916): 620-32. II. Technical English.

586. Harper, C. A. "College Teaching of English." Nation 95 (September 1912): 258-9. RG. Curriculum.

587. Harris, A. E. "Separation of Composition and Literature." Education 39 (May 1919): 559-65. RG. Literature and Composition.

588. Harris, A. V. "Outline for the First Grade: To Be Used as a Basis of Language and Reading." Journal of Education 80 (September 1914): 207+. II. Curriculum.

589. Harris, J. H. "Compositional Interests of Pupils in the Seventh and Eighth Grades." English Journal 2 (January 1913): 34-43. II. Composition.

590. Harris, J. H. "History and Status of the English Curriculum." School Review 10 (September 1902): 566-73. RG. History of Education.

591. Harris, J. H. "Social Aspects of Elementary English." Journal of Education 72 (September-October 1910): 291-3, 327-8. II. Curriculum.

592. Harris, L. H. "Proposed Course in Advanced Exposition for College Students." English Journal 5 (September 1916): 501-3. II. Curriculum.

593. Harris, L. H. "Study in the Relation of Latin to English Composition." School and Society 2 (August 1915): 251-2. RG.

594. Harrison, F. "On Style in English Prose." Nineteenth Century 43 (1898): 932. CLPI. Style.

595. Harrison, F. "Style in English." Nineteenth Century (1898): 932. PI. Style.

596. Harrison, F. "Style in English." Eclectic Magazine (1898): 327. PI. Style.

597. Harrison, J. B. "Preaching." Atlantic Monthly 44 (1879): 129. CLPI. Sermons.

598. Hart, J. M. "Approaches to English Language." Presbyterian Quarterly (1874): 434. PI.

599. Hart, J. M. "Cornell Course in Rhetoric and English Philology." Academy 6 (1891). AK. Curriculum.

600. Hart, J. M. "On the Approaches to the English Language." The Presbyterian Quarterly and Princeton Review ns 3 (1874): 434-56. AK.

601. Hart, J. M. "Outlook for English." School Review 2 (January 1894): 36-9. RG.

602. Hart, J. M. "Outlook for English in New York State; New Requirements at Cornell." School Review 1 (April 1893): 195-7. RG. Curriculum.

603. Hart, J. S. "English Language." Princeton Review (1868): 1. PI.

604. Hart, S. C. "English in the College." School Review 10 (May 1902): 364-73. RG, AK. Curriculum.

605. Hartog, P. J. "Teaching of Style in English and French Schools." Fortnightly Review 77 (June 1902): 1050-63. RG, PI. Style.

606. Hartshorn, H. E. "Don'ts for the Young English Teacher." Journal of Education 83 (March 1916): 293+. II. Teaching Methods.

607. Hartwell, C. S. "Need of More Instruction in High School." Journal of Education 80 (July 1914): 10-1. II. Curriculum.

608. Harvey, B. E. "Motivating English Composition." School Review 24 (December 1916): 759-63. RG. Teaching Methods.

609. Harvey, H. A. "Inspirational Theme-Grading." English Journal 2 (September 1913): 452-5. II. Evaluating Writing.

610. Harvey, P. C. "Analysis in Teaching the Short-Story." English Journal 8 (February 1919): 97-100. II. Literature.

611. Harvey, P. C. "Difference Between the Classes of the High School in Their English Work." English Journal 3 (June 1914): 386-8. II.

612. Hastings, T. S. "Oratorical and Rhetorical Style." Presbyterian Review (1889): 210. PI. Style.

613. Hatch, L. "Bolstering Up the National Exchequer: A Plea for a Tax Upon Literacy Pretentiousness." Century 87 (November 1913):94-6. RG.

614. Hatch, R. C. "Standard of Measurement in English Compostion." English Journal 9 (June 1920): 338-44. II. Evaluating Writing.

615. Hatfield, W. W. "Functional Tests." English Journal 5 (December 1916): 696-702. II. Testing.

616. Hatfield, W. W. "What the Graduates of Our High Schools Think." English Journal 2 (May 1913): 318-22. II.

617. Hathaway, E. V. "Building of an English Course of Study." English Journal 7 (October 1918): 526-32. II. Curriculum.

618. Hawk, H. W. "Fluency First, or Accuracy?" Nation 107 (July 1918): 97. RG. Grammar.

619. Hayles-MacQueen, L. "Teaching of English." Education 27 (March 1907): 393-6. RG. Teaching Methods.

620. Heath, W. R. "Demands of the Business World for Good English." English Journal 2 (March 1913): 171-7. II. Business English.

621. Hempl, G. "American Study of English Language." Chautauquan (1896): 436. PI.

622. Hendrickson, G. L. "Peripatetic Meaning of Style and the Three Stylistic Characters." American Journal of Philology (nd): 125. PI. Style.

623. Henneman, J. B. "Study of English in the South." Sewanee Review 2 (February 1894): 180-97. RG, AK.

624. "Heresies on Style." Academy (1906): 620. PI. Style.

625. Herr, C. B. "Co-operation in the Teaching of English Composition." English Journal 2 (March 1913): 185-7. II. Teaching Methods.

626. Herrick, R. W. "Effect of the Quarter System on Courses in English Composition." Educational Review (1894): 382. PI. Curriculum.

627. Herzberg, M. J. "Discipline of Expression." School Science and Math 20 (November 1920): 697-700. II.

628. Hetzel, M. H. "Value of English in Secondary Schools." Education 41 (June 1921): 673-80. RG. Curriculum.

629. Heydrick, A. "Narration." Chautauquan 36 (November 1902): 158-62. RG. Modes.

630. Heydrick, B. A. "Descriptive Writing." Chautauquan 36 (October 1902): 47-50. RG, PI. Modes.

631. Heydrick, B. A. "Exposition." Chautauquan 36 (December 1902): 270-3. RG, PI. Modes.

632. Heydrick, B. A. "Qualities of Style." Chautauquan 37 (April 1903): 43-6. RG, PI. Style.

633. Hickok, L. P. "Rhetoric: Determined and Applied." Bibliotheca Sacra 1 (1854). PI, CLPI. Rhetoric.

634. Higginson, T. W. "Hints on Speech-Making." Harper's Magazine 73 (1886): 952. CLPI. Speech.

635. "Higher Grammar." New York Review 2 (1838): 422. CLPI. Grammar.

636. "High-school Course in English." School Review 24 (March 1916): 233-5. RG. Curriculum.

637. Hill, A. S. "Colloquial English Language." Harper's Monthly Magazine (1889): 272. PI. Style.

638. Hill, M. G. "Another Word about Freshman English." English Journal 6 (April 1917): 264-5. II. Curriculum.

639. Hillegas, M. B. "Scale for the Measurement of Quality in English Composition by Young People." Teachers College Record 13 (September 1912): 331-84. II. Evaluating Writing.

640. Himes, C. "Better English Week." English Journal 7 (October 1918): 533-7. II. Error.

641. Hinchman, W. S. "Plea for the Infant Critics." Nation 86 (April 1908): 303-4. RG. Criticism.

642. Hinkley, M. A. "Motivating English Composition." English Journal 4 (April 1915): 266-9. II. Teaching Methods.

643. Hinkley, M. A. "Vexing Question of Correctness." English Journal 6 (December 1917): 686-8. II. Error.

644. Hinsdale, B. A. "Education in the U. S. in 1800-1900." Dial 1 (1900): 352. PI. History of Education.

645. "Hints on Speech-Making." Harper's Magazine 12 (1886). CSIGP. Speech.

646. "Historical Sketch of The Joint Conference on Entrance Requirements in English." School Review 16 (December 1908): 646-59. RG. Curriculum.

647. "History of Education in Ireland." North British Review (1871): 479. PI. History of Education.

648. Hitchcock, A. M. "Composition on Red Ink." English Journal 1 (May 1912): 273-7. II. Evaluating Writing.

649. Hitchcock, A. M. "Economy in Teaching Composition." Education 24 (February 1904): 348-55. RG.

650. Hitchcock, A. N. "Teaching." Education (1904): 348. PI.

651. Hodgson, E. "Orientation in English Composition." English Journal 3 (April 1914): 233-7. II.

652. Hollister, H. A. "Oral Composition in the Secondary School." English Journal 1 (October 1912): 497-501. II. Speech.

653. Hollister, R. D. T. "Common Faults in College Orations." Quarterly Journal of Speech Education 4 (May 1918): 311-23. RG. Speech.

654. Holzer, G. "Elementary English Grammar." School Review 12 (December 1904): 823-5. RG. Grammar.

655. Hooker, B. R. "Use of Literary Material in Teaching

Composition." School Review 70 (June 1902): 474-85. RG, PI, AK. Literature and Composition.

656. Hooper, C. L. "Existing Conditions." School Review 15 (April 1907): 261-74. RG.

657. Hooper, C. L. "Influence of the Study of Latin on the Student's Knowledge of English Grammar." English Journal 1 (September 1912): 393-404. II. Grammar.

658. Hopkins, E. M. "Can Good Composition Teaching be Done Under Present Conditions?" English Journal 1 (January 1912): 1-8. II. Curriculum.

659. Hopkins, E. M. "Cost and Labor of English Teaching." National Education Association (1915): 114-19. RG. Curriculum.

660. Hopkins, E. M. "Present Status of the English Teacher." Journal of Education 77 (February 1913): 178-9. II. Curriculum.

661. Hopkins, E. M. "Should English Teachers Teach?" Education 42 (September 1921): 12-18. RG.

662. Hopkins, E. M. "Wanted: A Bureau of Definition." English Journal 6 (March 1917): 131-45. II.

663. Hopplin, J. M. "Theory and Method of Preaching." New Englander 35 (1876): 311. CLPI. Sermons.

664. Horn, C. H. "(Reply) English Composition in the High School." School Review 7 (May 1899): 309-11. RG. Curriculum.

665. Hosic, J. F. "Advance Movement of Teachers of English." Education 34 (October 1913): 99-103. RG.

666. Hosic, J. F. "Advance Movement of Teachers of English." National Education Association (1913): 91-4. RG.

667. Hosic, J. F. "Committee on College-Entrance Requirements in English." National Education Association (1912): 707-13. RG. Curriculum.

668. Hosic, J. F. "Co-operation of All Departments in the Teaching of English Composition." School Review 21 (November 1913): 598-607. RG, AK. Curriculum.

669. Hosic, J. F. "Effective Ways of Securing Co-Operation of All Departments in the Teaching of English Composition." National Education Association (1913): 478-85. RG. Curriculum.

670. Hosic, J. F. "English in the Normal School." School and Society 5 (May 1917): 571-6. RG. Teacher Training

671. Hosic, J. F. "Essentials of Composition and Grammar." School and Society 1 (April 1915): 581-7. RG. Grammar.

672. Hosic, J. F. "Reorganization of English in Secondary Schools." U.S. Bureau of Education Bulletin 2 (1917): 1-181. RG. Curriculum.

673. Hosic, J. F. "Reorganization of English in Secondary Schools." Journal of Education 78 (August 1913): 181. II. Curriculum.

674. Hosic, J. F. "Separation of the Teaching of Literature and the Teaching of Composition in High School." Journal of Education 80 (December 1914): 656-7. II. Literature and Composition.

675. Hosic, J. F. "Some Recent Books in the Field of English." School and Society 3 (May 1916): 785-91. RG.

676. Hosic, J. F. "Waster in Education." Journal of Education 8 (July 1914): 69. II.

677. Hosmer, J. K. "Perspicuity the Prime Requisite of Style." Western (1878): 223. PI. Style.

678. House, R. T. "School Essays and Yellowbacks." School Review 20 (February 1912): 117-20. RG.

679. Houston, G. D. "Formal English Grammar: Its Uses and Abuses." Education 35 (April 1915): 447-88. RG. Grammar.

680. Howland, F. L. M. "Children and Good English." Outlook 56 (August 1897): 943-6. RG. Error.

681. Hudelson, E. "Rocking the Boat." English Journal 3 (February 1919): 122-3. II.

682. Hudelson, E. "Standard for the Measurement of English Composition in the Bloomington, Indiana Schools." English Journal 5 (November 1916): 590-7. II. Evaluating Writing.

683. Huling, R. G. "How English is Taught in One High School." National Education Association Proceedings 30 (1891): 632-40. RG. Curriculum.

684. Humphreys, E. B. "English Language." National Quarterly Review (1860): 401. PI.

685. Hunt, L. R. "Binghamton Conference of Principals of Secondary Schools to Confer Upon Work in English." School Review 1 (May 1893): 296-300. RG. Curriculum.

686. Hunt, T. W. "Rhetorical Science." The Presbyterian Quarterly and Princeton Review 3 (1874): 660-78. AK. Rhetoric.

687. Hunt, T. W. "Study and Teaching of English Language." Presbyterian Quarterly (1876): 535. PI. Teaching Methods.

688. Hunt, T. W. "The Study of English in American Colleges." Educational Review 12 (1896): 140-50. AK. Curriculum.

689. Hurlbut, B. S. "College Requirements in English Language." Academy (nd): 257. PI. Curriculum.

690. Hurlbut, B. S. "The Preparatory Work in English as Seen by a Harvard Examiner." Academy 6 (1891): 351-53. AK. Curriculum.

691. Illinois Association of Teachers of English. " Report on the Experiment in English Composition." The Illinois Association of English 1 (1914). HEW. Curriculum.

692. "Illinois Experiment." English Journal 3 (April 1914): 250-1. II. Curriculum.

693. Illinois State Teachers College, Macomb. "English in the Grades." The Military Tract Normal School Quarterly 10 (June 1911). HEW.

694. "Influence of the Uniform Entrance Requirements in English." English Journal 1 (February 1912): 95-121. II. Curriculum.

695. "Innovations in Style." Southern Literacy Messenger (1838): 322. PI. Style.

696. "Interim Report on the Teaching of English." School and Society 7 (June 1918): 679-80. RG. Curriculum.

697. Isaacs, A. S. "Literature and Language-Study." Education 27 (February 1907): 347-52. RG. Literature and Composition.

698. Ising, H. E. "Improving the Child's English." Journal of Education 72 (September 1910): 243-4. II.

699. Jackson, O. E. "Raw Material of Rhetoric." North American Review (1888): 467. PI. Rhetoric.

700. James, Henry. "The English Language." Booklover's Magazine (1905): 199. PI.

701. Jennings, F. H. "Elementary English and the High School." Educational Review 58 (June 1919): 8-14. RG. Curriculum.

702. Jervis, L. "Similitudes. " Westminster Review 154 (September 1900): 334-44. RG.

703. Jespersen, O. "Modern English Grammar." School Review 18 (October 1910): 530-40. RG. Grammar.

704. Jewell, F. S. "Art of Preaching and Study of Philosophy." Church Review (1888): 16. PI. Sermons.

705. Jewell, J. R. "Teaching of English in Secondary

Schools." School and Society 4 (November 1916): 731-5. RG. Curriculum.

706. "John S. Hart, Principal of the Philadelphia High School." American Journal of Education (1858): 91-106. AK.

707. Johnson, A. E. "Development of Education in New England." Andover Review (1890): 383. PI. History of Education.

708. Johnson, B. "Grammar, the Bane of Boyhood." Harper's Monthly 134 (December 1916): 122-7. RG. Grammar.

709. Johnson, B. "Well of English, and the Bucket." Century 90 (June 1915): 298-304. RG.

710. Johnson, E. H. "Use of English in Science Courses." School Science and Math 20 (January 1920): 14-19. II. Technical English.

711. Johnson, E. S. "Experiment in Teaching English." School Review 10 (November 1902): 666-74. RG. Curriculum.

712. Johnson, F. W. "Hillegas-Thorndike Scale for Measurement of Quality in English Composition by Young People." School Review 21 (January 1913): 39-49. RG. Evaluating Writing.

713. Johnson, H. C. "English Language; It's New Importance and Universality." National Education Association (1919): 606-9. RG.

714. Johnson, L. "Preaching During the Renaissance." Catholic World (1902): 334. PI. Sermons.

715. Johnson, M. E. "Helping Men to Help Themselves; Extension Course in English for Foreigners." English Journal 6 (November 1917): 613-14. II. TESOL.

716. Johnson, R. I. "Persistency of Error in English Composition." School Review 25 (October 1917): 555-80. RG. Error.

717. Johnson, R. I. "Value of a Mistake." English Journal 4 (May 1915): 311-14. II.

718. Johnson, W. H. "Deterioration of College English." Dial 22 (May 1897): 271-2. RG. Curriculum.

719. Johnson, W. H. "Deterioration of English Language." Dial (1897): 271. PI.

720. Johnson, W. H. "Taste vs. Rule in English Language." Nation (1906): 455. PI. Error.

721. Johnston, L. "Art of Preaching in Medieval Times." Catholic World (1902): 210. PI. Sermons.

722. Jones, A. L. "Dictionary in School." Education 80 (December 1914): 581-2. II.

723. Jones, L. H. "English Language and Composition." Education 71 (January 1910): 68-9. II.

724. Jones, R. "What The Colleges Want: College Entrance English." National Education Association Proceedings 36 (1897): 684-94. RG. Curriculum.

725. Joy, F. L. "Gleanings from the Class in Freshman English." English Journal 9 (April 1920): 201-9. II.

726. Kavana, R. M. "Constructive Side of English Study." School Review 10 (April 1902): 298-303. RG.

727. Kayfetz, I. "Critical Study of the Harvard-Newton Composition Scales." Pedagogical Seminary 23 (September 1916): 325-47. II. Evaluating Writing.

728. Kayfetz, I. "Critical Study of the Hillegas Composition Scale." Pedagogical Seminary 21 (December 1914): 559-77. II, HEW. Evaluating Writing.

729. Keary, C. F. "Style." Independent Review (1905): 363. PI. Style.

730. Keary, C. F. "Style." Eclectic Magazine (1905): 393. PI. Style.

731. Keary, C. F. "Style." Living Age (1905): 149. PI. Style.

732. Kelley, J. P. "Writing Good English." Nation 95 (August 1912): 123. RG. Style.

733. Kellogg, B. "On Teaching English." School Review 1 (February-March 1893): 96-105, 152-62. RG, AK. Teaching Methods.

734. Kellogg, M. D. "Study in Style." Education 21 (September 1900): 50-3. RG, PI. Style.

735. Kelly, F. F. "More About Speeding-Up." Bookman 43 (April 1916): 139-43. RG.

736. Kent, W. "Teaching of English Composition." Science ns 37 (June 1913): 942-3. RG. Composition.

737. Keyes, R. K. "Felicia, an Experiment in Descriptive Writing." English Journal 6 (November 1917): 615-19. II.

738. Keyes, R. K. "Literature and Composition for Commercial Pupils." English Journal 8 (February 1919): 81-9. II. Business English.

739. Keyser, R. S. "Some Misconceptions Regarding English Work." English Journal 4 (October 1915): 413-22. II.

740. Kiehle, D. L. "History of Education: What It Stands For." School Review (1901): 310. PI. History of Education.

741. Kingsbury, A. B. "Changes in Spoken English Language." New Science Review (1895): 428. PI.

742. Kingsley, M. E. "Examination Outline for English Work: Fourth Year in the High School." Education 36 (November 1915): 163-7. RG. Curriculum.

743. Kingsley, M. E. "Examination Outline for Language Work." Education 35 (December 1914; February - April 1915): 248-52, 366-70, 450-2, 511-15. RG.

Curriculum.

744. Kingsley, M. E. "Reorganization of English in Secondary Schools." Education 38 (February 1918): 478-82. RG. Curriculum.

745. Kingsley, M. E. "Rhetorical Programs for a Reading and Study Course in the Grammar Grades." Education 30 (September, November 1909): 52-5, 184-7. RG. Curriculum.

746. Kirby, T. J. "Grammar Test." School and Society 11 (June 1920): 714-19. RG. Grammar.

747. Kirchwey, M. F. "Language; Grade VI." Teachers College Record 8 (May 1907): 176-81. II.

748. Kirkpatrick, E. "Historical Development of Higher Education." Barnard's American Journal of Education (1877): 459. PI. History of Education.

749. Kirkus, W. "Preaching." New World (1902): 26. PI. Sermons.

750. Kittredge, G. L. "Ramsey's English Language and English Grammar." Nation (1892): 13. PI. Grammar.

751. Klapaper, P. "Teaching of English." English Journal 4 (October 1915): 548-50. II. Curriculum.

752. Knowlton, E. C. "Problem of Technical Composition." English Journal 6 (March 1917): 179-82. II. Technical English.

753. Knowlton, S. B. "Reaction in the Study of English." School Review 4 (November 1896): 682-6. RG, PI.

754. Krapp, G. P. "Modern English: It's Growth and Present Use (Review)." Forum 42 (September 1909): 277-82. RG.

755. Krapp, G. P. "Writing as a Fine Art." Forum 41 (March 1909): 234-41. RG.

756. Kurtz, B. "How to Preach." Evangelical Review

(1850): 524. PI. Sermons.

757. La Rue, D. W. "Philosophy of the Elementary Language Course." Education 30 (October 1909): 74-83. RG. Curriculum.

758. Lally, E. M. "Type Study in English Composition." Elementary School Journal 16 (May 1916): 469-74. RG.

759. Lamb, L. A. "A Standard Newspaper Style." Writer (1889): 13. PI. Style.

760. Lambuth, D. "Thinking on the Third Rail." Independent 87 (August 1916): 230. RG.

761. Lang, H. R. "Lost Motion in the Teaching of English." English Journal 3, 4 (December 1914; February 1915): 631-43, 99-112. II. Curriculum.

762. Lang, S. E. "Modern Teaching of Grammar." Educational Review 20 (October 1900): 294-302. RG, PI. Grammar.

763. "Language and Grammar." London Quarterly Review 2 (1859): 387. CLPI. Grammar.

764. "Language as an Asset for Our Foreign Born Citizens." Survey 22 (August 1909): 677-9. RG. TESOL.

765. Lathrop, H. B. "Unity, Coherence, and Emphasis." Univ. of Wisconsin Studies in Language and Literature 2 (1918): 77-98. AK. Rhetoric.

766. Laurie, S. S. "History of Early Education." School Review (1893): 263, 668. PI. History of Education.

767. Law, R. A. "New English Requirements." Nation 94 (May 1912): 461-2. RG. Curriculum.

768. Lawrence, I. "Children's Humor." English Journal 4 (October 1915): 508-12. II.

769. "Laws of Persuasion." Christian Review (1841): 30. PI. Modes.

770. Lawton, C. E. "Relations Between Grammar Schools and

High Schools." <u>Education</u> (1906): 103. PI. Curriculum.

771. Leacock, S. "English as She Is Taught." <u>Harper's Weekly</u> 62 (February 1916): 203. RG.

772. Leavitt, F. M. and E. Brown. "English for Prevocational Boys." <u>Elementary School Journal</u> 16 (September-October 1915): 22-31. RG. Business English.

773. Leddell, M. H. "English Historical Grammar." <u>Atlantic</u> 82 (July 1898): 98-107. RG. Grammar.

774. Ledwith, W. L. "The Imagination in Preaching." <u>Presbyterian and Reformed Review</u> (1901): 284. PI. Sermons.

775. Lee, H. A. "Student Newspaper Work." <u>English Journal</u> 5 (March 1916): 164-71. II.

776. Lee, J. M. "Has College English Improved?" <u>Dial</u> 31 (August 1901): 99. RG. Error.

777. Leggs, A. O. "Style." <u>Manchester Quarterly</u> (1882): 37. PI. Style.

778. Leighton, W. L. "Hints on Improving Instruction in English Composition." <u>Education</u> 32 (June 1912): 620-3. RG. Teaching Methods.

779. Leiper, M. A. "Teaching Language Through Agriculture and Domestic Science." <u>U. S. Bureau of Education Bulletin</u> (1819): 121-30. RG. Technical English.

780. Leonard, A. W. "Report of the Proceedings of the National Conference on Uniform Entrance Requirements in English." <u>English Journal</u> 1 (May 1912): 294-301. II. Curriculum.

781. Leonard, M. H. "English Future." <u>Journal of Education</u> 70 (November-December 1909): 543-4, 572. II.

782. Leonard, S. A. "As to the Forms of Discourse." <u>English Journal</u> 3 (April 1914): 201-11. II. Modes.

783. Leonard, S. A. "Correction and Criticism of Composition Work." English Journal 5 (November 1916): 598-604. II. Evaluating Writing.

784. Leonard, S. A. "In Praise of Prevision." English Journal 4 (October 1915): 500-7. II. Composition.

785. Leonard, S. A. "Old Purist Junk." English Journal 7 (May 1918): 295-302. II.

786. Leonard, S. A. "On Setting Up Composition Targets." English Journal 8 (September 1919): 401-11. II. Teaching Methods.

787. Leonard, S. A. "Two Types of Criticism for Composition Work." English Journal 5 (September 1916): 508-9. II. Evaluating Writing.

788. Lewis, C. L. "Neglected Side of English." English Journal 3 (May 1914): 282-9. II.

789. Lewis, E. H. "Hart on English Composition." School Review (1896): 105. PI. Composition.

790. Lewis, E. H. "Spalding on Problem of Elementary Composition." School Review (1897): 48. PI. Composition.

791. Lewis, F. W. "High School Course in English." Education 20 (January 1900): 277-83. RG. Curriculum.

792. Lewis, H. P. and Others. "Textbooks in Rhetoric and in Composition." School Review 14 (1906): 1-33. AK. Rhetoric.

793. Lewis, W. D. "Teaching of English." Outlook 94 (March 1910): 631-3. RG.

794. Lewis, W. D. "Test We Must Meet." English Journal 2 (September 1913): 417-21. II.

795. Liddell, M. H. "On the Teaching of English." Atlantic 81 (April 1898): 465-73. RG. Teaching Methods.

796. Liddell, M. H. "Teaching of English Language."

Atlantic Monthly (1898): 465. PI. Teaching Methods.

797. Lindsay, J. W. "English Language." Christian Review (1854): 529. PI.

798. Lindsay, J. W. "English Language." Eclectic Magazine (1850): 232. PI.

799. Lindsay, J. W. "English Language." Knickerbocker Magazine (1840): 89, 212. PI.

800. Lindsay, J. W. "English Language." London Quarterly (1867): 269. PI.

801. Lindsay, J. W. "English Language." Methodist Magazine (1821): 743. PI.

802. Lindsay, J. W. "English Language." Methodist Quarterly (1844): 543. PI.

803. Lindsay, J. W. "English Language." Methodist Quarterly (1861): 254. PI.

804. Lindsay, J. W. "English Language." North British Review (1850): 373. PI.

805. Lindsay, J. W. "English Language." Southern Literary Messenger (1837): 766. PI.

806. Linn, J. W. "Composition and Theory." New Republic 10 (March 1917): 194-6. RG. Composition.

807. Linn, J. W. "Random Thoughts of a Teacher of English. Univer. of Chicago M. 1 (May 1909): 285-91. RG.

808. Liscomb, W. S. "Shall and Will." Education 12 (March 1892): 413-22. RG. Grammar.

809. "Literary Style." Academy (1902): 23. PI. Style.

810. "Literature in the Grades." Journal of Education 78 (October 1913): 430-1. II. Literature.

811. Littell, P. "Teaching Children to Write English (Books and Things)." New Republic 3 (May 1915): 74. RG. Teaching Methods.

812. Lloyd, R. J. "English Language: Can It Be Preserved?" Westminster Review (1898): 286. PI. Grammar.

813. Locke, G. H. "Place of the Modern Languages in Secondary Education." School Review 11 (March 1903): 227-8. RG. Curriculum.

814. Lodge, M. "Composition as a Means of Cultivating Literary Appreciation." English Journal 1 (May 1912): 287-93. II. Literature and Composition.

815. Logan, J. D. "American Prose Style." Atlantic 87 (May 1901): 689-96. RG. Style.

816. Logan, J. D. "Postulates of a Psychology of Prose Style." Education 22 (December 1901): 193-201. RG. Style.

817. Logan, J. D. "Psychology of Prose Style." Education 22 (December 1901): 193-201. RG. Style.

818. Long, P. W. "Grades That Explain Themselves." English Journal 2 (October 1913): 488-93. II. Evaluating Writing.

819. Lounsbury, T. R. "Compulsory Composition in Colleges." Harper's Monthly 123 (November 1911): 866-80. RG, AK. Curriculum.

820. Lounsbury, T. R. "Correct English; Reply." Nation 93 (November 1911): 465. RG. Error.

821. Lounsbury, T. R. "Pedantic Usage." Harper's Monthly Magazine (1906): 739. PI.

822. Lounsbury, T. R. "Schoolmastering the Speech." Harper's Monthly Magazine (1906): 457. PI. Speech.

823. Lounsbury, T. R. "Standard of Usage." Harper's Monthly 111 (June 1905): 35-9. RG. Usage.

824. Lounsbury, T. R. "Uncertainties of Usage." Harper's Monthly Magazine (1905): 429. PI. Usage.

825. Lowell, D. O. S. "English in Secondary Schools." School Review 10 (May 1902): 351-63. RG. Curriculum.

826. Lyman, R. L. "Fluency, Accuracy, and General Excellence in English Composition." School Review 26 (February 1918): 85-10. RG. Composition.

827. Lyon, L. S. "Business-English Situation in the Secondary Schools." English Journal 7 (November 1918): 576-87. II. Business English.

828. Lyons, M. C. "My Experience With Business English." English Journal 2 (May 1913): 312-7. II. Business English.

829. Mackay, C. "Ascertainment of English Language." Nineteenth Century (1890): 131. PI. Grammar.

830. Mackay, C. "Ascertainment of English Language." Eclectic Magazine (1890): 267. PI. Grammar.

831. Mackay, C. "Ascertainment of English Language." Living Age (1890): 451. PI. Grammar.

832. MacMahon, K. "Hands Across the Sea." English Journal 7 (December 1918): 652-4. II.

833. MacMinn, G. R. "Pains and Palliatives in Teaching English Composition." Sewanee Review 26 (July 1918): 301-12. II. Composition.

834. Magee, H. B. "Inspiration in Freshman Composition." English Journal 7 (May 1918): 313-21. II. Composition.

835. Magee, H. B. "On the Value of Journal and Letter Writing as an Introduction to a Freshman Course in Exposition Writing." English Journal 8 (September 1919): 429-32. II. Teaching Methods.

836. Magee, H. B. "Prescribed English in College." Educational Review 45 (1913): 95-97. AK.

Curriculum.

837. Magoun, H. W. "Split Infinitive and Other Idioms." Bibliotheca Sacra 76 (January 1919): 61-83. II. Grammar.

838. Mahin, H. O. "Composition in the Open." English Journal 6 (February 1917): 103-7. II. Composition.

839. Mahin, H. O. "Study of English Composition as a Means to Fuller Living." English Journal 4 (September 1915): 445-50. II. Composition.

840. Mahoney, J. J. "Economy of Time in English." School and Society 2 (July 1915): 96-8. RG.

841. Mahy, M. C. "Differentiation of English Classes in the High School." Education 36 (May 1916): 575-80. RG. Curriculum.

842. "Making of English." Outlook 79 (April 1905): 1054-6. RG.

843. Manchester, F. A. "Freshman English Once More." English Journal 6 (May-June 1917): 295-307, 384-98. II.

844. Manchester, O. L. and Manchester, H. H. "What Modern Philology Offers Secondary Education." Educational Review 16 (1898): 262-74. AK. Grammar.

845. Manley, M. M. "English Problem and the Junior High School." Education 38 (December 1917): 208-14. RG. Curriculum.

846. Manson, E. "Art of Rhetoric." Westminster Review 148 (December 1897): 630-44. RG, CLPI, PI. Rhetoric.

847. Marble, A. P. "Study of English in the Public Schools." National Education Association Proceedings 33 (1894): 279-94. RG. Curriculum.

848. Marble, A. P. "Study of English in the Public Schools." School Review 1 (April 1893): 198-209. RG. Curriculum.

849. Marble, A. P. "Teaching Effective Use of English Language." Educational Review (1892): 22. PI. Usage.

850. March, F. A. "The Study of Anglo-Saxon." Report of the Commissioners of Education (1876-77): 475-79. AK. Curriculum.

851. Maris, F. "Shall the Teaching of English Be Commercialized?" Educational Review 58 (June 1919): 70-2. RG.

852. Mason, H. M. "Problem of Grammar." Western (1876): 352. PI. Grammar.

853. Masters, L. "Philosophy of Description." Writer (1889): 226. PI. Modes.

854. Mather, F. J. "A Wanted Style for the Times." Nation (1902): 185. PI. Style.

855. Mather, F. J. "Lafcadio Hearn on Style." Nation (1906): 478. PI. Style.

856. Mathewson, F. E. "English Composition for Industrial Pupils in the William L. Dickinson High School of Jersey City." Vocational Education 3 (January 1914): 173-85. II. Technical English.

857. Matthews, B. "Development of English Language." Munsey's Magazine (1904): 695. PI.

858. Matthews, B. "English Language in America." Scribner's Magazine 29 (March 1901): 360-9. RG.

859. Matthews, B. "Foreign Words in English Language." Harper's Monthly Magazine (1903): 476. PI.

860. Matthews, B. "Future of English Language." Munsey's Magazine (1899): 100. PI.

861. Matthews, B. "Persuasion and Controversy." Outlook (1906): 86. PI.

862. Matthews, B. "Several Ways of Telling a Story." Bookman 52 (January 1921): 290-8. RG.

863. Matthews, B. "Style from Several Angles." Outlook 128 (June 1921): 383-4. RG. Style.

864. Matthews, B. "Writing English." Independent 66 (March 1909): 579-80. RG.

865. Maxwell, W. H. "An Experiment in Correcting School Compositions." Educational Review (1894): 240. PI. Evaluating Writing.

866. Maxwell, W. H. "Curriculum of Grammar School." Educational Review (1892): 472. PI. Curriculum.

867. Maxwell, W. H. "English Grammar." National Education Association (1915): 565-73. RG. Grammar.

868. Maxwell, W. H. "Experiment in Correcting Compositions (abstract)." School Review 2 (September 1894): 450-1. RG. Evaluating Writing.

869. May, M. C. "Need for English Study By Kindergarten Students." National Education Association (1902): 425-9. RG. Curriculum.

870. McCarty, L. S. "Game of Correct English." English Journal 7 (November 1918): 588-91. II. Error.

871. McCaslin, D. "Our Rhetoric Slave." English Journal 5 (March 1916): 209-11. II. Rhetoric.

872. McClure, J. "High Priest and the Heretic." English Journal 7 (October 1918): 521-5. II.

873. McComb, E. H. K. "Separation of the Teaching of Composition from the Teaching of Literature." English Journal 6 (February 1917): 69-79. II. Literature and Composition.

874. McComb, E. H. K. "Social Motives for Composition." English Journal 3 (September 1914): 408-15. II. Composition.

875. McCoy, M. L. "Local Color." English Journal 7 (May 1918): 331-3. II.

876. McCrosky, C. B. "Administration of English in the High-School Curriculum." English Journal 7

(February 1918): 108-17. II. Curriculum.

877. McDonald, L. H. "Method in Assigning Theme Subjects." English Journal 6 (November 1917): 69-12. II. Teaching Methods.

878. McDonald, L. H. "Preparation for Assignment of Composition Subjects." English Journal 5 (April 1916): 233-6. II. Teaching Methods.

879. McElroy, J. G. R. "English in Secondary Schools." Academy 4 (1889): 244-55. AK. Curriculum.

880. McElroy, J. G. R. "English Language Grammar and Composition." Penn Monthly (1870): 882. PI. Composition.

881. McIlvaine, J. H. "Introduction to a New System of Rhetoric." Princeton Review (1871): 483. PI. Rhetoric.

882. McIntyre, C. F. "Out of the Mouths of Freshmen." English Journal 9 (February 1920): 96-102. II.

883. McIntyre, H. I. "Giving a Purpose to Students of High-School English." English Journal 6 (October 1917): 539-41. II. Teaching Methods.

884. McKee, M. F. "Three Examples of Motivation." English Journal 9 (October 1920): 457-62. II. Teaching Methods.

885. McKee, R. H. "Ancient vs. Modern Languages as a Preparation for English." Pedagogical Seminary 20 (March 1913): 45-7. II.

886. McKinney, I. "Motives for Composition Work in the Upper Elementary Grades." English Journal 2 (May 1913): 299-34. II. Teaching Methods.

887. McKitrick, M. "Adaptation of the Work in English to the Actual Needs and Interests of the Pupils." English Journal 2 (September 1913): 405-16. II. Teaching Methods.

888. McLaughlin, M. "English in Relation to Other Studies." Nation 86 (June 1908): 509-10. RG.

Curriculum.

889. McLaughlin, M. "Formal and Functional Grammar." English Journal 8 (October 1919): 50-2. II. Grammar.

890. McLean, L. M. "Rhetoric in Secondary Schools." Education (1898): 158. PI. Rhetoric.

891. McNary, S. J. "Few Reasons Why High-School Graduates Fall Short of Reasonable Requirements." English Journal 1 (June 1912): 351-8. II. Curriculum.

892. Mead, W. E. "Conflicting Ideals in Teaching English." Educational Review 25 (March 1903): 275-88. RG, PI. Curriculum.

893. Mead, W. E. "The Undergraduate Study of English Composition." Publications of the Modern Language Association 17 (ns 10) (1902): x-xxiv. AK. Curriculum.

894. Mead, W. E. "Undergraduate Study of English Composition." School Review 10 (May 1902): 317-31. RG, AK. Curriculum.

895. "Mechanics of Writing." English Journal 8 (February 1919): 105-21. II. Grammar.

896. "Melody in Speech." Longman's Magazine 9 (1886-7). CSIGP. Speech.

897. Mendenhall, T. C. "Characteristic Curves of Composition." Popular Science Monthly 65 (August 1904): 373-7. RG. Composition.

898. Merriam, H. G. "Inhibitions, Habits, and the Student's Right of Way." English Journal 7 (September 1918): 419-27. II.

899. Merrill, J. B. "Language Hint to Mothers." Kindergarten Primary Magazine 27 (December 1914): 115-6. II.

900. Merwin, H. C. "Style in Judicial Opinions." Green Bay (1897): 521. PI. Style.

901. Merwin, H. C. "Style in Judicial Opinions." Green Bay (1898): 7. PI. Style.

902. "Method and Delivery in Preaching." Christian Observer (1836): 289, 367. PI. Sermons.

903. Milburn, J. B. "Medieval Grammar Schools." Dublin Review (1899): 153. PI. History of Education.

904. Miles, D. "Composition as a Training in Thought." English Journal 2 (June 1913): 362-5. II. Composition.

905. Miles, D. "Supervision of English Teaching." English Journal 7 (April 1918): 229-36. II. Teacher Training.

906. Miller, E. L. "Description: How to Describe Effectively." Writer (1889): 32. PI. Modes.

907. Miller, E. L. "Rebuilding an English Course." National Education Association (1910): 483-7. RG. Curriculum.

908. Miller, E. L. "Separating Composition from Literature in the High School (With Discussion)." English Journal 3 (October 1914): 500-15. II. Literature and Composition.

909. Miller, E. L. "Separation of Literature and Composition." Journal of Education 80 (August 1914): 131. II. Literature and Composition.

910. Miller, E. L. "Subjects for Compositions: Shall We Draw Them from Literature or from Life?" National Education Association Proceedings 37 (1898): 696-700. RG. Literature and Composition.

911. Miller, E. L. "Week's Work in English." English Journal 1 (March 1912): 156-60. II.

912. Miller, R. D. "Coordination and the Comma." Publications of the Modern Language Association 2 (June 1908): 316-28. RG. Grammar.

913. Miller, R. D. "Teachers of English." Nation 94 (March 1912): 260. RG.

914. Miller, R. D. "Teaching of English." Nation 90 (March 1910): 208. RG. Teaching Methods.

915. Mills, L. J. "Bowling with Grammar." English Journal 9 (April 1920): 227-9. II. Teaching Methods.

916. Minnesota University. "An Investigation into the Amount of Improvement in the Ability to Write English Composition, 1918-1919. Bulletin 225 (February 1919). HEW. Evaluating Writing.

917. Minto, W. "Practical Talks on Writing English." Chautauquan (1891): 561. PI. Compostion.

918. Minto, W. "Practical Talks on Writing English." Chautauquan (1891): 6-273. PI. Composition.

919. Mitchell, M. A. G. "Wanted: A Higher Standard of Speech." English Journal 1 (May 1912): 284-6. II. Error.

920. Mitchill, T. C. "High School Courses in English." Educational Review 46 (November 1913): 387-9. RG. Curriculum.

921. "Modern Grammar." Spectator (1890): 622,692. PI. Grammar.

922. "Modern Preaching as an Art and an Influence." Dublin University Magazine 61 (1863): 131. CLPI. Sermons.

923. Moe, M. W. "Amateur Journalism and the English Teacher." English Journal 4 (February 1915): 113-15. II. Journalism.

924. Moffattt, J. H. "Boys in Composition." School Review 11 (October 1903): 636-46. RG, PI. Composition.

925. Monro, K. M. "Blackboard Work and the Card System." English Journal 7 (September 1918): 460-4. II. Teaching Methods.

926. Montmorency, J. E. G. de. "Future of the English

Language." Contemporary Review 100 (August 1911): 277-82. RG.

927. "Mood In Language." Bibliotheca Sacra 4 (1847): 68. CLPI.

928. Moon, G. W. "Common Errors in Speaking and Writing." Royal Soc. of Lit. Trans. 2 s. 11 (1878): 152. CLPI. Error.

929. Moore, E. C. "History of Education." School Review (1903): 350. PI. History of Education.

930. Moore, M. C. "Simple Grammar in Grades V and VI." School Review (1903): 771. PI. Grammar.

931. Moore, M. C. and P. Horne. "Report on Causes of Study in English for Public Schools." School Review 11 (November 1903): 746-76. RG. Curriculum.

932. Moore, S. "Robert Mannying's Use of Do as Auxiliary." Modern Language Notes 33 (November 1918): 385-93. II. Grammar.

933. Moran, M. L. "Teaching English to All." Kindergarten and First Grade 5 (January 1920): 21-3. II.

934. Moritz, R. E. "Characteristic Curves of Composition." Popular Science Monthly (1904): 132. PI.

935. Moritz, R. E. "Sherman Principles in Rhetoric." Popular Science Monthly 63 (October 1903): 534-42. RG. Rhetoric.

936. Moritz, R. E. "Significance of Characteristic Curves of Composition." Popular Science Monthly 65 (June 1904): 132-47. RG.

937. Morley, E. J. "Place of English Studies in National Life." Contemporary Review 116 (November 1919): 563-7. RG. Curriculum.

938. Morse, E. L. C. "From Grammar to High School." School Review 10 (October 1902): 620-5. RG.

Curriculum.

939. Mullen, S. M. "Baseball English." English Journal 8 (October 1919):496-9. II. Teaching Methods.

940. Mumford, A. D. "Aim of the High School Course in Composition." Education 28 (May 1908): 531-6. RG. Curriculum.

941. Munroe, H. K. "Experience with Oral Composition." English Journal 1 (June 1912): 359-63. II. Speech.

942. Myers, B. E. "Most Frequent Errors in Oral and Written English." Journal of Education 84 (November 1916): 467. II. Error.

943. "National Council of Teachers of English." English Journal 2:44-60. II.

944. Neal, R. W. "In the Book the Man." Amherst Graduates Quarterly 9 (1920): 81-82. AK.

945. "Neglect of Comparative Grammar." Classical Journal 3 (April 1903): 209-10. RG. Grammar.

946. Neilson, W. A. "What the College Has a Right to Expect of the Schools in English." School Review 16 (February 1908): 73-7. RG. Curriculum.

947. Newman, F. W. "English Language as Spoken and Written." Living Age (1878): 94. PI.

948. Newman, F. W. "English Language as Spoken and Written." Contemporary Review (1878): 689. PI.

949. Nightingale, A. F. "Discussion of Reports of Committee of Ten." National Education Association Proceedings 35 (1894): 155-60. RG. Curriculum.

950. Nisbet, J. F. "A Plea for Purer English Language." Academy (1898): 329. PI. Error.

951. Niven, F. "Note Upon Style." Bookman 51 (June 1920): 434-7. RG. Style.

952. Noble, A. B. "Preparation of College Teachers of English." English Journal 5 (December 1916):

665-70. II. Teacher Training.

953. Norris, F. A. "Incidental Teaching of English in School Shops." Manual Training 18 (September 1916): 13-15. RG. Technical English.

954. Norton, A. O. "Scope and Aims of History of Education." Educational Review (1904): 443. PI. History of Education.

955. Norton, E. L. "Psychological Basis of Grammar." Educational Review 35 (February 1908): 148-59. RG. Grammar.

956. Noyes, E. C. "Class Criticism in Teaching of English." School Review 13 (November 1905): 696-701. RG, PI. Teaching Methods.

957. Noyes, E. C. "Ideals Versus Realities in High-School English." National Education Association (1908): 653-6. RG. Curriculum.

958. Noyes, E. C. "Progress in Standardizing the Measurement of Composition." English Journal 1 (November 1912): 532-6. II. Evaluating Writing.

959. Nutter, C. R. "Subfreshmen Literary Stylists." Harvard Graduates' Magazine 15 (June 1907): 616-21. II. Style.

960. Nutting, E. "Composition as One of the Arts." English Journal 5 (December 1916): 671-9. II. Composition.

961. O'Brien, A. W. "Seed and Soil." Elementary School Teacher 5 (May 1905): 556-62. RG.

962. O'Conor, J. V. "The New Rhetoric." Catholic World (1881): 692. PI. Rhetoric.

963. Odell, R. M. "Problems in English Composition." English Journal 4 (December 1915): 647-52. II. Composition.

964. Oliver, F. E. "Conversation and Good English." Harper's Bazaar 46 (September 1912): 455. RG.

965. "On Teaching English." Fraser's Magazine 17 (1878): 18. CLPI. Teaching Methods.

966. Opdycke, J. B. "New Wine and Old Bottles." English Journal 5 (June 1916): 392-400. II.

967. Opdycke, J. B. "Reply to: Shall the Teaching of English Be Commercialized?" Educational Review 58 (September 1919): 161-6. RG.

968. Opdycke, J. B. "Teaching of Vocational English." Journal of Education 80 (September, October, November 1914): 181, 206-7, 236-7, 247-8, 466-7, 493-4, 521-2. II. Business English.

969. Opdycke, J. B. "Word for High School English." Journal of Education 79 (February 1914): 231-4. II.

970. "Oral English in Theory and Practice." English Journal 3 (September 1914): 458-60. II. Speech.

971. "Origin and Meaning of the Ancient Characters of Style." American Journal of Philology (1905): 249. PI. Style.

972. "Original Composition." Oxford Prize Essays (1836): 109. PI. Composition.

973. Orr, C. I. "Revolt and Its Consequences, Personal Experience in the Teaching of English Composition." English Journal 3 (November 1914): 546-52. II. Teaching Methods.

974. Osborne, E. "Method of Teaching English Composition to First Semester Freshmen in the High School." English Journal 7 (September 1918): 457-9. II. Teaching Methods.

975. Osgood, C. G. "American Ideals Through College English." English Journal 7 (May 1918): 344-5. II. Curriculum.

976. Osgood, C. G. "No Set Requirement of English Composition in the Freshman Year." English Journal 4 (April 1915): 231-5. II. Curriculum.

977. "Our Speech Drive." English Journal 8 (May 1919):

287-98. II. Speech.

978. Outcalt, I. E. "English Grammar in the Grades." School and Society 8 (November 1918): 650-1. RG. Grammar.

979. Outcalt, I. E. "Functional English for the Elementary School." School and Society 9 (March 1919): 328-30. RG. Grammar.

980. Owen, L. "Grammar in the Elementary Schools." Education 21 (June 1915): 85-91. RG, PI. Grammar.

981. Owen, W. B. "Educational Opportunity of High-School English." English Journal 1 (April 1912): 193-202. II.

982. Pafford, H. E. "Grading Composition." English Journal 5 (April 1916): 273-4. II. Evaluating Writing.

983. Painter, F. V. N. "What Proportion of Essay Subjects Shall Be Drawn from Literature?" National Education Association Proceedings 37 (1898): 693-6. RG. Literature and Composition.

984. Palmer, F. L. "Professor Genung's First Class at Amherst." Amherst Graduates' Quarterly 9 (1920): 82. AK.

985. Palmer, G. E. "Culture and Efficiency Through Composition." English Journal 1 (October 1912): 488-92. II. Composition.

986. Pancoast, H. S. "College Requirements in English Language." Educational Review (1892): 132. PI. Curriculum.

987. Park, E. A. Bibliotheca Sacra (1871): 566, 707. PI.

988. Park, E. A. "Rhetoric and Homiletics." Bibliotheca Sacra (1845): 12. PI. Sermons.

989. Park, E. A. "Structure of Sermon: The Text." Bibliotheca Sacra 30 (1873): 534, 697. CLPI. Sermons.

990. Parker, E. P. "Sixth-Grade English Unit: Development of the Topic Ships and Ship Building." Elementary School Journal 15 (October 1914): 82-90. RG. Teaching Methods.

991. Parker, F. E. and Parker, S. A. "Measurement of Composition in English Classes." English Journal 8 (April 1919): 23-17. II. Evaluating Writing.

992. Parker, R. G. "Teaching of Composition in Schools." American Institute of Instruction (1837): 181. PI. Curriculum.

993. Parker, S. C. "Bibliographies, Briefs, and Oral Exposition in Normal Schools." English Journal 2 (November 1913): 546-50. II. Speech.

994. Parkhill, R. P. "Vocational English." Industrial Arts Magazine 7 (August 1918): 303-4. RG. Technical English.

995. Parkinson, L. D. "Variety in Assignments for Written Composition." English Journal 7 (June 1918): 371-6. II. Teaching Methods.

996. Parmelee, E. W. "Comment on Demanding the Impossible." English Journal 5 (April 1916): 248-52. II.

997. Parsons, J. R. "Regents Work in English." School Review 1 (April 1893): 226-33. RG.

998. Pattee, G. K. "Some Neglected Models." English Journal 3 (October 1914): 463-9. II.

999. Pattee, G. K. "Unusual Course in Composition." English Journal 5 (October 1916): 549-55. II. Curriculum.

1000. Paul, H. G. "Methods of Amelioration." Nat'l Educ. Association of the United States Journal Proceedings and Addresses (1912): 755-758. HEW.

1001. Paul, H. G. "Supervising College Students' Use of English." English Journal 7 (December 1918): 648-51. II. Curriculum.

1002. Peabody, A. P. "Preaching." Chr. Exam. 33 (1843): 57. CLPI. Sermons.

1003. Peabody, A. P. "Style." Spectator (1890): 689. PI. Style.

1004. Peabody, A. P. "Style." Harvard Monthly 6 (1888): 1. PI. Style.

1005. Peabody, M. G. "Language; Grade V." Teachers College Record 8 (January 1907): 60-7. II. Curriculum.

1006. Pearson, H. C. "Is English Grammar a Practical Study?" Journal of Education 83 (Janaury 1916): 39-40. II. Grammar.

1007. Pease, C. "Distinctive Idea of Preaching." Bibliotheca Sacra 10 (1833): 366. CLPI. Sermons.

1008. Peck, H. T. "What is Good English? Review of Principles of English Grammar, by G. E. Carpenter." Bookman 7 (April 1898): 125-30. RG. Grammar.

1009. Peck, J. T. "Philosophy and Principles of Rhetoric." Universalist Quarterly Review (1863): 251. PI. Rhetoric.

1010. Peck, J. T. "Philosophy of Rhetoric." Methodist Quarterly (1843): 512. PI. Rhetoric.

1011. Pedersen, N. A. "Writing Themes for Magazines and Newspapers." Education 39 (December 1918): 217-24. RG.

1012. Pendleton, C. S. "New Teacher of English." English Journal 6 (November 1917): 575-83. II. Teacher Training.

1013. Penniman, J. H. "Study of English in School and College." School Review 1 (October 1893): 462-70. RG. Curriculum.

1014. Percival, M. "Evolution of Oral Composition." English Journal 4 (May 1915): 315-22. II. Speech.

1015. Perkins, A. F. "Difficulties in the Way of

Co-operation in English." Nation 87 (December 1908): 598-9. RG.

1016. Perkins, A. F. "Ineffective Teaching in English." Nation 85 (October 1907): 372-3. RG. Teaching Methods.

1017. Perrin, J. W. "Compulsory Beginnings in Education." Educational Review (1903): 240. PI.

1018. Perry, F. M. "Consideration of Proposed Changes in the College Entrance Requirements in English." Educational Review 39 (February 1910): 194-8. RG. Curriculum.

1019. Phelps, A. "Theory of Preaching." Bibliotheca Sacra 14 (1837): 282. CLPI. Sermons.

1020. Phillips, A. L. "Common Errors in English." Colorado State Teacher's Bulletin 17 (October 1918): HEW. Error.

1021. Phillips, J. N. "Plea for Accurate English Language." Writer (1900): 33. PI. Error.

1022. Pierce, C. S. "Ideas, Stray or Stolen, about Scientific Writing, No. 1, Edited by John Michael Krois." Philosophy and Rhetoric 11 (Summer 1978): 147-55. PS. Technical English.

1023. Pittenger, L. A. "Practice Work for Prospective Teachers of English in High Schools." English Journal 2 (April 1913): 254-5. II. Teacher Training.

1024. Pius, X. "Preaching and Popular Action." American Catholic Quarterly (1906): 744. PI. Sermons.

1025. Platt, F. J. "Alternative English III, Second Semester: A Course for Weak Juniors." English Journal 4 (September 1915): 468-70. II. Curriculum.

1026. "Plea For Greater Uniformity." Educational Review 7 (1894). CSIGP.

1027. "Pleasures of Composition." *Eclectic Review* (1811): 270, 350. PI. Composition.

1028. Plumbe, G. E. "Style in Composition." *University Quarterly* (1861): 94. PI. Style.

1029. Poland, W. "History of Education." *American Catholic Quarterly* (1902): 145. PI. History of Education.

1030. Poller, M. C. "A Stronger Foundation for and a Better Command of Spoken and Written English (A. in theElem. Sch.; B in the h.s. by J. H. Newton; C. in the Normal Schools by J. F. Hosic." *National Education Association of the U. S. Address and Proceedings* (1917): 690-707. HEW. Curriculum.

1031. Pope, E. H. "Linguistics as a Required Subject in College and in High School." *English Journal* 8 (January 1919): 28-34. II. Curriculum.

1032. Porter, B. F. "Principles of Rhetoric." *American Whig Review* (1849): 597. PI. Rhetoric.

1033. Porter, D. G. "English Language as Universal." *American Journal of Social Science* (1894): 117. PI.

1034. "Porter on Rhetorical Delivery." *United States Literary Gazette* (nd): 333. PI. Rhetoric.

1035. "Porter On Rhetorical Delivery." *American Monthly Review* (1832): 101. PI. Rhetoric.

1036. "Power to Think Straight." *Nation* 91 (October 1910): 333. RG.

1037. "Preliminary Report of the Grammar Subcommittee." *English Journal* 8 (March 1919): 179-89. II. Grammar.

1038. "Preliminary Report of the Special Committee on Freshman English." *English Journal* 7 (November 1918): 592-9. II. Curriculum.

1039. "Preparation of High-School Teachers of English, A Report of a Committee." *English Journal* 4 (May 1915): 323-32. II. Teacher Training.

1040. "Preparatory Course in English." School Review 5 (September 1897): 445-55. RG. Curriculum.

1041. "Prescribed English in College: Symposium." Educational Review 45, 46 (January-June 1913): 93-9, 187-92, 298-303, 407-9, 507-9, 46: 52-9. RG. Curriculum.

1042. Price, J. T. "Limitations of Early Education." New Church Review (1923): 21. PI.

1043. "The Property Prose Style." Academy (1899): 576. PI. Style.

1044. "Questionnaire on Material Available for Teaching English in Illinois Schools." English Journal 4 (September 1915): 475-9. II. Teaching Methods.

1045. Quiller-Couch, A. "On the Art of Writing (Reviewed by L. Gilman)." North American 204 (July 1916): 139-42. RG. Composition.

1046. Rankin, C. S. "After Pilgrim's Progress." English Journal 4 (March 1915): 196-200. II.

1047. Rankin, J. S. "Pedagogical Scrap-Iron, by a Normal-School Visitor." Elementary School Teacher 8 (January 1908): 233-43. RG.

1048. Rankin, J. S. "Weaknesses in the Teaching of English in Our Common Schools." Elementary School Teacher 7 (January 1907): 254-62. RG. Teaching Methods.

1049. Rankin, T. E. "Once More." English Journal 7 (November 1918): 570-5. II.

1050. Rapeer, L. W. "Outside of the Cup: Relative Values in High-School English." English Journal 5 (June 1916): 379-91. II.

1051. "Real Greatness of Composition." Literary World (1885): 28. PI. Composition.

1052. Reavis, W. C. "Experiment in the Teaching of High-School Composition." School Review 21 (October 1913): 538-41. RG. Curriculum.

1053. Redmond, D. W. "Study in the Correction of Dialectic English." English Journal 3 (October 1914): 480-3. II. Error.

1054. Reed, A. A. "English in the Grades." National Education Association (1904): 16-24. RG. Curriculum.

1055. "Reform in Grammatical Nomenclature in the Study of Languages; Symposium." School Review 19 (November 1911): 610-42. RG. Grammar.

1056. Reid, A. "Teaching of English in the Grades." Journal of Education 78 (December 1913): 639-40. II. Curriculum.

1057. "Rejoinder to Horn." School Review 7 (June 1899): 375-6. RG.

1058. "Reorganization of English in the Secondary Schools." School and Society 7 (January 1918): 13-14. RG. Curriculum.

1059. "Report of a Committee on Technical Grammar." Teachers College Record 12 (January 1911): 5-22. II. Grammar.

1060. "Report of the Committee on the Articulation of the Elementary Course in English with the Course in English in the High School." English Journal 3 (May 1914): 303-23. II. Curriculum.

1061. "Report of the Committee on the Preparation of College Teachers of English." English Journal 5 (January 1916): 20-32. II. Teacher Training.

1062. "Report of the Committee on Uniform Nomenclature in English Grammar." National Education Association (1913): 202-5. RG. Grammar.

1063. "Report of the Conference Committee on High School English." School Review 7 (February 1909): 85-8. RG. Curriculum.

1064. "Report of The Eighth Annual Meeting of The New England Association of College and Preparatory

Schools." School Review 1 (1893): 587-667. AK. Curriculum.

1065. "Report of the Joint Committee on Grammatical Nomenclature." National Education Association (1913): 205-8, 315-54. RG. Grammar.

1066. "Report on the Examinations in English for Admission to Harvard College." Educational Review 34 (June 1907): 97-100. RG. Testing.

1067. Reynolds, G. F. "For Minimum Standards in English." English Journal 4 (June 1915): 349-56. II. Testing.

1068. Reynolds, J. C. "Pure Speech." Christian Quarterly Review (1884): 559. PI.

1069. "Rhetoric in the College Course." Southern Literary Messenger (1849): 507. PI. Rhetoric.

1070. Ribot, T. "Evolution of Speech." Open Court (1899): 267. PI. Speech.

1071. Ribot, T. "Intermediate Forms of Speech." Open Court (1899): 349. PI. Speech.

1072. Ribot, T. "Origin of Speech." Open Court (1899): 202. PI. Speech.

1073. Rice, A. H. "One Year's Experience with Manuscript Work." School Review 11 (April 1903): 254-62. RG.

1074. Rice, J. M. "Need of a New Basis in Education." Forum 35 (January 1904): 440-57. RG. Curriculum.

1075. Rice, J. M. "The Futility of the Spelling Grind." The Forum 23 (1897): 163-72, 409-19. AK. Spelling.

1076. Richard, J. W. "Material and End of Preaching." Lutheran Quarterly Review (1887): 123. PI. Sermons.

1077. Rinaker, C. "Sentence Outlines for Exposition." English Journal 8 (December 1919): 610-16. II. Teaching Methods.

1078. Ringwalt, R. C. "Intercollegiate Debating." The Forum 22 (1897): 633-40. AK. Speech.

1079. Ripley, H. J. "Rhetorical Studies." Christian Review (1847): 369. PI. Rhetoric.

1080. Ripley, M. A. "The English Language." Education (1889): 537. PI.

1081. Robbins, I. E. "Language; Grade IV." Teachers College Record 8 (January 1907): 7-10. II. Curriculum.

1082. Roberts, A. E. "Easy Way of Correcting Compositions." Journal of Education 69 (February 1909): 158-9. II. Evaluating Writing.

1083. Robinson, A. T. "Question of Text-Books in Composition." Science ns 37 (January 1913): 60-2. RG, AK. Composition.

1084. Robinson, A. T. "Teaching of English in a Scientific School." Science ns 30 (November 1909): 657-64. RG. Technical English.

1085. Rogers, H. "History of English Language." Living Age (1851): 285. PI. Grammar.

1086. Rogers, H. "History of English Language." Edinburgh Review (1850): 293. PI. Grammar.

1087. Rogers, H. "Structure of English Language." Blackwood's (1837): 455. PI. Grammar.

1088. Rogers, H. "Structure of English Language." Edinburgh Review (1840): 221. PI. Grammar.

1089. Rogers, H. "Thoughts on Prose Composition." Good Words (1865): 453. PI. Composition.

1090. Rogers, H. "Thoughts on Prose Composition." Living Age (1865): 577. PI. Composition.

1091. "Round Table: Why College English Fails." English Journal 3 (February 1914): 118-23. II. Curriculum.

1092. Rounds, C. R. "English in the Normal School."

English Journal 3 (November 1914): 553-7. II. Curriculum.

1093. Rounds, C. R. "Uniform Terminology of Grammar." English Journal 3 (June 1914): 393-5. II. Grammar.

1094. Rounds, C. R. "Varying Systems of Nomenclature in Use in Our Texts in English Grammar." Educational Review 40 (June 1910): 82-8. RG. Grammar.

1095. Rounds, C. R. "Waste of Unlearning." English Journal 1 (April 1912): 214-20. II.

1096. Routh, J. "Method of Grading English Composition." English Journal 5 (May 1916): 341-5. II. Evaluating Writing.

1097. Routh, J. "Rhetoric in the Graduate School." South Atlantic Quarterly 14 (October 1915): 307-14. II. Rhetoric.

1098. Row, R. K. "Technical Grammar: When to Begin." Journal of Education 67 (June 1908): 691. II. Grammar.

1099. Rowsell, E. P. "How to Preach." Colburn's New Monthly Magazine (1857): 50-261. PI. Sermons.

1100. "Rules for Preaching." Christian Observer (1818): 496. PI. Sermons.

1101. "Rules for the Use of Shall and Will." Literary Digest 53 (October 1916): 1142. RG. Grammar.

1102. Rumbley, E. A. "Use for the Just-So Stories." English Journal 1 (December 1912): 642-4. II. Teaching Methods.

1103. Russell, J. E. "College Requirements in English Language." Educational Review (1892): 74. PI. Curriculum.

1104. Russell, L. M. "Experiments in Oral English in the High School." English Journal 3 (March 1914): 176-80. II. Speech.

1105. Sackett, L. W. "Comparable Measures of Composition." School and Society 5 (February 1917):233-9. RG. Evaluating Writing.

1106. Sampson, M. W. "Hart on English Composition." Dial (1896): 108. PI. Composition.

1107. Sarcey, F. "Compliments to the Grammarians." Living Age (1899): 794. PI. Grammar.

1108. Sayrs, W. C. "Standards in English." Education 37 (June 1917): 64-6. RG. Curriculum.

1109. "Schedule of English in St. Paul's School." English Journal 1 (October 1912): 505-8. II. Curriculum.

1110. Scheffield, A. D. "Rational Study of English Grammar." School Review 18 (November 1910): 618-26. RG. Grammar.

1111. Schuyler, W. "English as an Art Study." National Education Association (1904): 502-6. RG. Curriculum.

1112. "Scientific Standards in English Teaching; Report of Committee." English Journal 4 (January 1915): 28-34. II. Testing.

1113. Scott, E. H. "English Via Latin in the Grades; With Discussion." Classical Journal 11 (February 1916): 278-84. II.

1114. Scott, F. N. "Brief Catechism on Textbooks in English." Educational Review 37 (April 1909): 359-61. RG, AK. Curriculum.

1115. Scott, F. N. "College Entrance Requirements in English." Educational Review 20 (October 1900): 289-92. RG, AK. Curriculum.

1116. Scott, F. N. "College Entrance Requirements in English." School Review 9 (June 1901): 365-78. RG, AK. Curriculum.

1117. Scott, F. N. "Essay Correcting -- Can It Be Made a Joy Forever?" National Education Association Proceedings 37 (1898): 691-3. RG. Evaluating

Writing.

1118. Scott, F. N. "Our Problems." English Journal 2 (January 1913): 1-10. II.

1119. Scott, F. N. "Rhetoric Rediviva." College Composition and Communication 31 (December 1980): 413-19. PS. Rhetoric.

1120. Scott, F. N. "The Report on College-Entrance Requirements in English." Educational Review 20 (1900): 289-94. AK. Curriculum.

1121. Scott, F. N. "Training and Mistraining." English Journal 2 (September 1913): 456-8. II.

1122. Scott, F. N. "Undefended Gate." English Journal 3 (January 1914): 1-14. II.

1123. Scott, F. N. "What the West Wants in Preparatory English." School Review 17 (January 1909): 10-20. RG, AK. Curriculum.

1124. Scott, F. W. "Relation of Composition to the Rest of the Curriculum." English Journal 7 (October 1918): 512-20. II. Curriculum.

1125. Scripture, E. W. "Education as a Science." Pedagogical Seminary (1894): 111. PI.

1126. Searing, A. E. P. "Why College Graduates are Deficient in English." Educational Review 45 (1913): 407-409. AK. Curriculum.

1127. Sears, I. and Diebel, A. "Study of the Common Mistakes in Pupils' Oral English." Elementary School Journal 17 (September 1916): 44-54. RG. Error.

1128. Sedgwick, A. G. "Recent Books on Rhetoric, 1879." Nation (1879): 138. PI. Rhetoric.

1129. Sewell, J. W. "English Language." School Review (1900): 80. PI.

1130. Sewell, J. W. "Suggestions to Teachers." School Review 8 (February 1900): 80-6. RG. Teaching

     Methods.

1131. Shackford, M. H. "Partial Substitute for the Theme. <u>English Journal</u> 1 (April 1912): 208-13. II. Teaching Methods.

1132. Shackford, M. H. "Teaching Elementary English." <u>Educational Review</u> 30 (October 1905): 302-9. RG. Teaching Methods.

1133. "Shall Grammar Be Dropped?" <u>English Journal</u> 5 (May 1916): 360-1. II. Grammar.

1134. Shallies, G. W. "Waste in English." <u>Education</u> 31 (April 1911): 536-40. RG.

1135. Shaw, E. R. "Essentials of English Composition for Elementary Schools." <u>National Education Association Proceedings</u> 37 (1898): 87-94. RG. Curriculum.

1136. Shedd, W. G. T. "Fundamental Properties of Style." <u>American Presbyterian Review</u> (1864): 561. PI. Style.

1137. Shedd, W. G. T. "Relation of Style to Thought." <u>Bibliotheca Sacra</u> 8 (1851): 491. CLPI. Style.

1138. Sheffield, A. D. "Grammatical Concepts and Their Names." <u>School Review</u> 21 (March 1913): 180-6. RG. Grammar.

1139. Sheldon, E. "Oral Themes." <u>National Education Association</u> (1912): 718-21. RG. Speech.

1140. Shelley, M. E. "Concerning Mist--And a Whip." <u>English Journal</u> 3 (November 1914): 538-45. II.

1141. Shepard, L. "Prescribed English in College." <u>Educational Review</u> 46 (September 1913): 188-90. RG. Curriculum.

1142. Shepherd, H. E. "English Philosophy and English Literature in American Universities." <u>Sewanee Review</u> 1 (February 1893): 153-60. RG. Curriculum.

1143. Sheridan, B. M. "Analysis of the Common Errors in the Speech of Children." <u>Journal of Education</u> 82

(December 1915). 665-6. II. Error.

1144. Sheridan, B. M. "Language Games." <u>Journal of Education</u> 84 (November 1916): 489. II. Teaching Methods.

1145. Sheridan, B. M. "Problem of Spoken and Written English in the Elementary School." <u>Journal of Education</u> 82 (December 1915): 543-4+. II. Curriculum.

1146. Sheridan, S. S. "Speech Improvement Week in the New Haven High School." <u>English Journal</u> 5 (December 1916): 703-4. II. Error.

1147. Sherman, E. B. "Root and Foliage of Style." <u>Words to Wise and Others</u> (1907): 1-31. RG. Style.

1148. Sherman Principle in Rhetoric and Its Restrictions." <u>Popular Science Monthly</u> (1903): 534. PI. Rhetoric.

1149. Shute, K. H. "Composition." <u>Education</u> 12 (November 1891): 138-46. RG, PI. Composition.

1150. Shute, K. H. "Teaching of English in the Elementary Schools." <u>School Review</u> 10 (May 1902): 332-50. RG. Curriculum.

1151. Shute, K. H. "Teaching of the English Language." <u>Educational Review</u> 26 (November 1903): 415-20. RG. Teaching Methods.

1152. Shute, K. H. "Teaching of the English Language." <u>School Review</u> 10 (May 1902): 332-50. RG. Teaching Methods.

1153. Siebel, E. "Language-Exercise in Dramatization." <u>Elementary School Teacher</u> 9 (May 1904): 463-70. RG. Teaching Methods.

1154. "Significance of Recent Investigations in the Field of English; Symposium." <u>National Education Association</u> (1912): 747-65. RG, HEW. Curriculum.

1155. Item omitted.

1156. Simmons, P. "Coddling in English." <u>English Journal</u> 5 (December 1916): 659-64. II.

1157. Simmons, S. E. "Devices for Vitalizing Composition." English Journal 1 (December 1912): 628-37. II. Teaching Methods.

1158. Simons, S. E. "Imitative Writing in the High School." Pedagogical Seminary 17 (December 1910): 451-79. II. Teaching Methods.

1159. Skinner, T. H. "Delivery in Preaching." American Presbyterian Review (1864): 36. PI. Sermons.

1160. Slosson, P. W. "Prescribed English in College." Educational Review 45 (1913): 407-09. AK. Curriculum.

1161. Small, W. A. "Grammar School, 1700-1800." School Review (1906): 42. PI. Grammar.

1162. Small, W. A. "New England Grammar, 1635-1700." School Review (1902): 513. PI. Grammar.

1163. Smith, C. A. "Interpretive Syntax." Publications of the Modern Language Association ns 15 (1900): 97-113. RG. Grammar.

1164. Smith, E. W. "Advance Movement in English." English Journal 6 (January 1917): 12-19. II.

1165. Smith, H. P. "Check Sheet for English Composition." English Journal 6 (October 1917): 528-34. II. Teaching Methods.

1166. Smith, H. P. "Technical Points in Elementary English." Elementary School Journal 19 (September 1918): 54-68. RG. Curriculum.

1167. Smith, H. W. "Concerning Organization in Paragraphs." English Journal 9 (September 1920): 390-400. II. Paragraphs.

1168. Smith, J. F. "Report on English in Secondary Schools in England and Scotland." Educational Review 40 (October 1910): 266-92. RG. Curriculum.

1169. Smith, J. F. "Rhetorical Studies." Evangelical Review (1851): 547. PI. Rhetoric.

1170. Smith, M. E. "Those Long Themes." English Journal 5 (May 1916): 346-9. II.

1171. Smith, R. R. "English Expression in Its Relation to Teaching of Science." School Science and Math 20 (April 1920): 341-6. II. Technical English.

1172. Smith, S. C. "Poetic Triteness in Composition-Writing." English Journal 1 (November 1912): 547-51. II. Composition.

1173. Smith, S. W. "Fred Newton Scott as a Teacher." Michigan Alumnus (February 1933): 279-80. AK.

1174. Smyser, S. F. "The Lack of Scientific Work in Rhetoric." Dial 23 (1897): 141. AK. Rhetoric.

1175. Snell, A. L. F. "Freshman Composition." Nation 29 (January 1911): 9. RG. Curriculum.

1176. Snoddy, J. S. "English Composition in Elementary Schools." Education 20 (February-March 1900): 353-61, 423-30. RG. Curriculum.

1177. Snoddy, J. S. "English Grammar in Elementary Schools." Education 19 (May 1899): 522-32. RG, PI. Grammar.

1178. Snyder, F. "Use of Committees in the English Class." English Journal 9 (June 1920): 345-7. II. Teaching Methods.

1179. Snyder, F. B. "English a Once More." English Journal 9 (May 1920): 261-5. II.

1180. "Song of the English Teacher (Poem)." English Journal 7 (December 1918): 660-1. II.

1181. Sonnenschein, E. A. "Parallel Study of Grammar." Educational Review (1892): 450. PI. Grammar.

1182. Spence, A. M. "Our Inherited Bad Grammar." Poet Lore 7 (August 1895): 450-3. RG, PI. Grammar.

1183. Spencer, H. "Philosophy of Style." Eclectic Magazine (1853): 45. PI. Style.

1184. Spencer, H. "Philosophy of Style." <u>Westminster Review</u> (1852): 435. PI. Style.

1185. Spencer, H. "Philosophy of Style." <u>Writer</u> (1900): 113. PI. Style.

1186. Spencer, H. "Philosophy of Style." <u>Westminster Review</u> (1852): 435. PI. Style.

1187. Spencer, H. "Philosophy of Style." <u>Living Age</u> (1852): 401. PI. Style.

1188. Spencer, H. "Place of Grammar." <u>Facts and Comments</u> (nd): 280-91. RG. Grammar.

1189. Spencer, H. "Style." <u>Facts and Comments</u> (1902): 97-111. RG. Style.

1190. Spencer, H. "The Philosophy of Style." <u>Westminster Review</u> 114 (October 1852): 237-47. HR, PS. Style.

1191. Sperlin, O. B. "Working Plan for Conference Periods." <u>English Journal</u> 4 (November 1915): 582-5. II. Teaching Methods.

1192. Spilman, L. "Composition in the First and Second Years of High School." <u>English Journal</u> 5 (October 1916): 556-68. II. Curriculum.

1193. Squires, V. P. "English as It Is Abused." <u>Journal of Education</u> 68 (August 1908): 174-5. II. Error.

1194. St. John, C. M. "English in the Schools: A Parent's Point of View." <u>School Review</u> 1 (October 1893): 491-50. RG. Curriculum.

1195. Staley, G. L. "Elements of Preaching." <u>Mercersburg Review</u> (1869): 290. PI. Sermons.

1196. "Standards of Efficiency in the Teaching of English." <u>School Review</u> 23 (December 1915): 719-20. RG.

1197. Starch, D. and Elliott, E. C. "Reliability of the Grading of High-School Work in English." <u>School Review</u> 20 (September 1912): 442-57. RG. Testing.

1198. Stark, W. E. "Measurement of Eighth Grade

Composition." School and Society 2 (August 1915): 208-16. RG, HEW. Evaluating Writing.

1199. Stauffer, R. E. "Teacher of Composition as Literary Craftsman." English Journal 5 (April 1916): 225-32. II. Literature and Composition.

1200. Steeves, H. R. "Cultivation of Ideas in the College Writing Course." Educational Review 44 (June 1912): 45-54. RG. Curriculum.

1201. Steeves, H. R. "High-School English and College English." English Journal 6 (March 1917): 146-55. II. Curriculum.

1202. Stephens, K. "English Scheme Used in London, England." Journal of Education 72 (December 1910): 638-9. II. Curriculum.

1203. Stevens, A. A. "Question of English." Harper's Monthly 104 (January 1902): 287-91. RG.

1204. Stevens, W. L. "Co-operation in English Teaching." Nation 86 (April 1908): 303. RG.

1205. Stevenson, R. L. B. "On Style in Literature: Its Technical Elements." Contemporary Review 47 (1885): 548. CLPI. Style.

1206. Stobart, J. C. "Teaching of English." Living Age 304 (January 1920): 83-91. RG. Teaching Methods.

1207. Stoddard, H. H. "Uses of Rhetoric." Academy (1889): 395. PI. Rhetoric.

1208. Stoddard, W. E. "Comparison of the Hillegas and Harvard-Newton Scales in English Composition." Pedagogical Seminary 23 (December 1916): 498-501. II. Evaluating Writing.

1209. Stratton, C. "How Can the University Be of More Help to the Secondary School?" English Journal 1 (October 1912): 482-7. II.

1210. Straubenmuller, G. "Teaching Our Language to Non-English Speaking Pupils." National Education Association (1905): 413-21. RG. TESOL.

1211. "Stronger Foundation for, and a Better Command of, Spoken and Written English." National Education Association (1917): 690-707. RG. Curriculum.

1212. Struble, M. C. "Big Business-English Project." English Journal 9 (October 1920): 463-6. II. Business English.

1213. "Studies in Contemporary Style." Academy (1899): 379, 767. PI. Style.

1214. "Study of the English Language--Fitch's Lectures on Teaching, 1889." Macmillan's Magazine 15 (1866-7). CSIGP. Teaching Methods.

1215. "Style." Chambers's Edinburg Journal (1845): 321. PI. Style.

1216. "Style and Cleverness." Academy (1905): 685. PI. Style.

1217. "Style and Statecraft." Nation 77 (December 1903): 440-11. RG. Style.

1218. "Style in Writing." Dublin University Magazine (1865): 178. PI. Style.

1219. "Style in Writing." Dublin University Magazine (1871): 59. PI. Style.

1220. "Style of Modern Journalists." Academy (1901): 231. PI. Style.

1221. "Suggested Reforms." English Journal 8 (September 1919): 451-2. II. Curriculum.

1222. "Summary of the Forthcoming Report of the National Joint Committee on the Reorganization of High-school English." National Education Association (1916): 559-66. RG. Curriculum.

1223. Sutcliffe, E. G. "Enumerative Order." English Journal 4 (April 1915): 236-43. II.

1224. Sutcliffe, E. G. "How Shall the Crooked Be Made Straight?" English Journal 9 (December 1920):

584-7. II.

1225. Sutton, W. "Charm of Style." Irish Monthly (1884): 32. PI. Style.

1226. "Sweet's English Grammar." Athenaeum (1892): 120. PI. Grammar.

1227. Sykes, F. H. "English in Secondary Schools." School Review 14 (March 1906): 157-63. RG. Curriculum.

1228. Symmes, F. "English Teacher and the Spelling Question." School Review 13 (January 1905): 42-51. RG. Spelling.

1229. Sypherd, W. O. "English in High School and College." Delaware College Bulletins 4 (1908). HEW. Curriculum.

1230. Tafel, L. and Tafel, R. L. "Bopp's Comparative Grammar." Bibliotheca Sacra (1861): 771. PI. Grammar.

1231. Tarbell, R. W. and Metz, J. J. "English for Apprentices." Industrial Arts Magazine 7 (December 1918): 452-4. RG. Technical English.

1232. "Teachers of English." Nation 97 (November 1913): 433. RG.

1233. "Teaching English." Journal of Education 69 (February 1909): 212-13. II. Teaching Methods.

1234. "Teaching of English." Macmillan's Magazine (1818): 33. CSIGP, CLPI. Teaching Methods.

1235. "Teaching of English." Atlantic Monthly (1818): 98. CSIGP, CLPI. Teaching Methods.

1236. "Teaching of English at American Colleges and Universities." American Monthly Review of Reviews 10 (December 1894): 680. RG. Curriculum.

1237. "Teaching of English in College." Scientific American 73 (October 1895): 250. RG. Curriculum.

1238. "Teaching of English in the High Schools; Summary of

Report." School and Society 3 (June 1916): 941-5. RG. Curriculum.

1239. "Teaching of English Language." Dial (1897): 35. PI. Curriculum.

1240. "Teaching of English Language." Time (nd): 584. PI. Teaching Methods.

1241. Teaching of English Language in Preparatory Schools." Nation (1896): 364. PI. Curriculum.

1242. "Teaching of Grammar By the Sentence-Diagram." American Educational Review 13 (1897). CSIGP. Grammar.

1243. Teall, F. A. "Illogical Rhetoric." Writer (1896): 98. PI. Rhetoric.

1244. "Tendencies of Style." Edinburgh Review (1899): 356. PI. Style.

1245. Texas Department of Education. "Texas High Schools." Bulletin 83 (1918): 59-60. HEW. Curriculum.

1246. "Textbooks in Rhetoric and in Composition." School Review 14 (January 1906): 1-33. RG. Composition.

1247. Thach, C. C. "Essentials of English Composition to Be in Secondary Schools, with Discussion." National Education Association Proceedings 37 (1898): 94-103. RG. Curriculum.

1248. "Thackeray Among the Elements of Rhetoric." Bookman 36 (December 1912): 358-9. RG. Rhetoric.

1249. Thayer, W. M. "Use of English Language." Education (1893): 48. PI. Usage.

1250. "The Technique of Style." Spectator (1905): 382. PI. Style.

1251. Theisen, W. W. "Improving Teachers' Estimates of Composition Specimens with the Aid of the Traube Nassau County Scale." School and Society 7 (February 1918): 143-50. RG. Evaluating Writing.

1252. Thiergen, O. "English in the German Reform School." School Review 8 (October 1900): 441-8. RG. Curriculum.

1253. Thiergen, O. "English in the German Reform School." School Review 9 (March 1901): 150-9. RG. Curriculum.

1254. Tholuck, F. A. G. "Right Way of Preaching." Princeton Review (1870): 347. PI. Sermons.

1255. Thomas, C. E. "English for Industrial Pupils." English Journal 2 (April 1913): 241-6. II. Technical English.

1256. Thomas, C. S. "English Course in the High School: The New England View." English Journal 1 (February 1912): 84-94. II. Curriculum.

1257. Thomas, C. S. "Essential Principles in Teaching English." Education 31 (October 1910): 82-98. RG. Teaching Methods.

1258. Thomas, D. Y. "More About the Teaching of English." School and Society 5 (February 1917): 141-3. RG. Teaching Methods.

1259. Thomas, I. "English of School and College Graduates." Education 28 (June 1908): 639-45. RG.

1260. Thomas, J. M. "Do Thought-Courses Produce Thinking?" English Journal 5 (February 1916): 79-88. II. Teaching Methods.

1261. Thomas, J. M. "Inhibitory Instincts." English Journal 9 (January 1920): 1-12. II.

1262. Thomas, J. M. "Oral Composition in Its Relation to Written." English Journal 4 (October 1915): 487-99. II. Speech.

1263. Thomas, J. M. "Training for Teaching Composition in Colleges." English Journal 5 (September 1916): 447-57. II. Teacher Training.

1264. Thomas, R. W. "Hale's Constructive Rhetoric." School Review (1897): 402. PI. Rhetoric.

1265. Thompson, C. J. "Study of the Socialized Versus the Academic Method of Teaching Written Composition." School Review 27 (February 1919): 110-33. RG. Teaching Methods.

1266. Thompson, C. J. "Thought-Building in the Paragraph." English Journal 5 (November 1916): 610-19. II. Paragraphs.

1267. Thompson, R. S. "Movies and Topical Outlines." Journal of Education 82 (November 1915): 466. II. Film.

1268. Thompson, S. "Notebook System of Theme Correcting." English Journal 6 (January 1917): 28-33. II. Evaluating Writing.

1269. Thorndike, E. L. "Scale for Measuring the Merit of English Writing." Scientific American Supplement 72 (September 1911): 158-9. RG. Evaluating Writing.

1270. Thorndike, E. L. "Scale for Measuring the Merit of English Writing." Science ns 33 (June 1911): 935-8. RG. Evaluating Writing.

1271. Thorndike, E. L. "Significance and Use of the Hillegas Scale for Measuring the Quality of English Composition." English Journal 2 (November 1913): 551-61. II. Evaluating Writing.

1272. Thurber, C. H. "English as It Is Taught." School Review 6 (May 1898): 328-38. RG. Curriculum.

1273. Thurber, C. H. "English Language as It Is Taught." School Review (1898): 328. PI. Curriculum.

1274. Thurber, E. A. "College Composition." Nation 101 (September 1915): 328-9. RG. Curriculum.

1275. Thurber, E. A. "Composition in Our Colleges." English Journal 4 (January 1915): 9-14. II. Curriculum.

1276. Thurber, E. A. "English Journal as Textbook." English Journal 2 (September 1913): 445-50. II.

1277. Thurber, S. "Address to Normal School Teachers of English." School Review 8 (March 1900): 129-45. RG.

1278. Thurber, S. "Address to Teachers of English." Education 18 (May 1898): 515-26. RG, AK.

1279. Thurber, S. "Composition Topics." Academy (1891): 354, 459. PI. Composition.

1280. Thurber, S. "Conditions Needed for the Successful Teaching of English Composition." School Review 2 (January 1894): 13-21. RG, PI. Teaching Methods.

1281. Thurber, S. "English Situation." School Review 11 (March 1903): 169-86. RG.

1282. Thurber, S. "English Work in the Secondary Schools." School Review 1 (1893): 650-55. AK. Curriculum.

1283. Thurber, S. "Five Axioms of Composition Teaching." School Review 5 (January 1897): 7-17. RG, PI, AK. Teaching Methods.

1284. Thurber, S. "Limitations of the Secondary Teaching of English Composition." Education 14 (December 1893): 193-9. RG, PI. Teaching Methods.

1285. Thurber, S. "Some of the Main Principles of Secondary English Teaching." National Education Association Proceedings 37 (1898): 671-7. RG. Teaching Methods.

1286. Thurber, S. "Teaching of English Language." Education (1898): 515. PI. Teaching Methods.

1287. Tieje, R. E. and others. "Systematizing Grading in Freshman Composition at the Large University." English Journal 4 (November 1915): 586-97. II. Evaluating Writing.

1288. Tolman, A. H. "Revival of English Grammar." School Review 10 (February 1902): 157-65. RG, PI. Grammar.

1289. Towne, C. F. "Making a Scale for the Measurement of English Composition." Elementary School Journal 19

(September 1918): 41-53. RG. Evaluating Writing.

1290. Towne, C. F. "Organization of Lessons in English for Americanization Classes." School and Society 12 (September 1920): 183-6. RG. TESOL.

1291. Trabue, M. R. "Supplementing the Hillegas Scale." Teachers College Record 18 (January 1917): 51-84. II. Evaluating Writing.

1292. "Training of English Teachers: Report of the Committee of the New England Association of Teachers of English." Education 34 (April 1914): 473-90. RG. Teacher Training.

1293. Tressler, J. C. "Efficiency of Student Correction of Compositions." English Journal 1 (September 1912): 405-11. II. Evaluating Writing.

1294. Tressler, J. C. "Salvaging from the English Scrap-Heap." English Journal 8 (September 1919): 412-18. II.

1295. Trovillion, M. C. and Renard, H. E. "Cartooning Grammar." English Journal 6 (September 1917): 472-3. II. Grammar.

1296. Trueblood, T. C. "A Chapter on the Organization of College Courses in Public Speaking." Quarterly Journal of Speech 12 (1926): 1-11. AK. Speech.

1297. Tupper, F. "Study of the History of English Language." School Review (1902): 191. PI. Grammar.

1298. Tuttle, A. E. "Study of the English Language." School Review 14 (March 1906): 204-11. RG, PI.

1299. Tuttle, A. H. "Teaching Element in Preaching." Methodist Review (1898): 205. PI. Sermons.

1300. "Two Compositions." Journal of Education 65 (January 1907): 121. II.

1301. "Two Ways of Teaching English." Century Magazine 51 (1896): 793-94. AK. Teaching Methods.

1302. Tyler, J. M. "John Franklin Genung." *Amherst Graduates' Quarterly* 9 (1920): 65-70. AK.

1303. "Types of Organization of High-School English." *English Journal* 2 (November 1913): 575-96. II. Curriculum.

1304. "Uniform Grammatical Terms." *U.S. Bureau of Education Bulletin* 31 (1913): 57-8. RG. Grammar.

1305. "Unsatisfactory Results in English Composition." *Journal of Education* 76 (October 1912): 457. II. Curriculum.

1306. "Use of English Classical Literature in the Work of Education." *Macmillan's Magazine* 2 (1860). CSIGP. Literature.

1307. Utter, R. P. "Case Against Grammar." *Harper's Monthly* 140 (February 1920): 407-13. RG. Grammar.

1308. Valpy, A. J. "On Grammar." *Classical Journal* 36 (1827): 19. CLPI. Grammar.

1309. Van Cleve, E. M. "Language." *Journal of Education* 68 (September 1908): 280-1. II.

1310. Van Dyle, H. "Reading and Writing in the Teaching of English." *School Review* 15 (May 1907): 325-32. RG. Teaching Methods.

1311. Van Slyck, F. G. N. "High School and College Requirements." *School Review* 9 (May 1901): 316-23. RG. Curriculum.

1312. Van Wageman, M. J. "Accuracy with Which English Themes May Be Graded with the Use of English Composition Scales." *School and Society* 11 (April 1920): 441-5. RG. Evaluating Writing.

1313. Von Raumer, K. "History of Primary Education in Ireland." *Barnard's American Journal of Education* (1859): 413. PI. History of Education.

1314. "W. Raleigh on Style." *Academy* (1897): 104, 433. PI. Style.

1315. Waldo, D. "English for Peter." English Journal 6 (June 1917): 372-83. II.

1316. Walker, F. I. "Laboratory System in English." English Journal 6 (September 1917): 445-53. II. Teaching Methods.

1317. "Wanted: A Style For the Times." Nation 75 (September 1902): 185. RG. Style.

1318. Ward, C. C. "Unified Subject-Matter for Composition." English Journal 9 (June 1920): 318-30. II. Curriculum.

1319. Ward, C. H. "English Apparatus." Education 36 (November 1915): 172-81. RG. Teaching Methods.

1320. Ward, C. H. "Fluency First." Education 38 (October 1917): 102-9. RG.

1321. Ward, C. H. "Next C.G.N. Report." English Journal 8 (November 1919): 519-26. II.

1322. Ward, C. H. "Scale Illusion." English Journal 6 (April 1917): 221-30. II.

1323. Ward, C. H. "We Must Not Be Enemies." English Journal 5 (February 1916): 131. II.

1324. Ward, C. H. "What Is English?" Educational Review 51 (February 1916): 168-78. RG.

1325. Warfield, E. "Importance of English as the Vehicle of Expression." Education 21 (June 1901): 579-84. RG. Style.

1326. Warfield, E. D. "English Language as a Vehicle of Expression." Education (1901): 579. PI. Style.

1327. Warner, M. L. "Plea for More English Composition in Secondary Schools." Education 21 (November 1900): 163-70. RG. Curriculum.

1328. Watt, H. A. "Philosophy of Real Composition." English Journal 7 (March 1918): 153-62. II. Composition.

1329. Watt, H. A. "Protecting the Theme-Reader." English Journal 8 (March 1919): 164-73. II. Evaluating Writing.

1330. Waugh, A. "Tyranny of the Paragraph." Eclectic Magazine (1893): 474. PI. Paragraphs.

1331. Waugh, A. "Tyranny of the Paragraph." National Review (1893): 743. PI. Paragraphs.

1332. Weathers, J. R. "Some Remarks on Grammar." Education 16 (April 1896): 503-4. RG. Grammar.

1333. Weaver, R. M. "What Is Description?" English Journal 8 (February 1919): 63-80. II. Modes.

1334. Webster, E. and Allen, L. H. "An Experiment in Imaginative Writing." Records of the Education Society 32 (1918): 25. HEW. Curriculum.

1335. Webster, E. H. "Co-operation of Departments in English Instruction and Practice." Education 35 (March 1915): 409-21. RG. Curriculum.

1336. Webster, E. H. "Preparation in English for Business." English Journal 2 (December 1913): 613-7. II. Business English.

1337. Webster, E. H. "Teaching of English Composition Past and Present." Education 32 (March 1912): 414-22. RG. Composition.

1338. Webster, W. F. "Syllabus of a Course in English, with a Defense of the Same." National Education Association Proceedings 37 (1898): 681-90. RG. Curriculum.

1339. Wedgwood, H. "On the Use of Shall and Will." Philological Society London Proceedings 6 (1854): 1. CLPI. Grammar.

1340. Weeks, R. "Question of Good English." English Journal 2 (February 1913): 99-103. II. Error.

1341. Wendell, B. "English Work in the Secondary Schools." School Review 1 (1893): 638-50. AK. Curriculum.

1342. "Wendell on English Composition." Atlantic Monthly (1892): 129. PI. Composition.

1343. West, A. F. "Our Use of English." American Monthly Review of Reviews 60 (October 1919): 392-4. RG. Usage.

1344. Westcott, O. S. "How Shall We Teach Our Pupils the Correct Use of the English Language?" National Education Association (1900): 437-51. RG. Error.

1345. "What Lies Back of Co-operation in Teaching English." School Review 24 (January 1916): 75-7. RG. Curriculum.

1346. "Whately and Primary Education in Ireland." Dublin University Magazine (1850): 229. PI. History of Education.

1347. Whately, R. "Treatise on the Structure of a Sermon." Bibliotheca Sacra 5 (1848): 731. CLPI. Sermons.

1348. "Whately's Rhetoric." Littell's Museum of Foreign Literature (1829): 258. PI. Rhetoric.

1349. "Whately's Rhetoric." American Monthly Review (1832): 441. PI. Rhetoric.

1350. "Whately's Rhetoric." Blackwood's Magazine (1828): 885. PI. Rhetoric.

1351. "Whately's Rhetoric." Monthly Review (1825): 216. PI. Rhetoric.

1352. Wheeler, B. I. "Education as a Development." California University Chronicle (1906): 238. PI. Curriculum.

1353. Wheeler, D. H. "Conditions of Rhetoric." Methodist Review (1893): 91. PI. Rhetoric.

1354. Wheeler, E. "Color Similies." Current Literature 29 (September 1900): 277. PI. Rhetoric.

1355. Whelpley, J. D. "Style." American Whig Review (1845): 358. PI. Style.

1356. Whibley, C. "Language and Style." Fortnightly Review (1899): 10. PI, CLPI. Style.

1357. Whicher, G. F. "Genung's Rhetoric." The Nation 109 (1919): 658. AK. Rhetoric.

1358. Whicher, G. M. "Dr. Burton on the Future Tense." Bookman 3 (April 1896): 136-7. RG. Grammar.

1359. White, J. O. "English Work in a Private School." English Journal 2 (October 1913): 505-12. II. Curriculum.

1360. White, R. G. "English Language." Galaxy (1867): 62. PI.

1361. White, T. W. "Claims for English as a Study." Education 12 (January 1892): 273-8. RG. Curriculum.

1362. Whitney, W. D. "Comparative Grammar." North American Review (1870): 199. PI. Grammar.

1363. Wiley, M. C. "English Examination." English Journal 7 (May 1918): 327-30. II. Testing.

1364. Wilkinson, J. W. "Common Mistakes in English Language." Educational Review (1900): 77. PI. Error.

1365. Wilkinson, J. W. "Common Mistakes in Teaching English." Education 20 (October 1899): 77-87. RG. Teaching Methods.

1366. Wilkinson, J. W. "English Gerund." Education 15 (April 1895): 479-84. RG. Grammar.

1367. Williams, A. M. "Scottish School of Rhetoric." Education 13 (November 1892-April 1893): 142-50, 220-7, 281-90, 344-54, 427-34, 488-96. RG, PI. Rhetoric.

1368. Willing, M. H. "Measurement of Written Composition in Grades IV to VIII." English Journal 7 (March 1918): 193-202. II. Evaluating Writing.

1369. Willock, J. H. "Teaching of Elementary English." Education 31 (September 1910): 11-6. RG. Curriculum.

1370. Wilson, E. J. "Shall We Abolish Grammar?" English Journal 6 (May 1917): 308-13. II. Grammar.

1371. Winship, A. E. "In Literature and Language; By Their Fruits Ye Shall Know Them." Journal of Education 68 (June 1908): 16+. II. Literature.

1372. Wirick, C. M. "Text-Book English." School Science and Math 12 (May 1912): 364-9. II.

1373. Wiseman, N. "Gossip on Style." Monitor (1879): 217. PI. Style.

1374. Withers, S. "Spoken English--How Shall We Improve It?" Journal of Education 83 (January 1916): 95-7. II. Error.

1375. Wolfe, L. E. "English in the Elementary School." Educational Review 28 (September 1904): 152-63. RG. Curriculum.

1376. Wolverton, S. F. "Professional Scullery." Educational Review 60 (December 1920): 407-16. RG.

1377. Woodward, C. M. "Change of Front in Education." Science ns (1901): 474. PI.

1378. Woolley, E. C. "Admission to Freshman English in the University." English Journal 3 (April 1914): 288-44. II. Curriculum.

1379. Wright, J. G. "First Year English in the High School." School Review 1 (January 1893): 15-23. RG. Curriculum.

1380. Wright, T. H. "Style." Popular Science Monthly (1878): 340. PI. Style.

1381. Wright, T. H. "Style." Macmillan's Magazine (1878): 78. PI. Style.

1382. "Writers on English Composition." Adam's Plain Living. CSIGP. Composition.

1383. Young, W. H. "Grammar School from the High School Point of View." <u>Education</u> (1906): 606. PI. Curriculum.

1384. Zeitlin, J. "Parts of Speech: The Noun." <u>English Journal</u> 3 (March 1914): 137-45. II. Grammar.

1385. Ziegler, C. W. "Laboratory Method in English Teaching." <u>English Journal</u> 8 (March 1919): 143-53. II. Teaching Methods.

Books

Books

1386. Abbott, E. A. How to Parse. Little. Grammar. USC.

1387. Abbott, E. A. How to Tell the Parts of Speech. Little. Grammar. USC.

1388. Abbott, E. A. How to Write Clearly. Little. Composition. USC.

1389. Abbott, E. A. How to Write Clearly: Rules and Exercises on English Composition. Roberts, 1875. Composition. AC, AK.

1390. Abbott, E. A. Shakespearean Grammar. Macmillan. Grammar. USC.

1391. Abbott, E. A. and Seeley, J. R. English Lessons for English People. 1871. CLPI.

1392. Abbott, E. A. and Seeley, J. R. English Lessons for English People. Little, 1912. USC.

1393. Abbott, H. V. English Composition: Syllabus. Teachers College. Composition. USC.

1394. Accent and Rhythm Accent and Rhythm Explained. Edinburgh, 1888. Sound Patterns. BMI.

1395. Adams, E. Elements of the English Language. 1874. CLPI.

1396. Adams, F. A. Principles of Grammar. Christian Examiner, vol. 18. 1835. Grammar. CLPI.

1397. Adams, J. Q. Lectures on Rhetoric and Oratory. New York: Russell and Russell, 1962. Rhetoric. HR.

1398. Adams, J. Q. Lectures on Rhetoric and Oratory, Delivered to the Classes of Senior and Junior Sophisters in Harvard. 2 vol. Cambridge: Hilliard and Metcalf, 1810. Rhetoric. HR, PS, SIBP, CLPI, LLC, AK.

1399. Adams, W. J. *Up-to-Date Regents Questions in English Giving a Selection of Regents Questions To June, 1913, Classified and All the Questions Since 1914, By Examination.* Syracuse, NY: C. W. Bardeen, 1914. Testing. HEW.

1400. Addis, W. J. *Essay Writing.* Pitman's Civil Service Text-Books. 1916. Composition. BMI.

1401. Addis, W. J. *Exegesis of English Composition.* Dent, 1913. Composition. BMI.

1402. Addis, W. J. *Heuristic English Grammar.* Constable, 1915. Grammar. BMI.

1403. Addis, W. J. *Lessons in Prose and Verse Composition.* Dent, 1913. Composition. BMI.

1404. Addis, W. J. *Style in Composition.* London, 1904. Style. BMI.

1405. Adkins, F. J. *An English Course for Evening Students.* London: S. Sonnenschein and Co., LTD, 1909. English. Syllabi. HEW.

1406. *Advanced Composition, Reproduction and Supplementary Reading Cards.* Flanagan. Composition. USC.

1407. Agar, E. W. *Elementary Exercises in English Grammar.* Bogarte. Grammar. USC.

1408. Alabama English Association, Articulation Committee. *Report of Articulation Committee of the Alabama English Association.* Subject: English Composition for the First Eight Grades. Florence, AL: State Normal School, 1917. Curriculum. HEW, USC.

1409. Alabama Illiteracy Commission. *Textbook for Alabama Adult Schools.* Montgomery Brown Printing Co., 1918. Reading. HEW.

1410. Albert, E. *Practical Course in Intermediate English.* Harrap & Co., 1914. English Syllabi. BMI.

1411. Albright, E. M. Descriptive Writing. Macmillan, 1911. Composition. USC.

1412. Alden, H. M. Magazine Writing and the New Literature. New York: Harper Brothers, 1908. Journalism. BMI, LLC.

1413. Alden, J. Introduction to the Study of the English Language: Grammar and Rhetoric. A. Potter and Co., 1876. Grammar and Rhetoric. AC.

1414. Alexander, H. Common Faults in Writing English. Dodge, 1916. Error. USC.

1415. Alexander, W. J. and Mowat, A. Elementary Composition for Public School Grades. Toronto, 1912. Composition. BMI.

1416. Alford, H. Plea for the Queen's English. Macmillan, 1912. Usage. USC.

1417. Alford, H. The Queen's English. 1864. Usage. SIBP.

1418. Allbutt, T. C. Notes on the Composition of Scientific Papers. Macmillan, 1904. Technical English. USC.

1419. Allen, E. School Grammar of the English Language. Heath, 1900. Grammar. USC.

1420. Allen, E. A. Allen's Composition Books. Van Winkle, 1884. Composition. AC.

1421. Allen, E. A. Review of English Grammar for Secondary Schools. Heath, 1909. Grammar. USC.

1422. Allen, E. A. and Hawkins, W. J. School Course in English. 2 vol. Heath, 1905. English Syllabi. USC.

1423. Allen, E. and Hawkins, W. J. Grammar of the English Language. Heath, 1905. Grammar. USC.

1424. Allen, G. E. English Grammar. New York: G. E. Allen, 1914. Grammar. USC.

1425. Allen, G. E. English Rhetoric. New York: G. E. Allen, 1914. Rhetoric. USC.

1426. Allen, G. E. Studies in English. Hamilton Press, 1913. USC.

1427. Allen, I. S. Anglo: Being English Simplified. Cambridge, 1915. Grammar. BMI.

1428. Allen, J. C. Longman's English Course for Indian Schools. Bombay, 1913. TESOL. BMI.

1429. Allen, L. H. Outlines of a Course in Imaginative Composition Conducted at the Teacher's College, Sydney. Sydney: W. A. Gulleck, 1918. Composition. HEW.

1430. Alshouse, H. S. and Root, M. R. Brief English Grammar. Barnes, 1913. Grammar. USC.

1431. Alton, G. B. and Rankin, A. W. Exercises in Syntax. Northwestern School Supply Co., 1901. Grammar. USC.

1432. American Academy of Arts and Letters. Academy Papers; Addresses on Language Problems. Scribner, 1925. EGL.

1433. American Institute of Bankers. Studies in English. American Bankers Assn., 1916. Business English. USC.

1434. Analytical Question Series: Grammar. Flanagan. Grammar. USC.

1435. Anderson, E. Talks on Grammar. Macon, GA: J. W. Burke Co., 1918. Grammar. USC.

1436. Anderson, J. M. Sixty Composition Topics. Silver. Composition. USC.

1437. Andrews, A. L., ed. Specimens of Discourse. Holt, 1905. Readers. USC, AC.

1438. Andrews, G. P. Practical English for Use in Schools. Leeds, 1916. Grammar. BMI.

1439. Angus, J. Handbook of the English Tongue. 1862. Grammar. SIBP, AK.

1440. Ansley, E. A. Elements of Literature: An Introduction To Reading. 1849. Literature. SIBP.

1441. Apsinis et Longini Rhetorica. Oxford, 1912. Rhetoric. USC.

1442. Arelstrom, D. Pupil's Outline for Home Study in Connection with School Work Grammar. Brooklyn, NY: Jennings Publishing Co., 1909. Grammar. HEW.

1443. Arnold, F. S. New English Method. Rome, 1914. Teaching Methods. BMI.

1444. Arnold, H. Practice Parsing and Analysis. Little, 1906. Grammar. USC.

1445. Arnold, M. Essays in Criticism. London, 1895. Criticism. LC.

1446. Arnold, S. L. Outline of a Course to Accompany Mother Tongue. 2 vol. Ginn, 1901. English Syllabi. USC.

1447. Arnold, S. L. With Pencil and Pen. Ginn, 1906. USC.

1448. Arnold, S. L. and others. See and Say Series. 3 vol. Iroquois Publisher, 1913-1915. English Syllabi. USC.

1449. The Art of Punctuation. Colombo, 1894. Punctuation. BMI.

1450. Arts of Writing, Reading and Speaking. Dillingham. Rhetoric. USC.

1451. Ashmun, M. Composition in the High School: The 1st and 2nd Year. Madison: The University of Wisconsin, 1908. Composition. HEW, USC, AC.

1452. Ashmun, M. Prose Literature for Secondary Schools. Houghton Mifflin, 1908-1910. Literature. AC.

1453. Assoc. of High School Teachers of English of New York

City. <u>Reports of Committee</u>. 1915. Curriculum. HEW.

1454. Associated Academic Principals of the State of New York, Subcommittee on English. <u>Proposed Course of Study in English for the Secondary Schools of the State</u>. Syracuse, 1903. Curriculum. HEW.

1455. Atkinson, M. <u>First Aid to Essay-Writing</u>. Worker's Educational Assoc., 1914. Composition. BMI.

1456. Atkinson, W. W. <u>Art of Expression and the Principles of Discourse</u>. Progress Co., 1910. Composition. USC, AC.

1457. Atlantic Monthly. <u>Atlantic Classics</u>. 1st and 2nd ser. 2 vol. Little, 1916-18. EGL.

1458. Atlantic Monthly. <u>Essays and Essay Writing</u>. Atlantic Monthly Co., 1917. Composition. USC.

1459. Atteridge, W. H. <u>Primary School Certificate English</u>. Johannesburg, 1916. English Syllabi. BMI.

1460. Auerbach, J. S. <u>Essays and Miscellanies</u>. 3 vol. Harper, 1914-22. EGL.

1461. Austin, G. <u>Chironomia, Or a Treatise on Rhetorical Delivery</u>. London: T. Cadell and W. Davies, 1806. Rhetoric. HR, PS.

1462. Austin, R. <u>Lessons in English for Foreign Women</u>. New York: American Book, 1913. TESOL. USC, BMI.

1463. Avery, E. M. <u>Words Correctly Spoken</u>. Popular Publications. Usage. USC.

1464. Axelrad, P., ed. <u>How to Learn English</u>. 2 ser. Biblioteca Romana, 1918. TESOL. USC.

1465. Axelrad, P. ed. <u>How to Learn English Language; Grammar, Translator and Dictionary, English-Roumanian and Roumanian-English</u>. New York: P. Axelrad, 1914. TESOL. USC.

1466. Axelstrom, D. E. <u>Pupils' Outlines for Home Study in Connection with School Work: Grammar</u>. Brooklyn, NY:

Jennings Publishing Co., 1909. Grammar. USC.

1467. Aydelotte, F. College English. Oxford: Oxford, 1913. Curriculum. USC.

1468. Aydelotte, F. English and Engineering: A Volume of Essays for English Classes in Engineering Schools. 2 ed. McGraw, 1923. Technical English. EGL.

1469. Aydelotte, F. English and Engineering: A Volume of Essays for English Classes in Engineering Schools. New York: McGraw-Hill Book Company, Inc., 1917. Technical English. HEW, USC.

1470. Aydelotte, F. Oxford Stamp and Other Essays. Oxford: Oxford, 1917. EGL.

1471. Aydelotte, F., ed. Materials for the Study of English Literature and Composition. Oxford: Oxford, 1914. Literature and Composition. USC.

1472. Ayres, A. Some Ill-Used Words. Appleton, 1901. Usage. USC.

1473. Ayres, A. Verbalist. Appleton, 1907. Usage. USC.

1474. Ayres, A. Verbalist: Discussions of Right and Wrong Use of Words. Appleton, 1907. Usage. USC.

1475. Bachelor, J. M. and Henry, R. L., ed. Challenging Essays in Modern Thought. 1st and 2 ser. 2 vol. Appleton-Century, 1928-33. Readers. EGL.

1476. Bacon, J. H. Guide to English Composition. London, 1892. Composition. BMI.

1477. Bacon, J. H. Guide to English Composition. Pitman, 1912. Composition. USC.

1478. Baden, W. W. Principal Figures of Language and Figures of Thought in Isaeus and the Guardianship-Speeches of Demosthenes. Moscow: University of Idaho. Rhetoric. USC.

1479. Badlam, A. B. Suggestive Lessons in Language. Heath. English Syllabi. USC.

1480. Badlam, A. B. <u>Suggestive Lessons in Language and Reading</u>. Heath. Reading. USC.

1481. Bailey, J. C. <u>Continuity of Letters</u>. Oxford: Oxford, 1923. EGL.

1482. Bain, A. <u>An English Grammar</u>. 1863. Grammar. SIBP.

1483. Bain, A. <u>Autobiography</u>. Longmans, 1904. AK.

1484. Bain, A. <u>Brief English Grammar</u>. Holt. Grammar. USC.

1485. Bain, A. <u>Companion to the Higher English Grammar</u>. 1874. Grammar. CLPI.

1486. Bain, A. <u>Composition Grammar</u>. Holt. Composition. USC.

1487. Bain, A. <u>English Composition and Rhetoric</u>. 1874; 1887. Composition. CLPI.

1488. Bain, A. <u>English Composition and Rhetoric</u>. New York: Appleton, 1876. Composition. AC.

1489. Bain, A. <u>English Composition and Rhetoric</u>. New York: Appleton, 1888. Composition. AC.

1490. Bain, A. <u>English Composition and Rhetoric: A Manual</u>. New York: D. Appleton and Co., 1866. Composition. HR, PS, SIPB, AK.

1491. Bain, A. <u>English Composition</u>. London, 1887-88. AC.

1492. Bain, A. <u>English Grammar as Bearing Upon Composition</u>. Holt, 1877. Grammar. AC.

1493. Bain, A. <u>Higher English Grammar</u>. 1876. Grammar. CLPI.

1494. Bain, A. <u>Higher English Grammar</u>. Holt, 1879. Grammar. USC.

1495. Bain, A. <u>On Teaching English</u>. Appleton, 1887. Teaching Methods. AK.

1496. Baker, F. T. Course--English-Horace Mann School. New York: Columbia University Press, 1900. Curriculum. HEW.

1497. Baker, F. T. Syllabus of A Course Of Lectures On The Teaching of English In Elementary Schools. New York: Teacher's College, Columbia University, 1904. Curriculum. HEW.

1498. Baker, F. T. Teaching English in Elementary Schools. Teachers College. Curriculum. USC.

1499. Baker, F. T. and Abbott, H. V. English Composition. Holt, 1908. Composition. USC, AC.

1500. Baker, F. T. and Thorndike, A. H. Everyday English. 2 vol. New York: Macmillan, 1920. English Syllabi. USC.

1501. Baker, F. T. and Thorndike, A. H. Everyday English. 2 vol. Macmillan, 1912-13. English Syllabi. USC.

1502. Baker, F. T. and Thorndike, A. H. Teaching of English. Macmillan, 1920. Teaching Methods. USC.

1503. Baker, F. T. and Thorndike, A. H. The Teaching of English a Manual to Accompany Everyday English; Books One and Two. New York: The Macmillan Co., 1920. English Syllabi. HEW.

1504. Baker, G. P. Forms of Public Address. Holt, 1904. Speech. USC, CC.

1505. Baker, G. P. and Huntington, H. B. A College Manual of Rhetoric. 3rd ed. Longmans, 1904. Rhetoric. AK.

1506. Baker, G. P. and Huntington, H. P. Principles of Argumentation (Revised and Augmented). Ginn, 1895, 1905. Modes. AK.

1507. Baker, J. Correct English Daily Drill Book. Correct English Publisher. 1915. Usage. USC.

1508. Baker, J. T. Correct English. H. M. Rowe. Usage. USC.

1509. Baker, J. T. <u>Correct English Calendar Yearbook</u>. Progress Co. Usage. USC.

1510. Baker, J. T. <u>Correct Preposition: How To Use It</u>. Correct English Pub., 1911. Usage. USC.

1511. Baker, J. T. <u>Correct Word; How To use It</u>. Correct English Pub., 1911. Usage. USC.

1512. Baker, J. T. <u>Library of Correct English</u>. 9 vol. Progress Co. Usage. USC.

1513. Baker, J. T. <u>Literary Workshop--Helps for the Writer</u>. Correct English Pub., 1912. Usage. USC.

1514. Balch, W. S. <u>A Grammar of the English Language</u>. 1839. Grammar. SIBP.

1515. Baldwin, C. S. <u>Ancient Rhetoric and Poetic</u>. Macmillan, 1924. Rhetoric. AK.

1516. Baldwin, C. S. <u>College Composition</u>. Longmans, 1917. Composition. USC.

1517. Baldwin, C. S. <u>College Manual of Rhetoric</u>. Longmans, 1902. Rhetoric. AC.

1518. Baldwin, C. S. <u>College Manual of Rhetoric</u>. 4th ed. Longmans, 1912. Rhetoric. USC.

1519. Baldwin, C. S. <u>College Manual of Rhetoric</u>. London, 1902. Rhetoric. BMI.

1520. Baldwin, C. S. <u>Composition, Oral And Written</u>. Longmans, 1909. Composition. USC, AC, AK.

1521. Baldwin, C. S. <u>English Bible as a Guide to Writing</u>. Macmillan, 1917. Composition. USC.

1522. Baldwin, C. S. <u>Expository Paragraph and Sentence</u>. Longmans, 1912. Paragraphs. USC.

1523. Baldwin, C. S. <u>Expository Paragraph and Sentence: Elementary Manual of Composition</u>. Longmans, 1897. Paragraphs. AC, AK.

1524. Baldwin, C. S. <u>How to Write</u>. Macmillan, 1905.

Composition. USC.

1525. Baldwin, C. S. Writing and Speaking. 2 vol. Longmans, 1909, 1911. Composition. USC, AK.

1526. Baldwin, C. S. Writing and Speaking: Textbook of Rhetoric. New York: Longmans, 1909. Rhetoric. BMI, CC.

1527. Baldwin, C. S., ed. Specimens of Prose Description. Holt, 1895. Modes. USC.

1528. Baldwin, J. Harper's School Speaker. vol. 1. 1890-91. Speech. CC.

1529. Ball, M. Principles of Outlining, for Colleges and Advanced Classes in Secondary Schools. Sanborn, 1910. Outlining. USC, AC.

1530. Ballard, H. H. Composition Writing Made Easy. Hinds. Composition. USC.

1531. Ballard, H. H. Handbook of Blunders. Boston, 1885. Error. BMI.

1532. Ballard, H. H. Handbook of Blunders. Lothrop, 1912. Error. USC.

1533. Ballard, H. H. Model Composition Cards. Writers Pub., 1886. Composition. AC.

1534. Ballard, H. H. Pieces to Speak. 1897. AC.

1535. Balley, E. J. Course of Practical English. Bell and Sons, 1914. English Syllabi. BMI.

1536. Ballou, F. W. Scales for the Measurement of English Compositions. Harvard University Press, 1914. Writing Evaluation. USC, HEW.

1537. Bancroft, T. W. Method of English Composition. Ginn, 1884. Composition. AC.

1538. Bangs, J. E. Securing a Vocabulary. LaSalle Extension University, 1913. Vocabulary. USC.

1539. Banks, E. D. Original Recitations. 1902. AC.

1540. Banks, L. A. *Windows for Sermons: A Study of the Art of Sermonic Illustration*. New York, 1902. Sermons. BMI.

1541. Banks, M. L. *Graduated Passages for Reproduction*. Oxford: Oxford, 1912. Readers. USC.

1542. Barber, J. *A Grammar of Elocution*. New Haven: A. H. Maltby, 1830. Grammar. HR.

1543. Barber, J. *A Practical Treatise of Gesture*. Cambridge, MA: Hilliard and Brown, 1831. Speech. HR.

1544. Barber, J. *Exercises in Reading and Recitation Reduced to a System of Notation*. York, PA: J. Barber and C. Mason, 1825. Reading. HR.

1545. Barbour, F. A. *The Teaching of English Grammar, History, and Method*. Boston: Ginn and Co., 1901. History of Education. HEW, USC.

1546. Barclay, J. W. *Complete Dictionary of the English Language*. 2 vol. London. Dictionaries. CLPI.

1547. Bardeen, C. W. *Complete Rhetoric*. American Book. Rhetoric. USC.

1548. Bardeen, C. W. *Outlines of Sentence Making*. Bardeen, 1899. Composition. USC.

1549. Bardeen, C. W. *Outlines of Sentence-Making: Brief Course in Composition*. Barnes, 1884. Composition. AC.

1550. Bardeen, C. W. *Regents Questions in Elementary English 1895-1904*. Syracuse, NY: C. W. Bardeen, 1905. Testing. HEW.

1551. Bardeen, C. W. *Shorter Course in Rhetoric*. Barnes, 1885. Rhetoric. AC.

1552. Bardeen, C. W. *Shorter Course in Rhetoric*. American Book. Rhetoric. USC.

1553. Bardeen, C. W. *System of Rhetoric*. Barnes, 1884.

Rhetoric. AC.

1554. Bardeen, C. W. *Verbal Pitfalls*. Bardeen. Error. USC.

1555. Barnell, H. J. *Pitman's Illustrated Aids to Composition*. London, 1905. Composition. BMI.

1556. *Barnes' Language Lessons*. American Book. English Syllabi. USC.

1557. *Barnes' Picture Lessons in English*. American Book. English Syllabi. USC.

1558. *Barnes' Working Lessons in English*. American Book. English Syllabi. USC.

1559. Barnes, M. E. *Teaching English to Adult Foreigners*. Evanston, IL: The National WCTU Publishing House, 1919. TESOL. HEW.

1560. Barnes, W. *English in the Country School*. New York: Row, Peterson and Co., 1913. English Syllabi. USC, HEW.

1561. Barnes, W. *The New Democracy in the Teaching of English*. Pittsburg, PA: Board of Public Instruction, 1918. Curriculum. HEW.

1562. Barnett, P. A., ed. *Teaching and Organization with Special Reference to Secondary Schools; A Manual of Practice*. 1897. Teaching Methods. CC.

1563. Barrett, C. R. *Business English and Correspondence*. American School of Correspondence, 1914. Business English. USC.

1564. Barrett, J. *A Grammar of the English Language*. 2nd ed. 1819. Grammar. SIBP.

1565. Bartholomew, W. E. and Hurlbut, F. *Business Man's English, Spoken and Written*. Macmillan, 1920. Business English. USC.

1566. Bartlett, A. L. *Essentials of Language and Grammar*. Silver, 1900. Grammar. USC.

1567. Bartlett, A. L. *First Steps in English* [4th & 5th Grades]. Silver, 1906. English Syllabi. USC.

1568. Bartlett, A. L. and McBain, H. L. *Elements of English Grammar*. Silver, 1906. Grammar. USC.

1569. Bascom, J. *Philosophy of Rhetoric*. Woolworth and Ainsworth, 1872. Rhetoric. SIBP, AK.

1570. Bascom, J. *Philosophy of Rhetoric*. Putnam. Rhetoric. USC.

1571. Bascom, J. *Philosophy of Rhetoric*. A. Potter and Co. Rhetoric. AC.

1572. Bascom, J. *Philosophy of Rhetoric*. 1866. Rhetoric. SIBP.

1573. Bascom, L. *Elementary Lessons in English Idiom*. Appleton, 1920. Usage. USC.

1574. Baskervill, W. M. and Sewell. *School Grammar of English Language*. American Book, 1909. Grammar. USC.

1575. Baskervill, W. M. and Sewell, J. W. *English Grammar*. American Book. Grammar. USC.

1576. Batchelder, W. J. *Notes on the Teaching of English*. Macmillan, 1913. Teaching Methods. BMI.

1577. Bate, R. S. *English Composition*. Bell and Sons, 1914. Composition. BMI.

1578. Bates, A. *Talks on Writing English*. Houghton, 1901. Composition. USC, AK.

1579. Bates, A. *Talks on Writing English*. Houghton, Mifflin and Co., 1896. Composition. AC, AK.

1580. Beak, G. B. *Indexing and Precis Writing*. Macmillan, 1908. Precis. CC.

1581. Beare, C. *Development of English Prose*. McEvoy, 1910. Rhetoric. USC.

1582. Beare, C. *Development of the Essay*. McEvoy, 1910.

Rhetoric. USC.

1583. Beare, C. *Essentials of English Prose Composition*. McEvoy, 1910. Composition. USC.

1584. Bechtel, J. H. *Slips of Speech*. Penn. Error. USC.

1585. Beecher, H. W. *Yale Lectures on Preaching*. 3 ser. 1872-74. Sermons. SIBP, CLPI.

1586. Beeman, M. N. *Analysis of the English Language*. Flanagan, 1901. Grammar. USC.

1587. Beeton, F. *English Grammar*. 2nd ed. Lipp. Grammar. USC.

1588. Beglinger, N. J. *A Book for Soldiers Who Have Not Had Educational Advantages in English*. Battle Creek, MI: C. E. Spence, 1918. English Syllabi. HEW.

1589. Beglinger, N. J. *Book for Soldiers Who Have Not Had Educational Advantages in English*. Oshkosh, WI: N. J. Beglinger, 1918. English Syllabi. USC.

1590. Bell, A. R. *Principles of Elocution, with Exercises and Quotations*. Volta Bureau, 1887. Teaching Methods. CC.

1591. Bell, D. C. and Bell, A. R. *Standard Elocutionist*. Firak, 1911. Speech. CC.

1592. Bell, G. H. *Guide to Correct Language*. Southern Pub. Assn. Usage. USC.

1593. Bell, G. H. *Language Series*. Southern Pub. Assn. English Syllabi. USC.

1594. Bell, G. H. *Natural Method in English*. Review and H., 1915. Teaching Methods. USC.

1595. Bell, R. H. *Changing Values of English Speech*. Hinds, 1909. Speech. USC.

1596. Bell, R. H. *Worth of Words*. 3rd ed. Hinds, 1903. USC.

1597. Belloc, H. Conversation With an Angel and Other Essays. Harper, 1929. EGL.

1598. Bennett, A. How to Secure an Author; A Practical Guide. 1903. CC.

1599. Bennett, A. Things That Have Interested Me. 1st - 3rd ser. Doran. EGL.

1600. Bennett, T. New English Spelling and Dictionary Book. Blackie, 1912. Spelling. BMI.

1601. Bennett, T. Spelling Through Dictation. Harrap and Co., 1913. Spelling. BMI.

1602. Benson, A. C. Along the Road. Putnam, 1913. EGL.

1603. Benson, A. C. At Large. Putnam, 1908. EGL.

1604. Bent, S. A. Hints on Language. Lothrop. Composition. USC.

1605. Bent, S. A. Hints on Language in Connection with Sightreading and Writing in Primary Intermediate Schools. Boston: Lee and Shepherd, 1886. Composition. HEW.

1606. Bentham, J. Works. Edinburgh. 1843. CLPI.

1607. Berger. English Grammar for Poles. Stechert. TESOL. USC.

1608. Bergsten, N. Study on Compound Substantives in English. 1911. Grammar. BMI.

1609. Berkeley, F. C. College Course in Writing from Models. Holt, 1910. Composition. USC,CC,AC.

1610. Berlitz, M. D. English Method. Berlitz. English Syllabi. USC.

1611. Berlitz, M. D. Method for Children. Berlitz. English Syllabi. USC.

1612. Berlitz, M. D. Method for teaching Modern Languages; English Part First Book. Berlitz, 1918. English Syllabi. USC.

1613. Berlitz, M.D. English Idioms and Grammar. Berlitz, 1915. Grammar. USC.

1614. Bernon, A. Shall and Will. London, 1886. Grammar. BMI.

1615. Berry, L. B. Good English Program. 1920. English Syllabi. USC.

1616. Besant, W. The Pen and the Book: Advice to Young Authors. London, 1899. Composition. BMI.

1617. Beverley, C. Oral English. 2 vol. Atkinson, Mentzer and Co., 1914. Speech. USC.

1618. Bewsher, J. and Bennetts, H. J. T. English Grammar for Younger Forms. Longmans, 1920. Grammar. BMI.

1619. Bierce, A. Write It Right. Neale, 1909. Composition. USC.

1620. Bigelow, M. T. Mistakes in Writing English. Lothrop, 1912. Error. USC.

1621. Bigelow, M. T. Mistakes in Writing English and How to Avoid Them. Boston: Les and Sons, 1886. Error. AC, BMI.

1622. Bigsby, B. Elements of the English Language: Introduction to Grammar and Composition. Ginn, 1874. Grammar. AC.

1623. Birch, C. E. Methods of Teaching English. 2nd ed. Lawrence, KS: Birch, 1914. Teaching Methods. USC, HEW.

1624. Birkenhead, F. E. S. Law, Life, and Letters. 2 vol. Doran, 1927. EGL.

1625. Black, N. F. English for the Non-English. Regina, Canada: North West Pub. Co., 1913. TESOL. USC, HEW.

1626. Black, R. M., comp. Literatures for the Study of Language. Houghton, 1913. Literature. USC.

1627. Blackman, P. <u>Text Book of the English Language for Yiddish Students</u>. Mazin and Co., 1915. TESOL. BMI.

1628. Blackman, R. D. <u>Deacon's Composition and Style</u>. London, 1885. Composition. BMI.

1629. Blackstone, H., comp. <u>Best American Orations of Today</u>. 1903. Speech. CC.

1630. Blair, H. <u>Abridgment of "Lectures"</u>. Porter, 1876. Rhetoric. AC.

1631. Blair, H. <u>Abridgment of "Lectures"</u>. Lippincott, 1876. Rhetoric. AC.

1632. Blair, H. <u>An Abridgement of Lectures on Rhetoric</u>. Philadelphia: T. Ellwood Zell, 1854. Rhetoric. HR, CLPI.

1633. Blair, H. <u>Lectures on Rhetoric</u>. Funk, 1911. Rhetoric. USC.

1634. Blair, H. <u>Lectures on Rhetoric and Belles Lettres</u>. Charles Daly, 1839. Rhetoric. AK.

1635. Blair, H. <u>Lectures on Rhetoric and Belles-Lettres; With Questions By A. Mills</u>. G. R. Lockwood, 1876. Rhetoric. AC.

1636. Blair, H. <u>Lectures on Rhetoric and Belles-Lettres; With Questions by A. Mills</u>. Porter, 1876. Rhetoric. AC.

1637. Blaisdell, T. C. <u>English in the Grades</u>. American Book, 1905. Curriculum. USC, HEW.

1638. Blaisdell, T. C. <u>Steps in English: Composition-Rhetoric</u>. American Book, 1906. Composition. AC, USC, CC.

1639. Blaisdell, T. C. <u>Teacher's Handbook for 'Steps in English'</u>. American Book, 1912. Teaching Methods. USC.

1640. Blanton, A. W. <u>Review Outline and Exercises in English Grammar</u>. C. E. Merrill, 1909. Grammar.

USC.

1641. Blanton, A. W. *Supplementary Exercises in Punctuation and Composition.* C. E. Merrill, 1909. Composition. USC.

1642. Bleyer, W. G. *The High School Course in English.* 4th ed. Madison: The University of Wisconsin, 1911. Curriculum. HEW.

1643. Bleyer, W. G. *The High School Course in English 3rd.* Madison: The University of Wisconsin, 1909. Curriculum. HEW.

1644. Bloom, J. H. *Pulpit Oratory in the Time of James I, 1620-22.* 1831. Sermons. SIBP.

1645. Blount, A. *Intensive Studies in American Literature.* Macmillan, 1914. Literature. USC.

1646. Blount, A. and Northup, C. S. *Elementary English Grammar.* Holt, 1911. Grammar. USC.

1647. Blount, A. and Northup, C. S. *Elementary English Grammar, with Composition.* Holt, 1912. Composition. USC.

1648. Blount, A. and Northup, C. S. *English Composition for Grammar Grades.* Holt, 1913. Composition. USC.

1649. Blount, A. and Northup, C. S. *English Grammar.* Holt, 1914. Grammar. USC.

1650. Blount, A. and Northup, C. S. *Language Lessons for Intermediate Grades.* Holt, 1912. Grammar. USC.

1651. Boas, F. S. *Teachers and Modern Language Research.* Cambridge: Modern Humanities Research Association, 1919. Curriculum. BMI.

1652. Bobbit, A. *Elements of English Grammar.* 1833. Grammar. SIBP.

1653. Bolenius, E. M. *Elementary Lessons in Everyday English.* New York: American Book, 1920. Grammar.

USC, BMI.

1654. Bolenius, E. M. <u>Everyday English Composition</u>. New York: American Book, 1917. Composition. USC, BMI.

1655. Bolenius, E. M. <u>Teaching of Oral English</u>. 2nd ed. Lippincott, 1916. Speech. USC, HEW.

1656. Bolenius, E. M. <u>Teaching of Oral English</u>. 3rd ed. Lippincott, 1920. Speech. USC, HEW.

1657. Bonnell, J. M. <u>First Lessons in English Composition</u>. Morton, 1912. Composition. USC.

1658. Bonnell, J. M. <u>First Lessons in English Composition</u>. Morton, 1871. Composition. AC.

1659. Bonnell, J. M. <u>Manual of Prose Composition</u>. Morton, 1867. Composition. AC.

1660. Boone, R. G. <u>Education in the United States, Its History from the Earliest Settlements</u>. 1894. History of Education. CC.

1661. Booth, D. <u>Analytical Dictionary of the English Language</u>. London, 1835. Dictionaries. CLPI.

1662. Booth, D. <u>The Principles of English Grammar</u>. 1837. Grammar. SIBP.

1663. Boothe, I. H. <u>The Evolution of the Sentence</u>. Richmond, KY: Register Press, 1912. Sentences. HEW.

1664. Boston School Committee. <u>Outline of Work in English for Intermediate Classes in the Elementary Grades</u>. Boston: Printing Dept., 1916. Curriculum. HEW, USC.

1665. Bostwick, A. E. <u>Earmarks of Literature; The Things that Make Good Books</u>. McClurg, 1914. Literature. EGL.

1666. Bowden, T. R. <u>Blunders in Educated Circles Corrected</u>. New York, 1889. Error. BMI.

1667. Bowen, E. W. <u>Questions at Issues in Our English</u>

Speech. Broadway Pub., 1909. Usage. USC.

1668. Bower, H. J. *A Modern Civil Service and Commercial Manual for Spelling*. H. Russell, 1920. Spelling. BMI.

1669. Bowlin, W. R. and Marsh, G. L. *Vocational English*. Scott, 1918. Business English. USC.

1670. Bowman, J. C. ed. *Essays for College English*. 1 and 2 ser. 2 vol. Heath, 1915-18. Readers. EGL.

1671. Boyd, J. R. *Elements of English Composition*. Barnes, 1860. Composition. AC, AK.

1672. Boyd, J. R. *Elements of Rhetoric and Literary Criticism*. Harper. Rhetoric. AC.

1673. Boyd, J. R. *Elements of Rhetoric and Literary Criticism*. New York: Harper Brothers, 1844. Rhetoric. HR, AK.

1674. Boynton, H. W. *Journalism and Literature*. Boston, 1904. Journalism. LC.

1675. Boynton, P. H. *Principles of Composition*. Boston: Ginn, 1915. Composition. USC, BMI, AK.

1676. Brace, J. *The Principles of English Grammar*. 2 vol. 1939-40. Grammar. SIBP.

1677. Brackenbury, L. *The Teaching of Grammar*. J. Murray ed. 1908. Grammar. BMI.

1678. Bradley, H. *On the Relations Between Spoken and Written Language, with Special Reference to English*. Oxford, 1914. Speech and Writing. USC, BMI.

1679. Bradley, H. *On the Relations Between Spoken and Written Language with Special Reference to English*. Oxford, 1919. Speech and Writing. USC.

1680. Bradley, H. *The Making of English*. London. 1904. LC.

1681. Brautigan, I. M. and Others. *Progressive Composition Lessons*. Silver, 1914. Composition. USC.

1682. <u>Breaking the Spell: An Appeal to Common Sense</u>. Simplified Spelling Society, 1917. Spelling. BMI.

1683. Breed, F. S. and Frostic, F. W. <u>Scale for Measuring the General Merit of English Composition in the Sixth Grade</u>. Ann Arbor, MI: University of Michigan, 1917. Evaluating Writing. USC.

1684. Breitenbach, H.P. <u>Value of English to Practicing Engineer</u>. Univ. of Michigan, 1906. Technical English. USC.

1685. Brewer, J. M. <u>Oral English</u>. Ginn, 1916. Speech. USC.

1686. Brewster, W. T. <u>English Composition and Style</u>. New York: Century, 1912. Composition. USC, BMI, AK.

1687. Brewster, W. T. <u>Specimens of Prose Narration</u>. Holt. Modes. USC.

1688. Brewster, W. T. <u>Studies in Structure and Style; Based on 7 Modern English Essays</u>. Macmillan, 1896. Style. AC, AK.

1689. Brewster, W. T. <u>The Writing of English</u>. Home University Library, 1914. Composition. BMI, AK.

1690. Brewster, W. T. <u>Writing English Prose</u>. Holt, 1913. Composition. USC.

1691. Brewster, W. T., and Carpenter, G. R. <u>Studies in Structure and Style</u>. Macmillan. Style. USC.

1692. Brewster, W. T., ed. <u>Representative Essays on Theory of Style</u>. Macmillan, 1905. Style. USC.

1693. Briggs, L. R. <u>To College Teachers of English Composition</u>. Houghton, 1928. Teaching Methods. AK.

1694. Briggs, T. H. <u>Formal English Grammar as a Discipline</u>. New York: Teacher's College, Columbia University, 1913. Grammar. HEW, USC.

1695. Briggs, T. H. and McKinney, I. <u>First Book of</u>

       Composition for High Schools. Boston: Ginn, 1913. Composition. USC, BMI.

1696. Briggs, T. H., and McKinney, I. Second Book of Composition for High Schools. Boston: Ginn, 1919. Composition. USC, BMI.

1697. Briggs, T. H. and others. Junior High School English Books. Ginn, 1921. English Syllabi. USC.

1698. Bright, O.T. Graded Instruction in English. New York: D. Appleton and Co., 1883. English Syllabi. HEW.

1699. Bright, O.T. Graded Instruction in English. American Book. English Syllabi. USC.

1700. Brink, C.M. The Making of an Oration. Chicago: A. C. McClurg and Co., 1913. Speech. HEW.

1701. Brinkworth, M.G. A Business Speller. Boston, 1917. Spelling. BMI.

1702. Britton's Supplementary Leaflets for Class Use: 5th and 6th Grade Language. Britton Ptg. Co., 1914. USC.

1703. Britton's Supplementary Leaflets for Class Use: Grammar Exercises. Britton Ptg. Co., 1914. Grammar. USC.

1704. Broadus, J. A. A Treatise on the Preparation and Delivery of Sermons. New York: A.C. Armstrong and Son, 1870. Sermons. HR.

1705. Broadus, J. A. A Treatise on the Preparation and Delivery of Sermons. 2nd ed. 1871. Sermons. SIBP.

1706. Brockington, W. A. Elements of Prose. London, 1899. Composition. BMI.

1707. Bronxville, NY, Massee Country School. 500 Questions on English B. Bronxville, NY: Massee Country School, 1914. Testing. USC.

1708. Brookfield, F. First Book in Composition. Barnes,

1855. Composition. AC.

1709. Brookfield, W. *First Book in Composition*. Barnes. Composition. USC.

1710. Brooks, P. *Lectures on Preaching*. Dutton, 1877. Sermons. LLC,CLPI.

1711. Brooks, S. D. *English Composition*. American Book, 1911. Composition. USC.

1712. Brooks, S. D. *English Composition*. American Book, 1912. Composition. USC, BMI.

1713. Brooks, S. D. and Hubbard, M. *Composition on Rhetoric*. American Book, 1906. Composition. USC, AC.

1714. Brothers of the Christian Schools. *First Lesson in English Grammar*. La Salle Bureau, 1914. Grammar. USC.

1715. Brothers of the Christian Schools. *First Lesson in English Grammar*. W. H. Sadlier, 1912. Grammar. USC.

1716. Brothers of the Christian Schools. *Language Lessons*. W. H. Sadlier. Grammar. USC.

1717. Brothers of the Christian Schools. *Principals of English Grammar*. La Salle Bureau, 1914. Grammar. USC.

1718. Brown, A. and Sons. *Browns' Scholar's Own Composition*. London. Composition. BMI.

1719. Brown, G. *Brown's Elementary Grammar*. Wood, 1914. Grammar. USC.

1720. Brown, G. B. *Brown's Grammar Improved*. 1868. Grammar. SIBP.

1721. Brown, G. *First Lessons in Language and Grammar*. Wood. Grammar. USC.

1722. Brown, G. *First Lines of English Grammar*. Wood. Grammar. USC.

1723. Brown, G. Grammar of Grammars. Wood. Grammar. USC.

1724. Brown, G. Institutes of English Grammar. New York: Wood, 1914. Grammar. USC.

1725. Brown, G. The Grammar of English Grammars. Grammar. CLPI.

1726. Brown, G. The Grammar of English Grammars. 1851. Grammar. SIBP.

1727. Brown, G. P. "On the Teaching of English Elementary and High School," National Society and Scientific Study of Education. 1906. Teaching Methods. HEW.

1728. Brown, G. P. and De Garmo, C. Elements of English Grammar. American Books, 1900. Grammar. USC.

1729. Brown, J. American System of English Grammar. 1825. Grammar. CLPI.

1730. Brown, M. Humor or Bulls and Blunders. Small, 1906. Error. USC.

1731. Brown, M. F. Glimpse of Grammar-Land. Bardeen. Grammar. USC.

1732. Brown, R. W. Dean Briggs. Harper, 1926. AK.

1733. Brown, R. W. How the French Boy Learns to Write. Harvard University Press, 1915. Composition. USC.

1734. Brown, R. W. and Barnes, N. W. Art of Writing English. New York: American Book, 1913. Composition. USC, BMI, AK.

1735. Brown, R. W., ed. Writer's Art by Those Who Have Practiced It. Harvard University Press, 1921. Composition. USC.

1736. Brown, S. G. The Studies of an Orator. New York: Office of the American Biblical Repository and the American Eclectic, 1841. Speech. HEW.

1737. Brown, S. J. Suggested Course of Study and Syllabus

for Non-English Speaking Adults. Connecticut: Hartford Board of Education, 1918. TESOL. USC, HEW.

1738. Browning, O. Aspects of Education. 1892. CC.

1739. Browning, O. Introduction to the History of Education Theories. 1888. History of Education. CC.

1740. Brubacher, A. R. and Synder, D. E. English, Oral and Written. C. E. Merrill, 1914. Composition. USC.

1741. Brubacher, A. R. and Synder, D. E. High School English. Merrill, C. E., 1910. Curriculum. USC, AC.

1742. Brubacher, A. R. and Synder, D. E. High School English. C. E. Merrill, 1912. Curriculum. USC.

1743. Brubacher, A. R. and Synder, D. E. High School English. 2 vol. Merrill, 1917-1920. Curriculum. USC.

1744. Bruce, H. L. and Montgomery, G., ed. College Readings in English. Macmillan, 1920. Readers. USC.

1745. Bryan, W. F. and Crane, R. S., ed. The English Familiar Essay. Ginn, 1916. Modes. EGL.

1746. Bryan, W. F. and Denton, G. B. Manual for Theme Revision. Evanston, IL: W. F. Bryan., 1917. Composition. USC.

1747. Bryan, W. F. and Denton, G. B. Manual for Theme Revision. Evanston, IL: W. F. Bryan, 1914. Composition. USC.

1748. Bryan, W. F. and Denton, G. B. Manual for Theme Revision. Banta, 1920. Composition. USC.

1749. Bryant, F. E. On the Limits of Descriptive Writing Apropos of Lessing's Laocoon. Ann Arbor, MI. Modes. AC, AK.

1750. Bryant, H. W. Grammar and Correspondence. Chicago:

Bryant and Stratton. Grammar. USC.

1751. Bryant, J. H. *Plain English*. USC.

1752. Buchan, J. *Homilies and Recreations*. Houghton, 1926. Sermons. EGL.

1753. Buck, G. *A Course in Argumentative Writing*. Holt, 1899. Composition. AK.

1754. Buck, G. *Expository Writing*. Holt, 1899. Composition. USC.

1755. Buck, G. *Figures of Rhetoric: A Psychological Study*. F. N. Scott ed. Rhetoric. AK.

1756. Buck, G. *Make-Believe Grammar*. 1909. Grammar. USC, AK.

1757. Buck, G. *The Metaphor-A Study in the Psychology of Rhetoric*. F. N. Scott ed. Ann Arbor: Inland Press, 1899. Rhetoric. HR, PS, AK.

1758. Buck, G. *The Social Criticism of Literature*. Yale University Press, 1916. Criticism. AK.

1759. Buck, G. and Morris, E. W. *Course in Narrative Writing*. Holt, 1906. Composition. USC, AK.

1760. Buck, G. and Woodbridge, E. *Course in Expository Writing*. Holt, 1899. Composition. AC, AK.

1761. Buck, M. *Grammar and Analysis of English Language*. Hinds, 1900. Grammar. USC.

1762. Bucke, C. *A Classical Grammar of the English Language*. 1829. Grammar. SIBP.

1763. Buehler, H. G. *Modern English Grammar*. Newson. Grammar. USC.

1764. Buehler, H. G. *Modern English Grammar and Composition*. Newson, 1916. Composition. USC.

1765. Buehler, H. G. *Modern English Grammar Revised*. Newson, 1914. Grammar. USC.

1766. Buehler, H. G. Modern English Grammar with Composition. Newson. Composition. USC.

1767. Buehler, H. G. Practical Exercises in English. American Book, 1912. English Syllabi. USC.

1768. Buehler, H. G. Practical Exercises in English Arranged for Use with Hill's Foundations of Rhetoric. Harper, 1895. English Syllabi. AC.

1769. Buehler, H. G. Shorter English Grammar with Composition. Newson. Composition. AC.

1770. Buehler, H. G. and Hotchkiss, C. W. Modern English Lessons. Newson. USC.

1771. Bugbee, A. G. Exercises in English Syntax. Bardeen. Grammar. USC.

1772. Bugg, L. H. Correct English. 5th ed. Herder, 1912. Usage. USC.

1773. Buhlig, R. Business English. Heath. 1914. USC.

1774. Buhlig, R. First Year English. Heath, 1917. English Syllabi. USC.

1775. Bull, A. E. How to Write for the Papers. Pearson, 1912. Journalism. BMI.

1776. Bull, A. S. How to Write for the Papers. C. A. Pearson, 1918. Journalism. BMI.

1777. Bulley, M. W. The Universities' Mission English Primer. S. P. C. K., 1911. English Syllabi. BMI.

1778. Bullions, P. Analysis, Parsing and Composition. Sheldon, 1876. Composition. AC.

1779. Bullions, P. Practical English Grammar. American Book, 1912. Grammar. USC.

1780. Bullions, P. Practical Lessons in English Grammar. Sheldon, 1876. Grammar. AC.

1781. Bullions, P. School Grammar. American Book. Grammar. USC.

1782. Bullows, A. M. "The Need of Speech Work in the High Schools," <u>National Education Assoc. of the United States Journal of Proceedings and Addresses</u>. 1916. Speech. HEW.

1783. Bumby, M. T. <u>Minimum Essentials in English Grammar</u>. Atkinson, Mentzer, and Company, 1917. Grammar. USC.

1784. Bunce, O. B. <u>Don't</u>. Appleton. USC.

1785. Burgess, H. <u>Art of Preaching and Composition of Sermons</u>. 1881. Sermons. CSIGP.

1786. Burk, F. L. and McFadden, E. B. <u>Course of Study in Grammar</u>. State Normal Grammar School, 1908. Grammar. USC.

1787. Burke, M. <u>New Method of Teaching Writing to Infants</u>. G. Philip and Son, 1909. Composition. LC.

1788. Burleson, D. S. <u>Practical English Grammar</u>. National Book Company, 1919. Grammar. USC.

1789. Burnett, J. <u>Hints on Composition</u>. Benerman, 1876. Composition. AC.

1790. Burns, J. J. <u>How to Teach Reading and Composition</u>. New York: American Book, 1901. Composition. USC, BMI, AC.

1791. Burrell, D. J. <u>The Sermon. Its Construction and Delivery</u>. New York, 1913. Sermons. BMI.

1792. Burris, W. P. <u>A Course of Study in Elementary English</u>. Athens: Ohio University Press, 1906. English Syllabi. HEW.

1793. Burris, W. P. <u>Course of Study in Elementary English</u>. University of Cincinnati, 1912. English Syllabi. USC.

1794. Burroughs, J. <u>Literary Values and Other Papers</u>. Houghton, 1902. EGL.

1795. Burton, R. <u>Forces in Fiction, and Other Essays</u>.

Bobbs, 1902. EGL.

1796. Bush, M. G. *First School Days of the Non-English Child*. Wisconsin: Madison Dept. of Public Instruction, 1918. TESOL. USC.

1797. *Busy Work Language Cards*. Flanagan. Teaching Methods. USC.

1798. Butler, C. *Charles Butler's English Grammar*. 1910. Grammar. LC.

1799. Butler, G. P. *School English*. American Book. English Syllabi. USC.

1800. Butler, N. *A Practical and Critical Grammar of the English Language*. 1874. Grammar. SIBP.

1801. Butler, N. *Education in the United States*. 2 vol. 1900. History of Education. CC.

1802. Butler, N. *Introductory Grammar*. Morton. Grammar. USC.

1803. Butler, N. *New Practical Grammar*. Morton. Grammar. USC.

1804. Butler, N. *Practical and Critical Grammar*. Morton, 1912. Grammar. USC.

1805. Butler, N. *Practical Grammar*. Morton. Grammar. USC.

1806. Bygott, J. and Jones, A. J. *The Kings English*. Jarrolds, 1918. Usage. BMI.

1807. Bygott, J. and Jones, A. J. *The King's English and How to Write It*. London, 1903. Usage. BMI.

1808. Cabell, E. D. and Freeman, V. W. *English Taught Inductively*. Hall and McCreary, 1911. English Syllabi. USC.

1809. Cabell, E. D. and Freeman, V. W. *Suggestions for Teachers Using the Cabell-Freeman Series in English*. Hall and McCreary, 1912. Teaching Methods. USC.

1810. Cady, F. W. <u>Freshman Course in English</u>. Middlebury, VT: Middlebury College, 1914. English Syllabi. USC.

1811. Cairns, W. B. <u>Forms of Discourse</u>. Ginn, 1896, 1909. Rhetoric. USC, AC, AK.

1812. Cairns, W. B. <u>Introduction to Rhetoric</u>. Ginn, 1901, 1899. Rhetoric. USC, AC, AK.

1813. California Association of Teachers of English. <u>Cooperation in the Teaching of English</u>. Sacramento: California State Printing Office, 1915. Curriculum. HEW.

1814. California Association of Teachers of English. <u>Oral English in the High School, a Manual of Practical Suggestions</u>. Sacramento, CA: State Priniting Office, 1915. Curriculum. USC, HEW.

1815. California Commission of Immigration and Housing. <u>A Discussion of Methods of Teaching English to Adult Foreigners with a Report on Los Angeles County</u>. Sacramento: California State Printing Office, 1917. TESOL. HEW.

1816. Califronia Commission of Immigration and Housing. <u>Home Teacher</u>. Sacramento, 1915. TESOL. USC.

1817. Califronia Commission of Immigration and Housing. <u>Our Soldiers and English Language, a San Francisco Enterprise</u>. Sacramento: California State Printing Office, 1918. Business English. HEW.

1818. Call, R. E. <u>Correct English</u>. Sherwood Company, 1913. English Syllabi. USC.

1819. Call, W. T. <u>Little Grammar</u>. New York: Potterdon, 1906. Grammar. USC, HEW.

1820. Callandar, H. L. <u>System of Phonetic Spelling</u>. London, 1889. Spelling. BMI.

1821. Callaway, M. <u>The Incidental Teaching of English</u>. Austin, TX, 1909. Teaching Methods. HEW.

1822. Cambridge, Mass. School Com. <u>English, a Course of</u>

Study for Elementary Schools with Graded Standards. Cambridge, MA: School Com., 1915. English Syllabi. USC.

1823. Campagnac, E. T. Lectures on the Teaching of Composition. London: Constable and Company, 1912. Composition. HEW, BMI.

1824. Campagnac, E. T. Teaching of Composition. Houghton, 1912. Composition. USC, HEW.

1825. Campbell, B. J. and Vass, B. L. Essentials of Business English. 2nd ed. Jackson, MI: Business English Pub. Co., 1915. Business English. USC.

1826. Campbell, B. J. and Vass, B. L. Essentials of Business English. Ellis, 1910. Business English. USC.

1827. Campbell, G. Lectures on Pulpit Eloquence. 1824. Sermons. SIBP.

1828. Campbell, G. Philosophy of Rhetoric. Harper, 1875. Rhetoric. AC, AK.

1829. Campbell, G. Philosophy of Rhetoric. Funk, 1911. Rhetoric. USC.

1830. Campbell, G. The Philosophy of Rhetoric. 1823. Rhetoric. SIBP.

1831. Campbell, G. The Philosophy of Rhetoric. Lloyd F. Bitzer ed. Carbondale: Southern Illinois University Press, 1963. Rhetoric. HR.

1832. Canby, H. S. American Estimates. Harcourt, 1929. EGL.

1833. Canby, H. S. Better Writing. Harcourt, 1926. Composition. EGL.

1834. Canby, H. S. College Sons and College Fathers. Harper, 1915. EGL.

1835. Canby, H. S. Facts. Macmillan, 1917. USC.

1836. Canby, H. S. and Opdycke, J. B. Elements of

Composition for Secondary Schools. Macmillan, 1913, 1916. Composition. USC, BMI, AK.

1837. Canby, H. S. and Opdycke, J. B. Good English. Macmillan, 1918. Composition. USC.

1838. Canby, H. S. and others. English Composition in Theory and Practice. Macmillan, 1909. Composition. USC, AK.

1839. Canby, H. S. and others. Facts, Thought, and Imagination. Macmillan, 1917. USC.

1840. Canby, H. S. and Pierce, F. E. and others. English Composition in Theory and Practice. Macmillan, 1908-1910. Composition. AC.

1841. Canfield, D. F., and Carpenter, G. R. Elementary Composition. Macmillan, 1906. Composition. USC, AC.

1842. Cardozo, B. N. Law and Literature and Other Essays and Addresses. Harcourt, 1931. EGL.

1843. Carman, M. C. The Function of Words. Longmans, 1909. BMI.

1844. Carnagy, D. Public Speaking. New York: Association Press, 1920. Speech. HEW.

1845. Carnegie, A. "College-Bred Men in the Business World," Report of the Commissioner of Education. 1890. Curriculum. AK.

1846. Carpenter, G. R. Elements of Rhetoric. New York, 1900. Rhetoric. BMI.

1847. Carpenter, G. R. Elements of Rhetoric and English Composition. Macmillan, 1899. Composition. AC.

1848. Carpenter, G. R. Elements of Rhetoric and English Composition. 2 vol. Macmillan, 1912. Rhetoric. USC, BMI AK.

1849. Carpenter, G. R. English Grammar. Macmillan, 1906. Grammar. USC.

1850. Carpenter, G. R. *Exercises in Rhetoric.* New York, 1897. Rhetoric. BMI.

1851. Carpenter, G. R. *Exercises in Rhetoric and English Composition.* 6th ed. Macmillan, 1895. Composition. AC.

1852. Carpenter, G. R. *Exercises in Rhetoric and English Composition.* New York: Macmillan, 1896. Rhetoric. BMI, AC.

1853. Carpenter, G. R. *Exercises in Rhetoric and English Composition.* 3rd ed. Macmillan, 1895. Composition. AC, AK.

1854. Carpenter, G. R. *Exercises in Rhetoric and English Composition.* 2nd ed. Small, 1892. Composition. AC.

1855. Carpenter, G. R. *Model English Prose.* Macmillan, 1905. Readers. USC, AC.

1856. Carpenter, G. R. *Notes for Teachers of English Composition.* New York, 1901. Teaching Methods. BMI.

1857. Carpenter, G. R. *Principles of English Grammar for Use of Schools.* Macmillan, 1898. Grammar. USC.

1858. Carpenter, G. R. *Rhetoric and English Composition.* Macmillan, 1906. Composition. USC, AC, AK.

1859. Carpenter, G. R. *Teaching of English in the Elementary and the Secondary School.* J. E. Russell, 1903. Teaching Methods. BMI.

1860. Carpenter, G. R. and others. *Teaching of English in Elementary and Secondary School.* Longmans, 1903. Teaching Methods. USC.

1861. Carpenter, G. R. and others. *Teaching of English in the Elem. Secondary School.* Longmans, 1913. Teaching Methods. USC.

1862. Carpenter, G. R., Baker, F. T. and Scott, F. N. *The Teaching of English in the Elementary and Secondary Schools.* New York: Longmans, Green, and Co., 1903.

Teaching Methods. HEW, AK.

1863. Carpenter, J. H. *Fairy Grammar*. Dutton, 1920. Grammar. USC.

1864. Carson, L. C. *Handbook of English Composition*. World Book, 1905-1907. Composition. AC.

1865. Carson, L. C. *Handbook of English Composition*. World Book, 1910. Composition. USC.

1866. Carson, L. C. *Handbook of English Composition*. 2nd ed. World Book, 1919. Composition. USC.

1867. Chalmers, J. S. *The Primary School Grammar*. Glasgow. 1918. Grammar. BMI.

1868. Chancellor, W. E. *Reading and Language Lessons for Evening Schools*. American Book, 1904. English Syllabi. USC.

1869. Chancellor, W. E. *Reading and Language Lessons for Evening Schools*. American Book, 1912. English Syllabi. USC.

1870. Chancellor, W. E. *Standard Short Course for Evening Schools*. American Book, 1911. English Syllabi. USC.

1871. Chancellor, W. E. *Studies in English for Evening Schools*. American Book, 1904. English Syllabi. USC.

1872. Channing, E. T. *Lectures Read to the Seniors in Harvard College*. Dorothy I. Anderson and Waldo W. Braden. ed. Carbondale: Southern Ilinois University, 1968. Rhetoric. HR, PS, AK.

1873. Chaplin, A. *The Romance of Language*. London: Sidgwick and Jackson, 1920. HEW.

1874. Chapman, R. W. *Portrait of a Scholar, and Other Essays Written in Macedonia, 1918-19*. Oxford, 1920. EGL.

1875. Charles, W. W. and Miller, E. *A Course of Study--Grammar Based upon the Grammatical Errors of*

School Children of Kansas City, Missouri. Columbia, MO: University of Missouri, 1915. Grammar. HEW.

1876. Charters, W. W. and Miller, E. Course of Study in Grammar Based upon the Grammatical Errors of School Children of Kansas City, Missouri. University of Missouri, 1915. Grammar. USC.

1877. Chase, A. Illustrated Reproduction Stories. Readers. USC.

1878. Chester, M. Expository Paragraph and Sentence. Longmans. Paragraphs. USC.

1879. Chester, M. Illustrated Composition Outline Cards. Composition. USC.

1880. Chester, M. Writing and Speaking. Longman, 1909. Composition. USC.

1881. Chesterton, G. K. Generally Speaking. Dodd. 1929. EGL.

1882. Chicago Board of Education. High School English Syllabus, October 1920. Chicago, 1920. Curriculum. HEW.

1883. Child, F. J. Child Memorial Volume. Ginn, 1896. USC.

1884. Child Life Composition Pictures. Barnes, 1910. Teaching Methods. USC.

1885. Chittenden, L. A. Elements of English Composition. Griggs, 1884. Composition. AC.

1886. Choate, A. and Hartman, G. Exercises for Parsing and Analysis. Bryn Mawr, PA: Augusta Choate, 1909. Grammar. USC.

1887. Christinides, M. D. English for Immigrants. New York, 1914. TESOL. HEW.

1888. Chubb, P. Teaching of English in Elementary and Secondary Schools. Macmillan, 1902. Teaching Methods. USC, HEW.

1889. Claggett, R. *Elocution Made Easy*. Paine and Burgess. 1845. Rhetoric. AK.

1890. Clapp, H. L. and Huston, K. W. *Conduct or Composition Work in Grammar Schools*. Boston: Heath, 1902. Composition. USC, HEW, AC.

1891. Clare, M. C. *100 Test Papers in English Grammar*. Hong Kong, 1918. Grammar. BMI.

1892. Clare, M. C. *A Companion to English Grammar*. Hong Kong, 1918. Composition. BMI.

1893. Clare, M. C. *Analysis, Synthesis and Transformation of Sentences*. Hong Kong, 1918. Grammar. BMI.

1894. Clark, A. C. *Prose Rhythm in English*. Clarendon, 1913. Sound Patterns. LLC.

1895. Clark, G. *Self-Cultivation in Rhetoric*. New York: N. W. School Supply Co., 1916. Rhetoric. USC.

1896. Clark, G. E. *A Practical Guide to Essay Writing and Composition and Business Letter Writing*. 1916. Composition. BMI.

1897. Clark, G. E. *Guide to Essay Writing*. London, 1887. Composition. BMI.

1898. Clark, G. E. *Practical Guide to Dictation and Spelling*. 1915. Spelling. BMI.

1899. Clark, J. S. *Briefer Practical Rhetoric*. Holt, 1891. Rhetoric. USC, AC.

1900. Clark, J. S. *Exercises to Practical Rhetoric*. Holt, 1886. Rhetoric. AC.

1901. Clark, J. S. *Practical Rhetoric*. New York, 1891. Rhetoric. BMI.

1902. Clark, J. S. *Practical Rhetoric*. Holt, 1886. Rhetoric. AC, AK.

1903. Clark, M. G. *Motived Language*. 2 vol. Sioux City, IA. Ye Highe Schoole, 1917. USC.

1904. Clark, N. G. Outline of Elements of the English Language. Scribner. Grammar. USC.

1905. Clark, S. H. and Blanchard, F. M. Practical Public Speaking; A Textbook for College and Secondary Schools. 1905. Speech. CC.

1906. Clarke, G. H. and Ungold, G. T. English: A Modern Grammar. Marshall and Sons, 1913. Grammar. BMI.

1907. Clarke, W. E. C. and Muller, A. C. A Class Book of English Grammar. Capetown, 1911. Grammar. BMI.

1908. Clarke, W. E. C. and Muller, A. C. A Class Book of English Grammar. Capetown, 1917. Grammar. BMI.

1909. Classen, E. Lectures on Style and Composition. Macmillan, 1917. Composition. BMI.

1910. Claxton, P. P. and McGinniss, J. Effective English. Allyn, 1917. English Syllabi. USC.

1911. Cleaveland, E. W. Future Auxiliaries in English. New Haven, CT: Elizabeth W. Cleaveland, 1916. Grammar. USC.

1912. Clergyman of the English Church. The Art of Preaching. 1876. Sermons. SIBP.

1913. Clews, H. "College-Bred Men in the Business World," Report of the Commissioner of Education. 1890. Curriculum. AK.

1914. Clippinger, E. E. Illustrated Lessons in Composition and Rhetoric. Silver, 1915. Composition. USC.

1915. Clippinger, E. E. Illustrated Lessons in Composition and Rhetoric. Silver, 1912. Composition. USC.

1916. Clippinger, E. E. Written and Spoken English. Silver, 1917-1918. Composition. USC.

1917. Clodd, E. The Story of the Alphabet. McClure, 1904. Spelling. LLC.

1918. Cobbett, W. English Grammar. Grammar. USC.

1919. Cobbett, W. *Grammar of the English Language in a Series of Letters*. 1846. Grammar. CLPI.

1920. Cockayne, C. A., ed. *Modern Essays of Various Types*. Merrill, 1927. EGL.

1921. Cody, F. W. *A Freshman Course in English*. Middlebury, VT: Middlebury College, 1914. Freshman English. HEW.

1922. Cody, S. *100% Self-Correcting Course in English Language*. Sherwin Cody School Of English, 1919. Curriculum. USC.

1923. Cody, S. *Art of Writing and Speaking the English Language*. D. B. Clarkson, 1908-10. Composition. AC.

1924. Cody, S. *Art of Writing and Speaking the English Language*. 4 vol. Old Greek Press, 1912. Composition. USC, CC.

1925. Cody, S. *Brief Fundamentals*. Chicago School of English, 1917. USC, BMI.

1926. Cody, S. *Composition: Constructive Rhetoric*. Old Greek Press, 1905-07. Composition. AC.

1927. Cody, S. *Dictionary of Errors*. Old Greek Press. Error. USC.

1928. Cody, S. *English for Business Uses and Commercial Correspondence*. School of English, 1914. Business English. USC.

1929. Cody, S. *Literary Composition*. School of English, 1912. Composition. USC.

1930. Cody, S. *Literary Composition*. 2nd ed. McClurg, 1918. Composition. USC.

1931. Cody, S. *Short Term Grammar Drill*. Old Greek Press. Grammar. USC.

1932. Cody, S. *Story-Writing and Journalism*. Old Greek Press, 1905. Journalism. CC.

1933. Cody, S. *The Art of Writing and Speaking the English Language*. Chicago, 1903. Composition. BMI.

1934. Cody, S. *The Ideal Course in English for Vocational Students*. Chicago, 1914. Business English. HEW.

1935. Cody, S. *The Sherwin Cody Self-Correcting Course in English Language*. Rochester, NY: 1918. English Syllabi. BMI.

1936. Cody, S. *Word-Study for Schools*. Old Greek Press. USC.

1937. Cole, J. R. *Primary Writing Grammar*. T. Cushing and Co., 1874. Grammar. AC.

1938. Cole, R. E. *Every Day English for Every Coming American*. Cleveland, OH: Y. M. C. A., 1914. TESOL. USC.

1939. *College Entrance Exam*. Ginn, 1901-1905. Testing. USC.

1940. *College Entrance Requirements in English, 1909-1915*. American Book. Testing. AC.

1941. Collins, J. S. H. and Mugan, M. D. *New Graded Method in English Grammar, Letter Writing and Composition*. 5th ed. 3 vol. St. Louis, MO: Metropolitan Pub. Co., 1919. Composition. USC.

1942. Colonna, D. *Volere e' Potere*. 1912. USC.

1943. Colorado Teacher's Association Committee. *Report of the Committee on the Teaching of English in Colorado*. Denver, CO, 1902. Curriculum. HEW.

1944. *Columbia University Studies in the Teaching of English Grammar*. Teachers College, 1906. Grammar. USC.

1945. Committee on the Cost and Labor of English Teaching. *Report on the Cost and Labor of English Teaching*. Lawrence, KS: E. M. Hopkins, 1913. Teacher Training. USC.

1946. Comparative Experimental Teaching in Spelling. Teachers College, 1912. Spelling. USC.

1947. Composition Book: First Illustrated Composition Book. 1901. Composition. BMI.

1948. Composition Book: The Suggestive Composition Book. London, 1895. Composition. BMI.

1949. Compton, A. G. Some Common Errors of Speech. Putnam, 1898. Error. USC.

1950. Comstock, A. Practical Elocution; or, the Art of Reading. Uriah Hunt, 1830. Reading. AK.

1951. Conference on Speech Training in London Schools and Training College. London: March, 1916. Speech. HEW.

1952. Conferences of Teachers of English. Stratford-Upon-Avon, 1914. Curriculum. BMI.

1953. Conklin, B. Y. Complete Graded Course in English Grammar and Composition. Appleton, 1889. Composition. AC.

1954. Conklin, B. Y. Complete Graded Course in English Grammar and Composition. American Book. Composition. USC.

1955. Conklin, B. Y. Practical Lessons in Language. American Book. English Syllabi. USC.

1956. Conklin, G. W. Vest-Pocket Writing Desk Book. Saalfield ed. McKay. USC.

1957. Conklin, G. W., ed. Don'ts for Speakers and Writers. McKay. Usage. USC.

1958. Connecticut Board of Education. Report on the Study of English Language and Literature in Elementary and Secondary Schools. Hartford, 1904. Curriculum. HEW.

1959. Cook, A. S. Higher Study of English. Houghton, 1906. English Syllabi. USC, AK.

1960. Cook, L. B. Project Book in Business English. Holt, 1920. Business English. USC.

1961. Cook, W. A. and O'Shea, M. V. The Child and His Spelling. 1914. Spelling. BMI.

1962. Cooley, A. Language Teaching in the Grades. Boston, Chicago: Houghton, Mifflin, and Company, 1905. Teaching Methods. HEW.

1963. Cooley, A. W. Language Lessons from Literature. Houghton. Literature and Composition. USC.

1964. Cooley, A. W. Language Teaching in the Grades. Houghton, 1913. Teaching Methods. USC.

1965. Cooley, A. W. Webster-Cooley Two-Book Course in Language, Grammar and Composition. Houghton. Composition. USC.

1966. Cooley, A. W. and Webster, W. F. New Webster-Cooley Course in English. Houghton, 1909. Composition. USC.

1967. Coon, C. L. English and History in the Elementary School. Raleigh, NC: Office of the State Superintendent of Public Instruction, 1905. HEW.

1968. Cooper, F. T. Craftmanship of Writing. Dodd, 1911. Composition. CC.

1969. Cooper, L. Two Views of Education, with Other Papers Chiefly on the Study of Literature. Yale University Press, 1922. Literature. EGL.

1970. Cooper, L., ed. Theories of Style. Macmillan, 1907. Style. USC, AC.

1971. Copeland, C. T. and Rideout, H. M. Freshman English and Theme-Correcting in Harvard College. Silver, 1912. Freshman English. USC.

1972. Copeland, C. T. and Rideout, H. R. Freshman English and Theme-Correcting in Harvard College. Silver, 1901. Freshman English. CC, AK.

1973. Copeland, R. Freshman English and Theme-Correcting

in Harvard. Silver. Freshman English. AC.

1974. Coppee, H. Elements of Rhetoric. Butler, 1876. Rhetoric. AC.

1975. Coppens, C. Practical Introduction to English Rhetoric. Schwartz, Kirwin, and Fauss, 1912. Rhetoric. USC.

1976. Coppens, C. Practical Introduction to English Rhetoric. Catholic Publishers, 1886. Rhetoric. AC, AK.

1977. Coppens, C. The Art of Oratorical Composition. Schwartz, Kirwin, and Fauss, 1885. Speech. AC.

1978. Cornford, L. C. English Composition. London, 1900. Composition. BMI.

1979. Cornford, L. C. Essay-Writing for Schools. London, 1903. Composition. BMI.

1980. Cornwell, J. Complete Guide to English Composition. London, 1904. Composition. BMI.

1981. Corson, H. The Voice and Spiritual Education. New York: Macmillan, 1896. Sermons. HR, AK.

1982. Cortina, R. D. English in English. Cortina, 1906. USC.

1983. Cosad. English Composition. Crist, 1900-05. Composition. AC.

1984. Cosad, K. A. English Composition for Teachers' Training Classes. Crist, 1912. Composition. USC.

1985. Coster, J. Small English Grammar for Dutchmen. Stechert. TESOL. USC.

1986. Course of Study in Language and Grammar and Suggested Materials Grades 1-9. Cleveland, OH, 1916. Curriculum. HEW.

1987. Courses of Study. Washington., D. C., 1908. Curriculum. USC, HEW.

1988. Covert, M. The Study of the English Language as an Educational Force. Albany, NY: J. Munsell, 1866. English Syllabi. HEW.

1989. Cox, I. Arts of Writing, Reading and Speaking. Carleton, 1876. Rhetoric. AC.

1990. Cox, L. Arte or Crafte of Rhetoryke. Chicago: University of Chicago, 1901. Rhetoric. USC.

1991. Crafts, W. F., and Fisk, H. F. Rhetoric Made Easy. G. Sherwood, 1890. Rhetoric. AC.

1992. Cramp, W. The Philosophy of Language, Containing Practical Rules for Acquiring a Knowledge of English Grammar. 1838. Grammar. CLPI.

1993. Crandall, H. E. First Year English Book. Atkinson, M and G., 1908. English Syllabi. USC.

1994. Crawford, D. G. Study of English. Macmillan, 1919. USC.

1995. Croce, B. Conduct of Life. Harcourt, 1924. EGL.

1996. Crombie, A. The Etymology and Syntax of the English Language. 4th ed. 1836. Grammar. SIBP.

1997. Cromer, E. B. Political and Literary Essays. 3 vol. Macmillan, 1916. EGL.

1998. Cronson, B. Graded Lessons in Punctuation. New York, 1911. Punctuation. BMI.

1999. Crook, C. W. English Spelling and Pronunciation. Nisbet, 1918. Spelling. BMI.

2000. Crook, C. W. Essentials of English in Composition. Peter, 1919. Composition. BMI.

2001. Crosier, A. A. Digest of Infinitives and Participles. Flanagan. Grammar. USC.

2002. Cruikshank, J. Exercises in Analysis, Parsing and Composition. Sheldon, 1869. Composition. AC.

2003. Crumpton, C. Guide to Speech Week. Chicago:

National Council of Teachers of English, 1919. Speech. USC.

2004. Cruse, A. English Composition. H. Frowde, 1913. Composition. BMI.

2005. Cruse, A. English Composition Based on the Study of Literary Models. Oxford, 1913. Literature and Composition. USC.

2006. Cubberley, E. P. Readings in the History of Education: A Collection of Sources and Readings to Illustrate the Development of Educational Practice, Theory. Houghton, 1920. History of Education. LLC.

2007. Cubberley, E. P. The History of Education: Educational Practice and Progress Considered as a Phase of the Development and Spread of Western Civilization. Houghton, 1920. History of Education. LLC.

2008. Curl, M. J. Expository Writing. Houghton, 1919. Composition. USC.

2009. Curry, S. S. Imagination and Dramatic Instinct. Expression Co., 1896. CC.

2010. Curry, S. S. Province of Expression. Boston School of Expression, 1891. CC.

2011. Curry, S. S. The Province of Expression: A Search for Principles Underlying Adequate Method of Developing Dramatic and Oratoric Delivery. Boston: School of Expression, 1891. Rhetoric. HEW.

2012. Dabney, R. L. Lectures on Sacred Rhetoric. New York. Sermons. AC.

2013. Dale, R. W. Nine Lectures on Preaching. Sermons. CLPI.

2014. Dalgleish, W. S. Advanced Text-Book of English Composition. 1883. Composition. BMI.

2015. Dalgleish, W. S. Grammatical Analysis. American Book. Grammar. USC.

2016. Dalgleish, W. S. *Introductory Text-Book of English Composition*. Edinbourgh, 1882. Composition. BMI.

2017. Dana, M. *Grammar Made Easy*. E. J. Clode, 1919. Grammar. USC.

2018. Dann, H. E. *Oratoria in the High School*. 1914. Speech. HEW.

2019. Darby, A. *Mechanism of the Sentence*. Oxford, 1920. Sentences. USC.

2020. Darby, A. *The Mechanism of the Sentence*. Bombay, 1919. Sentences. BMI.

2021. Darlington, J. *Effective Speaking and Writing*. London, 1902. Composition. BMI.

2022. Davenport, H. C. *First Book in English*. Atkinson, Mentzer, and Co., 1914. English Syllabi. USC.

2023. Davenport, H. J., and Emerson, A. H. *Principles of Grammar*. Macmillan, 1898. Grammar. USC.

2024. David, A. A. *Notes on the Teaching of English in the Lower Middles*. Rugby, 1913. Teaching Methods. BMI.

2025. Davidson, H. A. *Guide to English Syntax*. Davidson, 1903. Grammar. USC.

2026. Davidson, W. *Intermediate English: Grammar and Syntax*. Schwartz, Kirwin, and Fauss. Grammar. USC.

2027. Davidson, W., and Alcock, J. C. *English Composition*. London, 1884. Composition. BMI.

2028. Davidson, W. and Alcock, J. C. *English Composition*. London, 1901. Composition. BMI.

2029. Davidson, W., and Alcock, J. C. *Key to English Composition*. London, 1884. Composition. BMI.

2030. Davidson, W. L. *Leading and Important English Words; Explained and Exemplified*. Longmans. USC.

2031. Davidson, W. and Alcock, J. *English Grammar and Analysis*. Schwartz, Kirwin, and Fauss. Grammar. USC.

2032. Davies, B. J. *How to Succeed as a Writer: or, Lessons on Journalism*. B. Davies, 1914. Journalism. BMI.

2033. Davies, E. L. *How to Write for the Press*. G. Pitman, 1910. Journalism. BMI.

2034. Davis, H. C., comp. *Commencement Parts; Valedictories, Salutatories, Orations, Class Poems, Joy Orations,Toasts, Also Original Speeches and Addresses for the National Holidays and Other Occasions*. 1898. Readers. CC.

2035. Davis, J. F. *English Composition and Business Correspondence*. Pitman, 1909. Business English. USC.

2036. Davis, R. *Practical Exercises in English*. Ginn, 1919. English Syllabi. USC, BMI.

2037. Davis, R., and Lingham, C. H. *Business English and Correspondence*. Ginn, 1914. Business English. USC.

2038. Davis, R. L. *Simplified English*. Oklahoma City, OK: R. L. Davis, 1916. English Syllabi. USC.

2039. Dawson, C. J. *Essays and Paraphrasing*. London, 1890. Paraphrasing. BMI.

2040. Dawson, J. *The Soul of the Sermon*. London, 1895. Sermons. BMI.

2041. Day, H. N. *Art of Discourse: System of Rhetoric*. Scribner, 1876. Rhetoric. AC, CLPI.

2042. Day, H. N. *Art of English Composition*. Scribner, 1876. Composition. AC.

2043. Day, H. N. *Elements of Rhetoric*. Barnes, 1876. Rhetoric. AC.

2044. Day, H. N. <u>Elements of the Art of Discourse</u>. 1850. Rhetoric. HR, SIBP.

2045. Day, H. N. <u>Introduction to the Study of English Literature</u>. New York, 1869. Literature. CLPI.

2046. Day, H. N. <u>Rhetorical Praxis</u>. Ivison, 1888. Rhetoric. AC.

2047. Day, H. N. <u>Rhetorical Praxis</u>. Wilstach, 1876. Rhetoric. AC.

2048. Day, H. N. <u>The Art of Discourse</u>. Charles Scribner and Co., 1867. Rhetoric. HR, PS, AK.

2049. Day, H. N. <u>The Young Composer: Guide to English Composition</u>. Scribner, 1876. Composition. AC.

2050. De Garmo, C. <u>Language Lessons</u>. American Book. English Syllabi. USC.

2051. De Mille, J. <u>Elements of Rhetoric</u>. Harper, 1878. Rhetoric. AC, SIBP, CLPI, AK.

2052. De Quincey, T. <u>Collected Writings</u>. 14 vol. Edinburgh, 1889-1890. CLPI.

2053. De Quincey, T. <u>De Quincey's Literary Criticism</u>. Helen Darbshire ed. London. Henry Frowde, 1909. Literary Criticism. PS.

2054. De Quincey, T. <u>De Quincey's Literary Criticism</u>. Oxford, 1909. Literary Criticism. USC.

2055. De Quincey, T. <u>DeQuincey's Essay on Style, Rhetoric, and Language</u>. F. N. Scott ed. Boston: Allyn and Bacon, 1893. Rhetoric. PS.

2056. De Quincey, T. <u>Essays on Style, Rhetoric, and Language</u>. Allyn. Rhetoric. USC.

2057. De Quincey, T. <u>Selected Essays on Rhetoric</u>. F. Burwick ed. Carbondale: Southern Illinois Press, 1967. Rhetoric. HR, PS.

2058. De Quincey, T. <u>Uncollected Writings</u>. 2 vol. London, 1890. CLPI.

2059. De Vinne, T. L. *Correct Composition*. Century, 1901. Composition. USC.

2060. Deffendall, P. H. *Practical Grammar for High Schools and Academies*. Ainsworth and Co., 1917. Grammar. USC.

2061. Deffner, M. *Elementary English Grammar for Greeks*. Stechert. TESOL. USC.

2062. Deming, A. G. *Games and Rhymes*. Beckley-Cardy, 1919. USC.

2063. Deming, A. G. *Language Games for All Grades*. Beckley-Cardy, 1914. Teaching Methods. USC.

2064. Deming, A. G. *Primary Language Stories*. Beckley-Cardy, 1916. Readers. USC.

2065. Dengler, W. E. *Lessons and Exercises in English*. Rowe. English Syllabi. USC.

2066. Denison, E. M. *Figures of Speech*. McEvoy. Rhetoric. USC.

2067. Denney, J. V. *American Public Addresses*. Scott Foresman, 1910. Speech. USC.

2068. Denney, J. V. *Two Problems in Teaching English, Contributions to Rhetorical Theory*. F. N. Scott ed. Inland Press. Rhetoric. AK.

2069. Denney, J. V. *Washington*. Scott Foresman, 1910. USC.

2070. Denney, J. V. , and Tobey, S. B. *English Grammar*. Berry, 1913. Grammar. USC.

2071. Denney, J. V., and Others. *Argumentation and Debate*. American Book, 1910. Rhetoric. CC.

2072. Dent, G. C. *Exercises in Prose Literature and Composition*. Oxford, 1915. Composition. USC, BMI.

2073. Department of Education Investigation and Measurement. *English Determining a Standard in*

Accurate Copying. Boston: Printing Dept., 1916. Curriculum. HEW, USC.

2074. Department of Educational Investigation and MeasurementEnglish. Determining the Achievement of Pupils in Letter Writing. Boston: Printing Dept., 1918. Curriculum. HEW, USC.

2075. Department of Public Instruction. Division of Secondary Schools. The Teaching of English Classes. Concord, NH: New Hampshire Department of Public Instruction, 1916-17. Teaching Methods. HEW.

2076. Detroit Board of Education. English Composition for Use in the Detroit Public Schools. Detroit, MI: Detroit Board of Education, 1917. Curriculum. USC.

2077. Detroit Public Library. Books for Foreigners Learning English. Detroit: Detroit Public Library, 1915. TESOL. HEW.

2078. Devlin, J. How to Speak and Write Correctly. Christian Herald, 1910. Composition. USC.

2079. Diebel, J. H. New Method with English Grammar. Flanagan, 1898. Grammar. USC.

2080. Diehl, A. T. Elecutionary Studies and New Recitations. 1892. Rhetoric. CC.

2081. Dietrich, N. Language Lessons, an Outline Suggestion Material and Methods for the Teaching of Language in the Elementary Grades. Lansing: Mich. Dept. of Public Instruction, 1919. Curriculum. USC, HEW.

2082. Dillion, C. Dillion's Desk Book3rd. Topeka, KS: Dillion, 1916. USC.

2083. Dillon, J. A. Technical Grammar. McVey, 1916. Grammar. USC, HEW.

2084. Discriminate; A Companion to "Don't". London, 1885. BMI.

2085. District of Columbia. Course of Study in English. Washington, D. C.: Board of Education, 1914. Curriculum. USC.

2086. Dixon, W. W., and Miller, M. M. Practical Aids in Teaching English Grammar. Eau Clare, WI: W. Dixon, 1916. Grammar. USC, HEW.

2087. Dobbs, E. M. The Teaching of English Analysis. 1912. Grammar. BMI.

2088. Dodd, L. H. Everyday Rhetoric. 2nd ed. Worcester, MA: David Press, 1915. Rhetoric. USC.

2089. Doddwell, H. H. Notes on Correct English. Madras, 1910. Usage. BMI.

2090. Doherty, H. An Introduction to English Grammar. 1841. Grammar. SIBP.

2091. Dole, N. H. The Mistakes We Make. New York, 1898. Error. BMI.

2092. Donnelly, F. P. Art of Interesting. Kenedy, 1920. USC.

2093. Donnelly, F. P. Imitation and Analysis. Allyn, 1902. USC.

2094. Donnelly, F. P. Model English. 2 vol. Allyn, 1919-1920. USC.

2095. Donnelly, F. P. Modern English. Allyn, 1919-1920. USC.

2096. D'Orsey, A. J. D. The Study of the English Language an Essential Part of a University Course. 1861. Curriculum. CLPI.

2097. Dow, H. P. Twenty Lessons on English For Non-English Speaking Women. Albany, NY: University of New York, 1919. TESOL. HEW.

2098. Doyle, F. C. Introduction to the Study of Rhetoric. London, 1893. Rhetoric. BMI, AC.

2099. Drew, B. Hints and Helps for Those Who Write, Print, or Read. Lee and Sons, 1889. AC.

2100. Drew, B. Pens and Types. Lee and Sons, 1889. AC.

2101. Driggs, H. R. Live Language Lessons. Nebraska: University Pub., 1913-1915. English Syllabi. USC

2102. Driggs, H. R. Live Language Lessons. Chicago: University Publishing Co., 1913-1914. English Syllabi. HEW.

2103. Driggs, H. R. Live Language Lessons, Elementary Book. Nebraska: University Pub., 1916. English Syllabi. USC.

2104. Driggs, H. R. Live Language Lessons; Advanced Book. Nebraska: University Pub., 1916. English Syllabi. USC.

2105. Driggs, H. R. Live Language Lessons; Grammar. University Publishing, 1920. English Syllabi. USC.

2106. Driggs, H. R. Live Language Lessons; Intermediate Book. University Publication, 1920. English Syllabi. USC.

2107. Driggs, H. R. Our Living Language--How to Teach It and How to Use It. Lincoln, OH: The University Publishing House, 1920. Teaching Methods. HEW, USC.

2108. Drummond, J. Lectures on the Composition and Delivery of Sermons. P. Green, 1910. Sermons. BMI.

2109. Drury, H. N. Pace Standardized Course in English. New York: Pace and Pace, 1914-1918. English Syllabi. USC.

2110. DuCygne, M. Ars Rhetorica. Murphy, 1876. Rhetoric. AC.

2111. Duluth, Minn. Americanization Committee. Night School Lessons. Duluth, MN: Americanization Committee Board of Education, 1920. English Syllabi. HEW.

2112. Duncan, C. S., and Others. Prose Specimens for Use with Classes in English Composition. Heath, 1913. Readers. USC.

2113. Duncan, P. G. *Lessons in Business English*. D. L. Musselman, 1914. Business English. USC.

2114. Duncan, P. G., and Musselman, T. E. *Musselman's Business English and Letter Writer*. Musselman, 1915. Business English. USC.

2115. Dunton, L., and Kelley, A. H. *Induction Course in English*. English Syllabi. USC.

2116. Dunton, L., and Kelly, J. H. *Graded Course in English*. Johnson, Blagden, and McTurnan, 1911. English Syllabi. USC.

2117. Durham, W. H. ed. *Critical Essays of the Eightenth Century 1700-1725*. Yale Univ. Press, 1915. Readers. EGL.

2118. Dye, C. *Letters and Letter Writing as Means to the Study and Practice of English Composition*. Bobbs, 1903. USC.

2119. Dyer, R. O. *Correlated Lessons in Language and Occupation Work*. Educational Publishing Co., 1913. USC, HEW.

2120. Earle, J. *English Prose*. Putnam. 1899. USC.

2121. Earle, J. *Simple Grammar of English Now in Use*. Putnam, 1898. Grammar. USC.

2122. Earle, S. C. *Theory and Practice of Technical Writing*. New York: Macmillan, 1911. Technical English. USC, BMI.

2123. Earle, S. C., and Others. *Sentences and Their Elements*. New York: Macmillan, 1911. Sentences. USC, BMI.

2124. Eason, J. L., and Weseen, M. H. eds. *English, Science, and Engineering*. Doubleday, 1918. Technical English. USC.

2125. Eastman, H. P. *Practical English Grammar*. Commerce, TX: H. P. Eastman. Grammar. USC.

2126. Eastman, H. P. *Primary Grammar*. Commerce, TX: H.

P. Eastman, 1907. Grammar. USC.

2127. Easy Language Lessons, for the Use of Catholic Schools and Academies. Benziger. English Syllabi. USC.

2128. Eberts, K. J. The Speaking Voice. Harper, 1908. Speech. CC.

2129. Eclectic Composition Book, No. 1. Van Antwerp, 1878. Composition. AC.

2130. Ederly, W. Emphasis and Analysis of the English Language. Ralston University. Grammar. USC.

2131. Edgar, H. C. Sentence Analysis by Diagram. Newson, 1915. Grammar. USC.

2132. Edmund, E. W. A Junior Course of English Composition. 1920. Composition. BMI.

2133. Edmunds, E. W. A Senior Course of English Composition, Etc. W. B. Clive, 1918. Composition. BMI.

2134. Edwards, A. M. Graded Lessons in Language. Bardeen. English Syllabi. USC.

2135. Edwards, J. A Primer of Homiletics. C. H. Kelly, 1913. Sermons. BMI.

2136. Edwards, L. Essay Lessons in English Grammar. Dublin, 1920. Grammar. BMI.

2137. Edwards, W. H. Parts of Speech. Liberty, MO, 1909. Grammar. USC.

2138. Eichbaum, F. A. G. More Scraps for Preachers and Teachers. West Malvern, 1904. Sermons. BMI.

2139. Eldrekin, B. Model Composition Exercises. London, 1888. Composition. BMI.

2140. Elementary English Composition. Macmillan, 1907. Composition. USC.

2141. Elements of English Grammar in Tamil for the Use of

Primary Classes. Trichinology, 1911. TESOL. BMI.

2142. Eliot, C. W. Educational Reform. Century, 1901. History of Education. LLC.

2143. Eliot, T. S. Sacred Wood; Essays on Poetry and Criticism. Knopf, 1921. Criticism. EGL.

2144. Eliot, T. S. Selected Essays 1917-1932. Harcourt, 1932. Criticism. EGL.

2145. Elliptical Exercises for Securing Accuracy in Spelling Words of Similar Sound. 1907. Spelling. BMI.

2146. Ellis, E. S. Common Errors in Writing and Speaking. Woolfall, 1894. Error. AC.

2147. Ellis, E. S. Common Errors in Writing and Speaking. Hinds. Error. USC.

2148. Ellis, J. By Way of Illustration: A Handbook for Preachers. London, 1902. Sermons. BMI.

2149. Eloquence of the Pulpit. 2 vol. 1823. Sermons. CSIGP.

2150. Elson, W. H., and Marsh, G. L. Good English, Oral and Written. 3 vol. Scott, 1918. Usage. USC.

2151. Elson, W. H., and Others. Good English, Oral and Written. Scott, 1917. Usage. USC.

2152. Elson, W. H., and others Manual for Good English. Scott, 1919. Usage. USC.

2153. Emerson, A. W. Composition and Criticism. Bardeen, 1912. Composition. USC.

2154. Emerson, A. W. Composition and Criticism. Bardeen, 1893. Composition. AC.

2155. Emerson, H. P., and Bender, I. C. Handbook to Accompany English Spoken and Written. Macmillan, 1917. Grammar. USC.

2156. Emerson, H. P., and Bender, I. C. Lessons in

Language for Primary Grades. New York: Macmillan, 1918. English Syllabi. HEW.

2157. Emerson, H. P., and Bender, I. C. Lessons in Language for Primary Grades. Macmillan, 1909. English Syllabi. USC.

2158. Emerson, H. P., and Bender, I. C. Lessons in Language, Literature, and Composition. Macmillan, 1908. Literature and Composition. USC.

2159. Emerson, H. P., and Bender, I. C. Modern English. 2 vol. New York: Macmillan. USC.

2160. Emerson, H. P., and Bender, I. C. Practical Lessons in English Grammar and Composition. Macmillan, 1910. Composition. USC.

2161. Emerson, H. P., and Bender, I. C. Teacher's Manual of Language, Composition and Grammar. Macmillan, 1916. Teaching Methods. USC.

2162. Emery, I. C. Constructive English for the Higher Grades of the Grammar School. Scribner, 1915. English Syllabi. USC.

2163. England Joint Committee on Grammatical Terminology. Summary of Grammatical Terms for Use in English. Kegan Paul, 1919. Grammar. BMI.

2164. England Standing Committee on Grammactical Terminology. Grammatical Terminology. Murray, 1914. Grammar. BMI.

2165. England Standing Committee on Grammatical Reform. Report on the Terminology and Classification of Grammar. Oxford, 1920. Grammar. BMI.

2166. English, a Course of Study for Elementary Schools With Graded Standards. Cambridge: Chopple, 1915. English Syllabi. USC, HEW.

2167. English as She is Wrote. London, 1884. BMI.

2168. English Association. Essays and Studies. 2 vol. Oxford, 1910-1911. USC.

2169. English Association, London. <u>English Papers in Examination for Pupils of School Age in England and Wales</u>. London, 1917. Testing. HEW.

2170. English Association, London. <u>Essays and Studies by Members of the Association</u>. 18 vol. London: Oxford, 1910-1933. EGL.

2171. English Association, London. <u>The Essentials of English Teaching by Members of the English Association</u>. London: Longmans, Green, and Co., 1919. Teaching Methods. HEW.

2172. <u>English Composition for Use in Detroit Public Schools</u>. Detroit, 1917. Composition. HEW.

2173. <u>English Composition in Theory and Practice</u>. Macmillan, 1912. Composition. USC.

2174. <u>English Composition Through Picture and Object Lesson</u>. London, 1901. Composition. BMI.

2175. <u>English Grammar</u>. Benziger. Grammar. USC.

2176. Eno, J. N. <u>Compendium of English Grammar</u>. Silver. Grammar. USC.

2177. Erasmus, D. <u>Ciceronianus</u>. Teachers College, 1908. Rhetoric. USC.

2178. Erskine, J., and H. <u>Written English</u>. Century, 1910. Composition. USC, AC.

2179. Erskine, J., and H. <u>Written English</u>. Century, 1913. Composition. USC.

2180. Esenwein, J. B. <u>Lippincott's New Picture Composition Book</u>. Lippincott, 1914. Composition. USC.

2181. Esenwein, J. B., and Carnagey, D. <u>The Art of Public Speaking</u>. 1915. Speech. BMI.

2182. Espenshade, A. H. <u>Essentials of Composition and Rhetoric</u>. Heath, 1909. Composition. CC.

2183. Espenshade, A. H. <u>Essentials of Composition and Rhetoric</u>. Heath, 1913. Composition. USC.

2184. Espenshade, A. H. Essentials of Composition and Rhetoric. Heath, 1904. Composition. USC, AC, AK.

2185. Espenshade, A. H. Essentials of Composition and Rhetoric. London, 1905. Composition. BMI.

2186. Espenshade, A. H., ed. Forensic Declamations. 1909. USC.

2187. Essentials of English. Ellis ed. English Syllabi. USC.

2188. Evans, L. B. Elements of English Grammar. American Book, 1908. Grammar. USC.

2189. Evans, T. New Stories for Composition. London, 1890. Readers. BMI.

2190. Evans, W. M. Manual of Grammar. Bardeen, 1899. Grammar. USC.

2191. Evenson, O. K. Lessons in Sentence Analysis. H. M. Rowe. Sentences. USC.

2192. Ewart, J. A., and Others. Civil Services Manual. 2 vol. Home Correspondence School, 1908. Business English. USC.

2193. Ewings, F. C. Outline for Review in First-Year English. Bardeen, 1905. English Syllabi. USC.

2194. Excelsior Studies in Grammar. Sadlier. Grammar. USC.

2195. Fables, Anecdotes and Stories for Teaching Composition. Boston, 1890. AC.

2196. Fansler, H. E. Manual of Principles of English Form and Diction. Row, Peterson, and Company. USC.

2197. Fearn, J. Anti-Tooke; or, An Analysis of the Principles and Structure of Language, Exemplified in the English Tongue. 2 vol. 1824-1827. Grammar. CLPI, SIBP.

2198. Feasey, J. E. Teaching Composition. New York:

Pitman and Son, 1912. Teaching Methods. HEW, USC.

2199. Fee, M. H. _A Textbook in English Composition_. Boston: Ginn and Company, 1912. Composition. HEW.

2200. Feeney. _Manual of Sacred Rhetoric_. Herder, 1900-05. Rhetoric. AC.

2201. Fellow, A. N. _First Steps in English Grammar_. American Book. Grammar. USC.

2202. Fernald, J. C. _Connectives of English Speech_. Funk, 1904. USC.

2203. Fernald, J. C. _English Grammar Simplified_. Funk, 1916. Grammar. USC, BMI.

2204. Fernald, J. C. _Expressive English_. Funk, 1918. USC, BMI.

2205. Fernald, J. C. _Working Grammar of the English Language_. Funk, 1908. Grammar. USC.

2206. Feuuo, F. H. _Science and the Art of Elocution_. 1878. CC.

2207. Fewsmith, W. _Elementary Grammar_. Sower. Grammar. USC.

2208. Fewsmith, W. and Singer, E. A. _Standard English Grammar_. Sower, 1905. Grammar. USC.

2209. _Final Draft Paper_. Macmillan, 1900. Composition. USC.

2210. Finch, R. J. _How to Teach English Composition_. London: Evans Brothers, 1919. Teaching Methods. HEW, BMI.

2211. Finlay, T. A. _Principles and Practice of English Composition_. 1897. Composition. BMI.

2212. Firman, S. G. _Progressive Lessons in English_. Appleton. USC.

2213. Fish, H. C. _Pulpit Eloquence of the 19th Century_. 1874. Sermons. SIBP.

2214. Fisher, A. and Call, A. D. *English for Beginners*. Ginn, 1917. USC.

2215. Fisk, F. W. *Manual of Preaching; Lectures on Homiletics*. 1884. Sermons. CLPI.

2216. Fitzgerald, J. *Pitfalls in English*. Commonwealth Co. USC.

2217. *Five Hundred Mistakes Corrected; in Speaking, Pronouncing and Writing the English Language*. Moss, 1876. Error. AC.

2218. Fletcher, C. R. L. *Development of English Prose Style*. Oxford, 1881. Style. BMI.

2219. Fletcher, J. B. and Carpenter, G. R. *Introduction to Theme Writing*. 1893. Composition. CC.

2220. Fletcher, J. B. and Carpenter, G. R. *Introduction to Theme-Writing*. Allyn, 1912. Composition. USC.

2221. Fletcher, J. B. and Carpenter, G. R. *Introduction to Theme-Writing*. Allyn and B., 1894. Composition. AC, AK.

2222. Fletcher, R. H. *Principles of Composition and Literature*. Barnes, 1914. Literature and Composition. USC.

2223. Flint, L. N. *Editorial*. Appleton, 1920. USC.

2224. Flounders, G. W. *English Grammar*. Sower. Grammar. USC.

2225. Flounders, G. W. *Standard English Language and Grammar*. Sower, 1906. Grammar. USC.

2226. Foerster, N. *Outlines and Summaries*. Holt, 1915. Outlining. USC, HEW.

2227. Foerster, N. and Steadman, J. M. *Sentences and Thinking*. Houghton, 1919. Sentences. USC.

2228. Foerster, N. and Steadman, J. M., Jr. *Sentences and Thinking*. Chapel Hill, NC, 1918. Sentences. USC.

2229. Forbes, A. W. H. <u>Practical Essay Writing</u>. London, 1888. Composition. BMI.

2230. Foster, J. E. <u>Lessons in Oratory</u>. J. F. Spriggs, 1912. Speech. BMI.

2231. Foster, L. C. <u>Syllabus of English Grammar</u>. Macmillan. Grammar. USC.

2232. Foster, W. T. <u>Argumentation and Debating</u>. Houghton, 1908. Modes. CC.

2233. Foster, W. T. <u>Essentials of Composition and Argument</u>. Houghton, 1911. Composition. USC, HEW.

2234. Fowler, H. W. <u>Sentence Analysis for Lower Forms of Public Schools</u>. Oxford, 1906. Sentences. USC.

2235. Fowler, H. W. <u>The King's English</u>. Oxford: Clarendon Press, 1906. HEW.

2236. Fowler, H. W. and F. G. <u>King's English</u>. 2nd ed. Oxford, 1912. USC.

2237. Fowler, J. H. <u>A Manual of Essay Writing</u>. London, 1899. Composition. BMI.

2238. Fowler, J. H. <u>English Exercises for Middle Forms</u>. Macmillan, 1918. BMI.

2239. Fowler, J. H. <u>First Course of Essay-Writing</u>. London, 1902. Composition. BMI.

2240. Fowler, J. H. <u>Manual of Essay Writing</u>. London, 1905. Composition. BMI.

2241. Fowler, J. H. <u>Manual of Essay-Writing</u>. A. and C. Black, 1914. Composition. BMI.

2242. Fowler, J. H. <u>The Teaching of English Composition</u>. 1910. Teaching Methods. BMI.

2243. Fowler, W. C. <u>English Grammar. The English Language in Its Elements and Forms</u>. 1860. Grammar. CLPI.

2244. Fowler, W. C. <u>English Grammar, the English Language</u>

in its Elements and Forms. 1855. Grammar. CLPI.

2245. Fowler, W. C. English Grammar, the English Language in its Elements and Forms, with a History of its Origin and Development. 1851. Grammar. SIBP.

2246. Franciscan Sisters of Perpetual Adoration. Sixty Lessons in English for the Grades. La Crosse, WI, 1915. USC.

2247. Frank, M. M. Constructive Exercises in English. Longmans, 1909. USC.

2248. Frank, M. M. Elements of High School English. Longmans, 1915. USC.

2249. Frank, M. M. High School Exercises in Grammar. Longmans, 1911. Grammar. USC.

2250. Fransler, H. E. and D. S. Exercises in English Form and Diction. Row, Peterson, and Company. USC.

2251. Fraser, J. I. 1. Modern Methods of Teaching English in Germany. 2. Educational Studies at the St. Louis Exposition. 3. Physical Laboratories in Germany. India: Government Printing, 1906. TESOL. HEW.

2252. Fraser, J. N. The First Steps in Teaching English by the Direct Method. Bombay, 1917. Teaching Methods. BMI.

2253. Freeman, H. Speech Formation as the Basis for Spelling. London, 1886. Spelling. BMI.

2254. Frenald, J. C. Better Say. Funk, 1907. USC.

2255. French, R. C. English, Past and Present. London: George Rutledge and Son, Ltd. HEW.

2256. Frink, H. A. and Phelps, A. Rhetoric, its Theory and Practice. Scribner. Rhetoric. USC.

2257. Froebel, F. The Education of Man. W. N. Hailmann trans. Appleton, 1887. LLC.

2258. Frost, H. Good Engineering Literature. Chicago, 1911. USC.

2259. Frost, S. A. How to Write a Composition. Flanagan. Composition. USC.

2260. Fry, R. J. Salvation of Jemmy Slang. Spokane, WA, 1920. USC.

2261. Frye, P. H. Romance and Tragedy. Jones, Marshall, 1922. EGL.

2262. Fulcher, P. M., ed. Foundations of English Style. Crofts, 1927. Style. EGL.

2263. Fulton, E. English Prose Composition. Holt, 1911. Composition. USC.

2264. Fulton, E. English Prose Composition. Holt, 1910. Composition. USC.

2265. Fulton, E. Rhetoric and Composition. Holt, 1906. Composition. USC, AC, AK.

2266. Fulton, M. G. College Life, its Condition and Problems. Macmillan, 1914. USC, HEW.

2267. Fulton, M. G., comp. and ed. Expository Writing. Macmillan, 1912. Composition. USC, BMI.

2268. Fulton, R. I. and Trueblood, T. C. Essentials of Public Speaking for Secondary Schools. 1909. Speech. CC.

2269. Funk and Wagnalls. Faulty Diction as Corrected by the Funk and Wagnalls New Standard Dictionary of the English Language. Funk and Wagnalls, 1915. USC.

2270. Fyfe, W. T. Lessons in Rhetoric. London, 1883. Rhetoric. BMI.

2271. Gaines, J. T. and Theiss, O. B. Inductive Grammar. Morton. Grammar. USC.

2272. Gairdner, W. T. On the Function of Articulate Speech. 1866. SIBP.

2273. Galbraith, E. Composition in the School-Room. Putnam, 1885. Composition. AC.

2274. Gales, R. L. Studies in Arcady, and other Essays from a Country Parsonage. Simpkin, 1910-1912. EGL.

2275. Gallagher, O. C. Teaching of English in Commercial Courses. Houghton, 1914. Business English. USC, HEW.

2276. Gallagher, O. C. and Moulton, L. B. Practical Business English. Houghton, 1918. Business English. USC.

2277. Ganoe, W. A. English of Military Communciations. Banta, 1918. Military English. USC.

2278. Garber, J. P. Annals of Educational Progress in 1910; A Report upon Current Educational Activities Throughout the World. Lippincott, 1911. History of Education. CC.

2279. Gardiner, J. H. Forms of Prose Literature. Scribner, 1900. Modes. USC, AK.

2280. Gardiner, J. H. and others. Elements of English Composition. Ginn, 1902. Composition. USC.

2281. Gardiner, J. H., Kitteredge, G. L., Arnold, S. L. Manual of Composition and Rhetoric. Ginn, 1907. Composition. AC, CC, USC, AK.

2282. Gardner, A. Tales for Composition. Manchester, 1885. Readers. BMI.

2283. Gardner, J. H. The Mother Tongue. Boston, 1902. BMI.

2284. Garig, M. M. Drill in English. Baton Rouge: Louisiana State Univ., 1912. USC, HEW.

2285. Garnett, J. M. English in the Preparatory Schools. West Virginia, 1890. English Syllabi. HEW.

2286. Garrsion, C. L. Manual and Diagrams to Metcalf's Grammar. American Book. Grammar. USC.

2287. Gass, S. B. English Composition. Scott, 1910. Composition. USC, AC.

2288. Gates, A. F. *Practical English*. Waterloo, I. A. F. Gates, 1915. USC.

2289. Gay, R. M. *Facts, Fancy, and Opinion; Examples of Present Day Writing*. Little, 1923. Readers. EGL.

2290. Gay, R. M. *Writing Through Reading*. Atlantic Monthly Press, 1920. Literature and Composition. USC.

2291. Gayley, C. M. and Bradley, C. B. *Suggestions to Teachers of English in the Secondary Schools*. 2nd ed. California: University of California, 1906. Teaching Methods. USC.

2292. Gayley, C. M. and Bradley, C. B. *Suggestions to Teachers of English in the Secondary Schools*. Berkeley: The University Press, 1894. Teaching Methods. HEW.

2293. Gemmill, E. *Essentials of English Grammar*. 2nd ed. Harcourt, 1920. Grammar. USC.

2294. Gemmill, E. *New Grammar Drill*. Nobel, 1917. Grammar. USC.

2295. Gemmill, E. *New Grammar Drill*. Cranford, NJ: Elsie Gemmill, 1917. Grammar. USC.

2296. Genung, J. *Outlines of Rhetoric*. Ginn, 1912. Rhetoric. USC.

2297. Genung, J. *Practical Elements of Rhetoric*. Ginn, 1912. Rhetoric. USC.

2298. Genung, J. F. *Handbook of Rhetorical Analysis*. Ginn, 1889. Rhetoric. AC, AK.

2299. Genung, J. F. *Handbook of Rhetorical Analysis*. Ginn, 1888. Rhetoric. USC.

2300. Genung, J. F. *Outlines of Rhetoric*. Ginn, 1893. Rhetoric. AC, AK.

2301. Genung, J. F. *Practical Elements of Rhetoric*. Ginn, 1887. Rhetoric. AC.

2302. Genung, J. F. Practical Elements of Rhetoric, with Illustrated Examples. 1902. Rhetoric. CC.

2303. Genung, J. F. Study of Rhetoric in the College Course. Heath, 1887. Rhetoric. AC, AK.

2304. Genung, J. F. The Practical Elements of Rhetoric. 2nd ed. Boston: Ginn and Co., 1886. Rhetoric. HE, AK.

2305. Genung, J. F. The Practical Elements of Rhetoric. Amherst: J. E. Williams, 1885. Rhetoric. HR, PS.

2306. Genung, J. F. The Study of Rhetoric in the College Course. Boston: D. C. Heath and Co., 1892. Rhetoric. HEW.

2307. Genung, J. F. and Hanson, C. L. Outlines of Composition and Rhetoric. Ginn, 1915. Composition. USC, BMI, AK.

2308. Genung, T. Working Principles of Rhetoric. Ginn, 1901. Rhetoric. USC, BMI, AC, AK.

2309. Gerrish, C. M. and Cunningham, M. Practical English Composition. Heath and Co., 1915. Composition. BMI.

2310. Gerrish, C. M. and Cunningham, M. Practical English Composition. Heath, 1912. Composition. USC.

2311. Getty, J. A. Elements of Rhetoric. Littell, 1831. Rhetoric. AK.

2312. Gideon, E. Exercises in English. Hinds, 1904. USC.

2313. Gideon, E. Lessons in Language. Hinds. USC.

2314. Giffin, W. M. Language Reading lessons. Flanagan. USC.

2315. Giffin, W. M. Suggestive Questions in Language. March. USC.

2316. Giles, E. Studies in Preparatory English. Bardeen. USC.

2317. Gillan, S. Y. Language Lessons. Gillan. USC.

2318. Gilmore, J. H. Outlines of Art of Expression. Ginn, 1876. AC.

2319. Gilmore, J. H. Outlines of Rhetoric for Schools and Colleges. Leach, 1891. Rhetoric. AC, AK.

2320. Gist, E. T. Lessons in English: Composition, Grammar, and Rhetoric Combined. Sherwood, 1888. Composition. AC.

2321. Gjerset, K. English Grammar. Luth, 1908. Grammar. USC.

2322. Glover, W. J. Practical Course of English Composition for Middle and Upper Forms. G. Philip, 1920. Composition. BMI.

2323. Glover, W. J. The New English Books: Graduated Course of English Composition, for Primary and Secondary Schools. G. Philip, 1919. Composition. BMI.

2324. Godde, F. On the History and Use of the Suffixes -ery (-ry), -age, and -ment in English. 1910. Grammar. LC.

2325. Goggin, D. J. and Morgan, S. A. High School English Grammar. Toronto, 1913. Grammar. BMI.

2326. Goldberger, H. H. How to Teach English to Foreigners. New York: A. G. Seiler, 1918. TESOL. USC, HEW.

2327. Goldberger, H. H. Teaching English to the Foreign Born: A Teacher's Handbook. Washington: Government Printing Office, 1920. TESOL. HEW.

2328. Goldberger, H. H. and Brown, S. J. Course of Study and Syllabus for Teaching English to Non-English Speaking Adults. Scribner, 1919. TESOL. USC, HEW.

2329. Golden, W. E. Brief English Grammar. New York: W. E. Golden, 1911. Grammar. USC.

2330. Goldsmith, A. M. <u>Report Writing</u>. New York: President Inst., 1913. Reports. USC.

2331. Goldwasser, I. E. <u>Method and Methods in the Teaching of English</u>. Heath, 1913. Teaching Methods. USC, HEW.

2332. Goltman, R. <u>How to Speak and Write English Correctly</u>. Montreal, 1903. Composition. BMI.

2333. Goodrich, C. A. <u>Select British Eloquence</u>. New York: Harper and Brothers, 1852. HR, PS, AK.

2334. Goodwin, M. L. and Guill, K. G. <u>Student's Handbook of Composition</u>. Macmillan, 1917. Composition. USC.

2335. Goodwin, M. L. and Guill, K. G. <u>Student's Handbook of Composition</u>. Macmillan, 1918. Composition. USC.

2336. Goodyear, R. A. H. <u>Golden Hints for Writers</u>. Scarborough, 1916. BMI.

2337. Gordon, K. H. <u>Reformed Spelling</u>. London, 1883. Spelling. BMI.

2338. Gordy, W. F. and Mead, W. E. <u>Grammar Lessons</u>. Scribner, 1904. Grammar. USC.

2339. Gordy, W. F. and Mead, W. E. <u>Language Lessons: A First Book in English</u>. Scribner, 1903. USC.

2340. Gough, H. B. <u>Suggestions on the Preparation and Delivery of Biographical Speeches</u>. Chicago: American Bureau of Public Speaking, 1914. Speech. USC.

2341. Gould, E. S. <u>Good English</u>. 1859. CLPI.

2342. Gowdy, C. <u>English Grammar</u>. Allyn, 1909. Grammar. USC.

2343. Gowdy, C. and Dexheimer, L. M. <u>Lessons in English</u>. Allyn, 1913-1915. USC.

2344. Gowdy, E. and Thompson, L. G. <u>Teachers' Manual to

Accompany a Gateway into English for Chinese Students. Silver, 1919. TESOL. USC.

2345. Gowers, E. A. Plain Words: Their ABC. New York. HEW.

2346. Goyen, P. Key. Macmillan, 1894. AC.

2347. Goyen, P. Key Principles of Composition. London, 1894. Composition. BMI.

2348. Goyen, P. Principles of English Composition. London, 1894. Composition. BMI.

2349. Goyen, P. Principles of English Composition Through Analysis and Synthesis. Macmillan, 1894. Composition. AC.

2350. Graham, W. Notes for Young Writers. Harper, 1918. USC.

2351. Grammar Lessons. Longmans. Grammar. USC.

2352. Grandgent, C. H. Old and New; Sundry Papers. Harvard, 1920. LLC.

2353. Grant, C. E. The Teacher's Book of Word Building. Kingsway Series., 1916. BMI.

2354. Grant, F. M. Primary Reproduction Stories. Flanagan. USC.

2355. Great Britain. Memorandum on the Teaching of Engish in Scottish Primary Schools. London: Wyman and Sons, 1907. Teaching Methods. HEW.

2356. Green, R. The First Use of a Latin Element in English Style. Oxford, 1915. Style. BMI.

2357. Greene, H. R. Inductive Language Lessons: Elementary Grammar and Composition. A. Lovell, 1888. Composition. AC.

2358. Greene, H. R. Language Half Blanks. Simmons. USC.

2359. Greene, S. S. A Treatise on the Structure of the English Language. Cooperthwait, 1869. Grammar. AK.

2360. Greene, S. S. Analysis of the English Language. Cooperthwait, 1875. AK.

2361. Greene, S. S. English Grammar. American Book. Grammar. USC.

2362. Greene, S. S. Introduction to English Grammar. American Book. Grammar. USC.

2363. Greene, S. S. New Analysis of the English Language. American Book. USC.

2364. Greenough, C. N. English A: Manual of Instruction and Exercises for 1913-1914. Cambridge: C. N. Greenough, 1913. English Syllabi. USC.

2365. Greenough, C. N., and Hersey, F. W. C. English Composition. Macmillan, 1917. Composition. USC, BMI.

2366. Greenough, C. N., and others. Report on Examinations in English for Admission to Harvard. Harvard University, 1907. Testing. USC.

2367. Greenough, J. B., and Kittredge, G. L. Words and their Ways in English Speech. Macmillan, 1901. USC.

2368. Greenwood, J. M. Elements of Language and Grammar. Silver. Grammar. USC.

2369. Greenwood, J. M. Studies in English Grammar. Silver. Grammar. USC.

2370. Greenwood, J. M., ed. Normal Courses in English. Silver. English Syllabi. USC.

2371. Greever, G. War Writing. Century, 1919. USC.

2372. Greever, G., and Jones, E. S. Century Handbook of Writing. Century, 1918. Grammar. USC.

2373. Gregg, E. L. Studies in English Grammar. 3rd ed. Torch Press, 1912. Grammar. USC.

2374. Gregg, E. L. Studies in English Grammar. 4th ed. Cedar Falls, IA: Cross and Company, 1914. Grammar. USC.

2375. Gregory, B. O. The Foundation of English. Chelsea, MA, 1905. HEW.

2376. Grierson, F. Celtic Temperament, and Other Essays. Lane, 1913. EGL.

2377. Grierson, H. J. C. Rhetoric and English Composition. 2nd ed. Folcroft, PA: Folcroft Library, 1973. Composition. HR.

2378. Griffin, C. S. Daily Lessons Plans in English. Educational, 1914. English Syllabi. USC.

2379. Griffin, J. T., and Moraff, F. English by Grades. 2 vol. Hinds, 1914. USC.

2380. Griffin, N. E. English Language. Teachers College. USC.

2381. Grose, H. B. Specimens of English Composition. Scott, 1909. Readers. USC.

2382. Grove, G. A. One Hundred Lessons in English. Packard, 1904. USC.

2383. Guide to Composition. London, 1890. Composition. BMI.

2384. Guide to the English Language - Bain's Education as a Science. 1889. CSIGP.

2385. Guingrich, R. L. H. Daily Lessons Plans in Language for Second and Third Grades. Flanagan, 1912. English Syllabi. USC.

2386. Gwillan, W. J. Grammar Combined with Composition. Manchester, 1901. Composition. BMI.

2387. Gwynne, P. Word to the Wise: Hints on Current Improprieties of Expression in Writing and Speaking. Dutton, 1882. Error. AC.

2388. Haes, D. E. A Concentric Grammar Course. G. Bell,

       1916. Grammar. BMI.

2389. Hagar, H. A. <u>Applied Business English</u>. Gregg, 1909. Business English. USC.

2390. Hagar, H. A., and So Relle, R. P. <u>Applied Business English and Correspondence</u>. Gregg Pub., 1914. Business English. USC.

2391. Hailmann, W. N. <u>Twelve Lectures on the History of Pedagogy</u>. 1874. Teaching Methods. CC.

2392. Hale, C. B. and Tobin, J. E. <u>Contrast and Comparison: A Book of Essays</u>. Prentice Hall, 1931. EGL.

2393. Hale, E. E., Jr. <u>Constructive Rhetoric</u>. Holt, 1912. Rhetoric. USC.

2394. Hale, E. E., Jr. <u>Constructive Rhetoric</u>. Holt, 1896. Rhetoric. AC, AK.

2395. Hall, F. <u>Modern English</u>. 1873. CLPI.

2396. Hall, F. M. <u>A-B-C of Correct Speech and the Art of Conversation</u>. Harper, 1916. Speech. USC.

2397. Hall, H. <u>Composition Outlines</u>. Flanagan, 1887. Composition. AC.

2398. Hall, H. <u>Composition Outlines</u>. Flanagan, 1912. Composition. USC.

2399. Hall, J. L. <u>English Usage</u>. Scott, 1917. Usage. USC.

2400. Hall, W. D. <u>Rand-McNally Practical English Grammar</u>. Rand, 1898. Grammar. USC.

2401. Hamill, S. S. <u>New Science of Elocution</u>. 1886. Speech. CC.

2402. Hamilton, F. W. <u>Word Study and English Grammar</u>. 1918. Grammar. USC.

2403. Hammond, H. W. and Herzberg, M. J. <u>Style Book of Business English</u>. Pitman, 1916. Business English.

USC.

2404. Hammond, J. M. *Language and Composition by Grades*. Beckley-Cardy Co., 1915. Composition. USC.

2405. Hammond, J. M. and Isler, L. M. *Graded Language and Composition*. Owen, 1920. Composition. USC.

2406. *Handbook for Writers and Artists*. London. 1898. BMI.

2407. Haney, J. L. *Good English*. Philadelphia: Egerton, 1917. USC.

2408. Haney, J. L. *Good English*. Egerton Press, 1915. USC.

2409. Hanson, C. L. *English Composition*. Ginn, 1908. Composition. USC, AC.

2410. Hanson, C. L. *Two Years' Course in English Composition*. Ginn, 1912. Composition. USC.

2411. Hardman, J. *Preliminary Self-Help Exercises in English*. Pitman, 1916. Grammar. BMI.

2412. Hardman, J. *Self-Help Exercises in Essay Writing*. Pitman, 1919. Composition. BMI.

2413. Hardy, I. *Elementary Composition Exercises*. Holt, 1912. Composition. USC.

2414. Hardy, I. *Elementary Composition Exercises*. Holt, 1890. Composition. AC.

2415. Harper, M. J. *Practical Composition*. Scribner, 1876. Composition.

2416. Harper, W. R. and Burgess, I. B. *Inductive Studies in English Grammar*. American Book. Grammar. USC.

2417. Harper's Monthly Magazine. *Harper Essays*. Harper, 1927. EGL.

2418. Harrington, H. F. and Frankenberg, T. T. *Essentials in Journalism*. Boston, 1912. Journalism. BMI.

2419. Harris, A. V. and Gilbert, C. B. *Guide Books to English*. Silver, 1907. USC.

2420. Harris, J. *Hermes, or A Philosophical Inquiry Concerning Universal Grammar*. 1806. Grammar. CLPI.

2421. Harris, J. H. *Course of Study and Teachers' Manual in Elementary English*. Northwestern School, 1909. English Syllabi. USC.

2422. Harris, T. G. *Spiral Course in English*. Heath, 1907. USC.

2423. Harris, W. T. *Advanced English Grammar*. Globe School Book, 1903. Grammar. USC.

2424. Harris, W. T. *Advanced English Grammar*. World Book, 1914. Grammar. USC.

2425. Harrison, F. *Literary Estimates*. Macmillan, 1900. EGL.

2426. Harrison, M. *Rise, Progress, and Present Stucture of the English Language*. 1848. Grammar. SIBP.

2427. Hart, J. M. *Essentials of Prose Composition*. Hinds. Composition. USC.

2428. Hart, J. M. *Handbook of English Composition*. Eldredge, 1895. Composition. AC, AK.

2429. Hart, J. M. *Handbook of English Composition*. Hinds. Composition. USC.

2430. Hart, J. S. *A Manual of Composition and Rhetoric*. Eldredge, 1876. *Composition*. AC, AK.

2431. Hart, J. S. *Composition and Rhetoric*. Hinds. Composition. USC.

2432. Hart, J. S. *Elementary Grammar*. Hinds. Grammar. USC.

2433. Hart, J. S. *First Lessons in Composition*. Eldredge, 1875. Composition. AC.

2434. Hart, J. S. First Lessons in Composition. Hinds. Composition. USC.

2435. Hart, J. S. Grammar of the English Language. Hinds, 1910. Grammar. USC.

2436. Hart, J. S. Language Lessons for Beginners. Hinds. USC.

2437. Hartley, C. Everyone's Handbook of Common Blunders in Speaking and Writing. London, 1897. Error. BMI.

2438. Hartog, P. J., and Langdon, A. H. Writing of English. Oxford, 1908. USC, HEW.

2439. Harvard University, Board of Overseers. Report of the Committee on Composition and Rhetoric to the Board of Overseers of Harvard College. 1892-1897. Composition. HEW, AK.

2440. Harvard-Cleveland Course in English for Junior and Senior High Schools. Harvard University Press, 1920. English Syllabi. USC.

2441. Harvey, T. W. Elementary Grammar. American Book, 1900. Grammar. USC.

2442. Harvey, T. W. Elementary Grammar and Composition. Van Antwerp, 1880. Grammar. AC.

2443. Harvey, T. W. Elementary Lessons in Language and Grammar. American Book. Grammar. USC.

2444. Harvey, T. W. First Lessons in the English Language. American Book. USC.

2445. Harvey, T. W. New English Grammar for Schools. American Book. Grammar. USC.

2446. Harvey, T. W. New Language Lessons. American Book. USC.

2447. Harvey, T. W. Practical Grammar of the English Language. American Book. Grammar. USC.

2448. Hatfield, W. W. Business English Projects.

Macmillan, 1921. Business English. USC.

2449. Hathaway, B. A. <u>1001 Questions and Answers on English</u>. Hinds. USC.

2450. Hathaway, B. A. <u>Bad English Corrected</u>. Hinds. Error. USC.

2451. Hauck, M. E. <u>Reproduction Stories for the Primary Grades</u>. Flanagan. USC.

2452. Haven, E. O. <u>Rhetoric and Text Book</u>. 1878. Rhetoric. SIBP. AC.

2453. Haven, E. O. <u>Rhetoric, for Schools, College and Private Study</u>. Harper, 1876. Rhetoric. AC, AK.

2454. Hazen, M. W. <u>First Book of Observation, Thought and Expression</u>. Silver. USC.

2455. Hazen, M. W. <u>Second Book of Observation, Thought and Expression</u>. Silver, 1899. USC.

2456. Head, Sir E. W. <u>"Shall" and "Will": or, Two Chapters on Future Auxiliary Verbs</u>. Grammar. CLPI.

2457. Heath, F. R. <u>Manual of Language Lessons</u>. 1908. USC.

2458. Heath, N. L. <u>Elementary Lessons in English</u>. Ginn. USC.

2459. Heath, N. L. <u>Parts of Speech and How to Use Them</u>. Ginn. Grammar. USC.

2460. Heatley, H. R. <u>Gradatim, Stories for Beginners</u>. Allyn. USC.

2461. Heimbach, C. C. <u>Drill Book in Business English</u>. Philadelphia: Lasher, 1912. Business English. USC.

2462. Henderson, B. L. K., and Freeman, A. <u>Manual on Essay Writing</u>. Bell and Son, 1915. Composition. BMI.

2463. Henderson, G. E. <u>Exercises in Composition for Fourth and Fifth Classes</u>. Toronto, 1898. Composition.

BMI.

2464. Henderson, G. W. <u>English Grammar by Parallelism and Comparison</u>. 1910. Grammar. USC, AC.

2465. Henderson, G. W. <u>English Grammar by Parallelism and Comparison</u>. Columbus, OH: Henderson, 1912. Grammar. USC.

2466. Hennesy, J. A. <u>Dictionary of Grammar</u>. Funk, 1917. Grammar. USC, BMI.

2467. Henry, V. <u>Short Comparative Grammar of English and German</u>. Macmillan. Grammar. USC.

2468. Hepburn, A. D. <u>Manual of English Rhetoric</u>. Van Antwerp, 1875. Rhetoric. AK.

2469. Hepburn, A. D. <u>Manual of English Rhetoric</u>. Wilson and Company. Rhetoric.

2470. Herlihy, C. M. <u>Beginner's Course in English for Non-English Speaking Men Illiterate in Their Native Language</u>. Washington: Government Printing Office, 1917. TESOL. HEW.

2471. Herlihy, C. <u>Advanced Course in English for Foreign-born Men Literate in Their Native Language</u>. Washington: Government Printing Office, 1919. TESOL. HEW.

2472. Hermann, E. P. <u>Effectiveness in Business English Study</u>. 1915. Business English. USC.

2473. Herrick, and Damon. <u>Composition and Rhetoric for the Schools</u>. Scott F. and Company, 1902. Composition. AC, AK.

2474. Herrick, R., and Damon, L. T. <u>Composition and Rhetoric for Schools</u>. Scott, F. and Company, 1899. Composition. AC.

2475. Herrick, R., and Damon, L. T. <u>New Composition and Rhetoric for School</u>. Scott, 1911. Composition. USC, AK.

2476. Hervey, G. W. <u>A System of Christian Rhetoric</u>. 1873.

Rhetoric. AK.

2477. Hervey, G. W. *System of Christian Rhetoric for Preachers and Other Speakers*. Harper. Sermons. AC

2478. Hewitt, E. *Ease in Conversation*. Jacobs, 1907. Speech. USC.

2479. Hewlett, M. H. *Extemporary Essay*. Oxford, 1922. Composition. EGL.

2480. Heydrick, B.A. *Short Studies in Composition*. Hinds, 1905. Composition. USC, AC.

2481. Heydrick, B. A. *Familiar Essays of Today*. Scribner, 1930. EGL.

2482. Hicks, W. E. *New Champion Spelling Book*. New York, 1920. Spelling. BMI.

2483. Higginson, T. W. *Hints on Writing and Speech-Making*. Longmans, 1912. Composition. USC.

2484. Higginson, T. W. *Hints on Writing and Speechmaking*. Lee and Sons, 1890. Composition. AC.

2485. Hill, A. *Foundations of Rhetoric*. American Book, 1912. Rhetoric. USC.

2486. Hill, A. S. *Beginnings of Rhetoric and Composition*. American, 1902. Composition. USC, CC, AC, AK.

2487. Hill, A. S. *Foundations of Rhetoric*. Harper, 1892. Rhetoric. AC, AK.

2488. Hill, A. S. *Our English*. Harper, 1888. AK.

2489. Hill, A. S. *Our English*. American Book, 1912. USC.

2490. Hill, A. S. *Principles of Rhetoric*. American Book, 1912. Rhetoric. USC.

2491. Hill, A. S. *Principles of Rhetoric and Their Application*. Harper, 1885. Rhetoric. AC.

2492. Hill, A. S. *The Principles of Rhetoric*. New York, 1881. Rhetoric. BMI.

2493. Hill, A. S. The Principles of Rhetoric and Their Application. New York, 1878. Rhetoric. HR, PS SIBP, AC, CLPI, AK.

2494. Hill, A. S. The Principles of Rhetoric and Their Application. New York: American Book, 1895. Rhetoric. HR, AC, AK.

2495. Hill, A. S., and Others. Twenty Years of School and College English. Harvard, 1896. AK.

2496. Hill, A. S. and Others. Twenty Years of School and College English. Harvard, 1912. USC.

2497. Hill, D. The Elements of Rhetoric and Composition. Sheldon, 1878. Composition. AK.

2498. Hill, D. J. Elements of Rhetoric and Composition. American Book, 1906. Composition. USC, AC.

2499. Hill, D. J. Elements of Rhetoric and Composition. Sheldon, 1884. Composition. AC.

2500. Hill, D. J. Science of Rhetoric. American Book, 1912. Rhetoric. USC.

2501. Hill, D. J. The Science of Rhetoric. New York: Sheldon, 1877. Rhetoric. HR, PS, AC, AK.

2502. Hillegas, M. B. Scale for the Measurement of Quality in English Composition by Young People. 1912. Evaluating Writing. USC, HEW.

2503. Hindale, B. A. Teaching the Language Arts. Appleton, 1912. Teaching Methods. USC.

2504. Hindale, B. A. Teaching the Language Arts; Speech, Reading Composition. New York: Appleton and Company, 1897. Teaching Methods. HEW.

2505. Hindale, B. A. Teaching the Language Arts; Speech Reading Composition. New York: Appleton and Company, 1896. Teaching Methods. HEW.

2506. Hitchcock, A. M. Composition and Rhetoric. Holt, 1913. Composition. USC.

2507. Hitchcock, A. M. *Composition and Rhetoric.* Holt, 1917. Composition. USC.

2508. Hitchcock, A. M. *Junior English Book.* Holt, 1920. USC.

2509. Hitchcock, A. M. *New Practice Book in English Composition.* Holt, 1914. Composition. USC.

2510. Hitchcock, A. M. *Practice Book in English Composition.* Holt, 1906, 1909. Composition. USC, AC.

2511. Hitchcock, A. M. *Rhetoric and the Study of Literature.* Holt, 1913. Literature and Composition. USC.

2512. Hitchcock, A. M. *Theme-Book in English Composition.* Holt, 1910. Composition. USC, CC.

2513. Hitchcock, A. M. *Words and Sentences.* Holt, 1908. Composition. USC.

2514. Hitchcock, A. M. *Words, Sentences, and Paragraphs.* Holt, 1915. Composition. USC.

2515. Hitchcock, G. S. *Sermon Composition.* Burns and Oates, 1908. Sermons. BMI.

2516. Hobbes, T. *English Works.* London, 1839-1845. CLPI.

2517. Hockenberry, H. J. *Essentials of English Grammar.* Silver. Grammar. USC.

2518. Hockenberry, H. J. *Textbook of English Grammar.* Portland, OR: Hockenberry, 1918. Grammar. USC.

2519. Hodge, L. F., and Lee, A. *Elementary English Written and Spoken.* Merrill, 1920. USC.

2520. Hodgson, C. H. *Hints on Essay Writing for Schools.* London, 1902. Composition. BMI.

2521. Hodgson, W. B. *Errors in the Use of English.* Edinburgh, 1881. Error. BMI, CLPI.

2522. Hoenshel, E. J. *Advanced Grammar*. American Book. Grammar. USC.

2523. Hoenshel, E. J. *Complete English Grammar for Common and High Schools*. American Book, 1907. Grammar. USC.

2524. Hoenshel, E. J. *Key and Manual for Complete Grammar*. American Book. Grammar. USC.

2525. Hoenshel, E. J. *Language Lessons and Elementary Grammar*. American Book. Grammar. USC.

2526. Hoenshel, E. J. *Manual of Elementary and Advanced Grammar*. American Book. Grammar. USC.

2527. Hoenshel, E. J. *Progressive Course in English*. American Book, 1912. USC, BMI.

2528. Holbrook, A. *New English Grammar*. American Book. Grammar. USC.

2529. Holbrook, A. *Training Lessons in English Grammar*. American Book, 1900. Grammar. USC.

2530. Holland, R. W. *English Composition Precis Writing*. Longmans, 1911. Composition. USC.

2531. Holliday, C. *Grammar of Present Day English*. Laird, 1919. Grammar. USC.

2532. Holmes, H. W., and Gallagher, O. C. *Composition and Rhetoric*. Appleton, 1917. Composition. USC.

2533. Holtz, M. E. *Constructive English Grammar*. Century, 1914. Grammar. USC.

2534. Hooton, M. B. *Correlation of Vocational and Liberal Education Through English Language and Literature*. Lincoln, NE: Long and Co., 1918. USC, HEW.

2535. Hooton, M. B. *Course of Study in English Language and Literature for Junior and Senior High Schools*. Lincoln, NE: Long and Co., 1917. USC.

2536. Hope, M. B. *The Princeton Text Book in Rhetoric*. Princeton, NJ: Robinson, 1859. Rhetoric. HR, PS,

AK.

2537. Hosic, J. F. Business English: A Summary of Principles. National Education Association of United States Journal of Proceedings and Addresses. 1916. Business English. HEW.

2538. Hosic, J. F. Elementary Course in English. Chicago: Chicago Press, 1917. USC.

2539. Hosic, J. F. The Elementary Course in English; A Syllabus for Teachers. Chicago: The Chicago Normal School Press, 1908. English Syllabi. HEW.

2540. Hosic, J. F. The Elementary Course in English; A Syllabus with Graded Tests and Reference. Chicago: University of Chicago Press, 1911. English Syllabi. HEW.

2541. Hosic, J. F., and Hooper, C. L. Composition for Elementary Schools. Rand, 1919. Composition. USC.

2542. Hosic, J. F., and Hooper, C. L. Composition for Elementary Schools; A Child's Composition Book. Rand, 1916. Composition. USC.

2543. Hosic, J. F., and Hooper, C. L. Composition for Elementary Schools; A Composition Grammar. Rand, 1916. Composition. USC.

2544. Hotchkiss, G. B. Business English. 1916. Business English. USC, HEW.

2545. Hotchkiss, G. B., and Kilduff, E. J. Handbook of Business English. 1915. Business English. USC.

2546. Hotchkiss, G. B., and Kilduff, E. J. Handbook of Business English. Harper, 1920. Business English. USC.

2547. Hotchkiss, G. R., and Drew, C. A. Business English. American Book, 1916. Business English. USC.

2548. Hotten, M. B. Course of Study in English Language and Literature for Junior and Senior High School. Lincoln, NE: Woodruff Press, 1917. English Syllabi. HEW.

2549. Houghton, F. *First Lessons in English for Foreigners in Evening Schools*. American Book Co., 1911. TESOL. HEW.

2550. *How to Speak with Elegance and Ease*. Hurst, 1876. Speech. AC.

2551. *How to Teach Grammar - Teacher's Manual of the Science and Art of Teaching*. 1879. Grammar. CSIGP.

2552. *How to Write: Pocket Manual of Composition and Letter Writing*. Wells, 1857. Composition. AC, CLPI.

2553. *How to Write a Composition*. Dick, 1912. Composition. USC.

2554. *How to Write a Composition*. Dick and F., 1876. Composition. AC.

2555. *How to Write English*. Dundee, 1903. Composition. BMI.

2556. *How to Write for the Magazines*. London, 1900. Journalism. BMI.

2557. *How to Write for the Press*. London, 1899. Journalism. BMI.

2558. *How to Write for the Press*. London, 1904. Journalism. BMI.

2559. Howe, M. A. *Wendell and His Letters*. Atlantic Monthly, 1924. AK.

2560. Howe, W. D., and others. *Gate to English*. Longmans, 1915. USC.

2561. Howland, G. *Elementary Lessons in English*. McClurg, 1910. USC.

2562. Howland, G. C. *Advanced Lessons in English*. McClurg, 1910. USC.

2563. Hoyt, C. O. Studies in the History of Modern Education. Silver, 1908. History of Education. CC.

2564. Hudelson, E. Hudelson English Composition Scale. World Book, 1920. Evaluating Writing. USC.

2565. Huffcut, E. W. English in the Preparatory Schools. Heath, 1912. English Syllabi. USC.

2566. Huffcut, E. W. English in the Preparatory Schools. Boston: Hinth and Co., 1892. English Syllabi. HEW.

2567. Hughes, J. L. and Kleenin, L. R. Progress of Education in the Century. Liuscott, 1907. History of Education. CC.

2568. Hughs, G. S. Grammar of English. Chicago, 1910. Grammar. USC.

2569. Hughs, G. S. Grammar of English; on the Theory that This Is the First. Chicago: Hughs, 1910. Grammar. USC.

2570. Hunt, J. Manual of the Philosophy of Voice and Speech, Especially in Relation to the English Language and the Art of Public Speaking. 1859. Speech. CLPI.

2571. Hunt, J. N. Elementary-School Speller. New York, 1920. Spelling. BMI.

2572. Hunt, T. W. Principles of Written Discourse. Doran. Composition. USC.

2573. Hunt, T. W. Principles of Written Discourse. Armstrong, 1884. Composition. AC, BMI, AK.

2574. Hunt, T. W. Studies in Literature and Style. New York, 1890. Style. BMI, CLPI, AK.

2575. Hunt, T. W. Studies in Literature and Style. Doran, 1912. Style. USC.

2576. Huntington, T. F. Elementary English Composition. Macmillan. Composition. USC.

2577. Huntington, T. F. Elements of English Composition. Macmillan, 1904. Composition. USC, AC, BMI.

2578. Huston, W. H. One Hundred Lessons in Composition. N. E. Pub., 1889. Composition. AC.

2579. Hutton, W. A. and Leigh, T. N. First Steps in Composition. Toronto, 1896. Composition. BMI.

2580. Hyde, M. F. Lessons in English. Heath. USC.

2581. Hyde, M. F. Practical Course in English. Heath, 1917. USC.

2582. Hyde, M. F. Practical English Grammar. Heath. Grammar. USC.

2583. Hyde, M. F. Two Book Course in English. Heath, 1906. USC.

2584. Illinois Assocation of Teachers of English. Report on the Experiment in English Composition. Urbana, IL, 1914. Composition. USC.

2585. Indianapolis Board of School Commissioners. Illustrative Compositions and Letters Written by Pupils 2B to 8A. Indianapolis, IN: Harrington and Folger, 1907. Composition. HEW.

2586. Inland Empire Council of Teachers. Minimal Essentials in Composition and Grammar Schools Grades I to VIII. Missoula, MT: Missoulian Publishing Co. 1920. Composition. HEW.

2587. Inland Empire Council of Teachers of English Minimum Requirements in the Mechanics of English Composition for use in the High School's of the Inland Empire. Missoula, MT: The Inter-Mountain Educator, 1920. Composition. HEW.

2588. International Library of Technology. International Textbook Co. USC.

2589. Iowa, University. Minimum Essentials of English Composition. Iowa: Iowa University, 1920. Composition. HEW.

2590. Irish, F. V. Grammar and Analysis by Diagrams. American Book. Grammar. USC.

2591. Jackson, A. V. W. English and Its History Syllabus. New York. Grammar. USC.

2592. Jackson, H. Eighteen Nineties; A Review of Art and Ideas at the Close of the Nineteenth Century. Knopf, 1922. EGL.

2593. Jackson, M. H. Helps to the Study of "A Book of English Essays". Cape Town, 1913. Teaching Methods. BMI.

2594. Jackson, M. H. Tuta's University English Course. Cape Town, 1915. English Syllabi. BMI.

2595. Jackson, M. H. Tuta's University English Course. Cape Town, 1918. English Syllabi. BMI.

2596. Jackson, T. C. Practical Outline in English Composition. London, 1897. Composition. BMI.

2597. Jacobs, T. E. Civil Service Essay Writer. London, 1895. Business English. BMI.

2598. Jacoby, F. C. Grammar Handbook. Crane and Co., 1901. Grammar. USC.

2599. James, H. Questions of Our Speech. Houghton, 1905. Speech. USC.

2600. Jameson, H. W. Rhetoric and Elocution. I. H. Brown, 1889. Rhetoric. AC.

2601. Jameson, H. W. Rhetorical Method. Barnes, 1879. Rhetoric. AC, AK.

2602. Jamieson, A. Grammar of Rhetoric and Polite Literature. Mason, 1876. Grammar. AC.

2603. Jamieson, A. Grammar of Rhetoric and Polite Literature. 1820. Grammar. HR, PS.

2604. Jamieson, A. Grammar of Rhetoric and Polite Literature. Maltby, 1842. Grammar. AK.

2605. Jelliffe, R. A. Handbook of Exposition. Macmillan, 1914. Composition. USC.

2606. Jeschke, H. Beginners' Book in Language. Ginn, 1918. USC.

2607. Jewell, F. S. Grammatical Diagrams Defended. Bardeen. Grammar. USC.

2608. Johansen, F. O. Projects in Action English; Socialized Recitations in Composition and Grammar. Boston: R. G. Badger, 1920. Composition. HEW, USC.

2609. Johnson, B. Essaying the Essay. Little, 1927. Composition. EGL.

2610. Johnson, F. L. Correct English. Publicity. Usage. USC.

2611. Johnson, H. The Ideal Ministry. Revell, 1908. Sermons. CC.

2612. Johnson, R. The Alphabet of Rhetoric. New York: Appleton, 1903. Rhetoric. BMI, CC, AC, USC.

2613. Johnson, R. I. Mechanics of English. Allyn, 1921. Mechanics. USC.

2614. Johnson, S. Dictionary of the English Language. London, 1827. Dictionaries. CLPI.

2615. Joint Committee on the Reorganization of High-School English. A Brief Summary of the Forthcoming Report of the National Joint Committee on the Reorganization of High-School English. 1916. Curriculum. HEW.

2616. Joint Committee on the Reorganization of High-School English. Reorganization of English in Secondary Schools. Washington: Government Printing Office, 1917. Curriculum. HEW, USC.

2617. Jones, B. L. Outline Studies in English Composition. Michigan, 1912. Composition. USC.

2618. Jones, F. W. Unscientific Essays. Longmans, 1924. EGL.

2619. Jones, H. S. V. Words and Sentences. Holt, 1919. Grammar. USC.

2620. Jonson, B. English Grammar. 1838. Grammar. CLPI.

2621. Jonson, B. English Grammar. Strugis and Walton, 1909. Grammar. USC.

2622. Jordan, M. A. Correct Writing and Speaking. Barnes, 1904. Composition. USC.

2623. Journal of Opthalmology, Otology, and Laryngology. 1916. HEW.

2624. Joyce, P. W. English Composition. Dublin, 1887. Composition. BMI.

2625. Judd, C. H. Introduction to the Scientific Study of Education. Ginn, 1918. Teaching Methods. LLC.

2626. Junnings, M. W. Rules on English Prose Composition for Hindustani Students. Bombay, 1903. TESOL. BMI.

2627. Kames, Lord, H. H. The Elements of Criticism. Branes, 1855. Criticism. BMI.

2628. Kapper, P. Teaching of English. Appleton, 1915. Teaching Methods. USC, HEW, BMI.

2629. Kaufman, P. Points of View for College Student. Doubleday, Poran. 1926. EGL.

2630. Kavana, R. M. Elements of English Composition. Badger, 1920. Composition. USC.

2631. Kavana, R. M. and Beatty, A. Composition and Rhetoric Based on Literary Models. Rand. Composition. USC.

2632. Kayfetz, I. Critical Study of the Harvard-Newton Composition Scales. Brookland, NY, 1916. Evaluating Writing. USC.

2633. Keagy, J. M. Essay on Mode of Teaching English Composition. Fortescue, 1852. Teaching Methods. AC.

2634. Keating, J. F. English Grammar Condensed. Herrick Book, 1903. Grammar. USC.

2635. Keefe, J. English Composition and Essay Writing. London, 1893. Composition. BMI.

2636. Keeler, H. L. and Adams, M. E. High School English. Allyn, 1906. English Syllabi. USC.

2637. Keeler, H. L. and Davis, E. C. Studies in English Composition. Allyn. Composition. USC.

2638. Keller, L. Historical Outlines of English Syntax. London, 1892. Grammar. LC.

2639. Kelley, A. R. Pulpit Equipment: A Primer For Local Preachers. New York, 1903. Sermons. BMI.

2640. Kelley, J. P. Workmanship in Words. Little, 1916. USC, HEW.

2641. Kellner, L. Historical Outline of English Syntax. Macmillan, 1912. Grammar. USC.

2642. Kellogg, A. M. How to Teach Composition Writing. Kellogg. Teaching Methods. AC.

2643. Kellogg, A. M. How to Teach Composition Writing. Flanagan, 1912. Teaching Methods. USC.

2644. Kellogg, A. M. Writing of Composition. Flanagan. Composition. USC.

2645. Kellogg, B. A Text-Book on Rhetoric. Maynard, 1889. Rhetoric. AC.

2646. Kellogg, B. A Text-Book on Rhetoric. Clark and Maynard, 1880. Rhetoric. AK.

2647. Kellogg, B. English Composition. Maynard and Co. Composition. AC.

2648. Kellogg, B. English Composition. Merrill, 1906.

Composition. USC.

2649. Kellogg, B. <u>Text-Book on Rhetoric</u>. Merrill, 1912. Rhetoric. USC.

2650. Kellogg, B. <u>Text-Book on Rhetoric</u>. Maynard, 1892. Rhetoric. AC.

2651. Kellow, H. A. <u>Practical Training in English</u>. Heath, 1912. English Syllabi. USC.

2652. Kemble, C. S. <u>Preacher's English</u>. Madison, NJ.: Correspondence School of Theology, 1912. Sermons. USC.

2653. Ken, D. L. <u>Notes on Parsing and Analysis</u>. Nelson, 1920. Grammar. BMI.

2654. Kendall, G. <u>Essay-Writing</u>. Longmans, 1915. Composition. USC.

2655. Kendall, G. <u>Essay-Writing: A Guide to the Practice of English Composition</u>. Arnold, 1915. Composition. BMI.

2656. Kendrick, W. <u>New Dictionary of the English Language</u>. London, 1773. Dictionaries. CLPI.

2657. Kennedy, W. W. and Bridges, T. B. <u>Effective English and Letter Writing</u>. Ellis, 1918. Composition. USC.

2658. Kerl, S. <u>Common School Grammar of the English Language</u>. American Book. Grammar. USC.

2659. Kerl, S. <u>Elements of Composition and Rhetoric</u>. Ivison, 1869. Composition. AC.

2660. Kerl, S. <u>Elements of Composition and Rhetoric</u>. American Book, 1912. Composition. USC.

2661. Kerl, S. <u>First Lessons in English Grammar. American Book</u>. Grammar. USC.

2662. Kern, A. A. and Noble, S. G. <u>First Book in English</u>. Dallas, TX: Southern, 1916. English Syllabi. USC.

2663. Kerney, M. J. *Abridgment of Murray's English Grammar.* Murphy, 1911. Grammar. USC.

2664. Kersey, J. A. *Ethics of Literature.* Marion, IN, 1894. Literature. LC.

2665. *Key to Composition: Or How to Write A Book.* Hurst, 1876. Composition. AC.

2666. Keyes, A. M. *Elementary Grammar.* Schwartz, Kirwin, and Fauss, 1914. Grammar. USC.

2667. Keyser, C. J. *Mole Philosophy and Other Essays.* Dutton, 1927. EGL.

2668. Kidd, A. S. *The Evolution of English According to the New Syllabus.* Grahamstown, 1916. English Syllabi. BMI.

2669. Kidd, R. *New Evolution and Vocal Outline.* 1883. English Syllabi. CC.

2670. Kiddle, H. *3,000 Grammar Questions with Answers.* Bardeen. Grammar. USC.

2671. Kimball, G. S. *Business English.* Bobbs, 1911. Business English. USC.

2672. Kimball, L. G. *Elementary English Books.* American Book, 1911. English Syllabi. USC, BMI.

2673. Kimball, L. G. *English Grammar.* American Book, 1912. Grammar. USC, BMI.

2674. Kimball, L. G. *Structure of the English Sentence.* American Book, 1900. Sentences. USC, AK.

2675. Kimpsten, A. *English Composition.* Shaldon, 1904. Composition. BMI.

2676. Kinard, J. P. *English Grammar for Beginners.* Macmillan, 1906. Grammar. USC.

2677. Kinard, J. P. *English Grammar for Beginners.* New York, 1910. Grammar. BMI.

2678. King, M. *Language Games.* 1909. English Syllabi.

USC.

2679. King, W. J. <u>Normal Outlines of Language</u>. March. English Syllabi. USC.

2680. Kingsley, M. E. <u>Outlines of Grammar</u>. Palmer Company. Grammar. USC.

2681. Kinnear, G. <u>Use of Words</u>. Dutton, 1904. Usage. USC.

2682. Kirkham, S. <u>A Compendium of English Grammar</u>. Thompson, 1823. Grammar. AK.

2683. Kirkham, S. <u>English Grammar in Familiar Lectures</u>. Steele, 1829. Grammar. AK.

2684. Kirkland, E. S. <u>1000 Composition Subjects</u>. Barnes, 1889. Composition. AC.

2685. Kirkland, E. S. <u>1000 Composition Subjects</u>. Hinds, 1912. Composition. USC.

2686. Kirkland, E. S. <u>One Thousand Composition Subjects</u>. Hinds, 1899. Composition. AC.

2687. Kirkland, E. S. <u>One Thousand Composition Subjects; or, What Shall We Write About?</u> Barnes, 1891. Composition. AC.

2688. Kirkland, E. S. <u>Speech and Manners for Home and School</u>. McClurg. Speech. USC.

2689. Kirkland, E. S. <u>What Shall We Write About? 1000 Composition Subjects</u>. Fergus, 1889. Composition. AC.

2690. Kirkland, W. M. <u>View Vertical, and Other Essays</u>. Houghton, 1920. EGL.

2691. Kirkpatrick, J. <u>Handbook of Idiomatic English as Now Written and Spoken</u>. Heidelburg, 1914. Grammar. BMI.

2692. Kirwan, G. R. <u>Primer of English Grammar</u>. Longmans. Grammar. USC.

2693. Kitchener, E. E. Exercises in English Composition for Juniors Forms. Murray, 1920. Composition. BMI.

2694. Kittredge, G. L. and Arnold, S. L. Mother Tongue Book. New York: Ginn. USC.

2695. Kittredge, G. L. and Farley, F. E. Advanced English Grammar with Exercises. Ginn, 1913. Grammar. USC, BMI.

2696. Kittredge, G. L. and Farley, F. E. Concise English Grammar. Ginn, 1918. Grammar. USC, BMI.

2697. Klapper, P. Teaching of English. Appleton, 1915. Teaching Methods. USC, HEW, BMI.

2698. Kleiser, G. Fifteen Thousand Useful Phrases. New York: Funk Wagnalls, 1917. Dictionaries. HEW.

2699. Kleiser, G. Helpful Hints on Writing and Reading. Funk Wagnalls, 1911. Composition. USC.

2700. Kleiser, G. How to Argue and Win. Funk Wagnalls, 1910. Rhetoric. CC.

2701. Kleiser, G. How to Develop Power and Personality in Speaking. Funk Wagnalls, 1909. Speech. CC.

2702. Kleiser, G. Miscellaneous Studies in Prose. Funk Wagnalls, 1911. USC.

2703. Kleiser, G. Models for Study. Funk Wagnalls, 1911. Readers. USC.

2704. Kleiser, G. Study of Words. Funk Wagnalls, 1911. Vocabulary. USC.

2705. Kleiser, G. The Philosophy of Rhetoric. Funk Wagnalls, 1911. Rhetoric. USC.

2706. Kleiser, G. Vital English for Speakers and Writers. Funk Wagnalls, 1919. English Syllabi. USC.

2707. Kleiser, G. P. How to Speak in Public. Funk, 1906. Speech. CC.

2708. Knight, G. C. *American Mercury*. Readings from the American Mercury. Knopf, 1926. USC.

2709. Knight, G. C, ed. *Readings from American*. Knopf, 1926. Readers. EGL.

2710. Knight, M. *Practice Work in English*. Longmans, 1914. English Syllabi. USC.

2711. Knight, M. *Primer of Essentials in Grammar and Rhetoric for Secondary Schools*. American Book, 1905. Rhetoric. USC, AC.

2712. Knowies, A. *Oral English*. Heath, 1916. Speech. USC.

2713. Knox, Rev. S. *Compendious System of Rhetoric*. 1809. Rhetoric. CLPI.

2714. Koch, C. O. *Contributions to an Historical Study of the Adjectives of Size in English*. 1906. Grammar. BMI.

2715. Krapp, G. P. *Elements of English Grammar*. Scribner, 1908. Grammar. USC.

2716. Krapp, G. P. *English Language and Grammar: Syllabus*. Teachers College. Grammar. USC.

2717. Krapp, G. P. *Modern English, Its Growth and Present Use*. Scribner, 1909. Grammar. USC.

2718. Kurtz, B. P. and Others. *Essays in Exposition*. Ginn, 1914. Composition. USC.

2719. Lacey, W. I. *Illustration of the Principles Rhetoric*. Pittsburgh, 1834. Rhetoric. CC.

2720. Lakewood Ohio Board of Education. *Course of Study in English*. Lakewood Public School, 1918. Curriculum. HEW.

2721. Lamb, J. B. *Practical Hints on Writing for the Press*. London, 1897. Journalism. BMI.

2722. Lamont, H. *English Composition*. Scribner, 1906. Composition. USC, AC, AK.

2723. Lamont, H. Specimens of Exposition. Holt, 1894. Modes. USC.

2724. Lamonte, A. English Self-Taught for the French. Ottenheimer, 1914. TESOL. USC.

2725. Lang, S. E. Advanced English Grammar. Toronto, 1915. Grammar. BMI.

2726. Lang, S. E. Introductory English Grammar. Toronto, 1915. Grammar. BMI.

2727. Language and Composition Picture Portfolio. Flanagan. Composition. USC.

2728. Language for Men of Affairs. Ronold, 1920. Business English. USC.

2729. Language Lessons for Common Schools. Concordia. English Syllabi. USC.

2730. Lansing, J. H. Child's Book of Language. American Book. USC.

2731. Larrabee, W. H. Helps to Speak and Write Correctly. Tibbals, 1876. Usage. AC.

2732. Latham, R. G. Handbook of the English Language. 1864. Grammar. CLPI.

2733. Latham, R. G. The English Language. 1864. CLPI.

2734. Latham, R. G. The English Language. 1850. SIBP.

2735. Lathron, H. R. Freshman Composition. Century, 1920. Composition. USC.

2736. Laug, H. A. Great Teachers of Your Centuries. 1893. CC.

2737. Law, F. H. English that Makes Money. New York, 1920. BMI.

2738. Law, F. H. Modern Essays and Stories. Appleton-Century, 1922. Literature. EGL.

2739. Law, W. H. *The English Language*. 1901. LC.

2740. *Laws of Speech--Wilson's Studies in Life and Sense*. 1887. CSIGP.

2741. Lay, E. J. S. *The Pupils' Class Book of English Composition*. Macmillan, 1918. Composition. BMI.

2742. Laycock, C. and Scales, R. L. *Argumentation and Debate*. 1905. Rhetoric. CC.

2743. Le Row, C. B. *English as She is Taught*. Century, 1901. USC.

2744. Leathes, Sir S. M. *The Teaching of English at the Universities*. Oxford: Hart, 1913. Teaching Methods. HEW, BMI.

2745. Lee, A. *Lessons in English*. Merrill, 1917. English Syllabi. USC.

2746. Lee, A. *Lessons in English*. Merrill, 1918. English Syllabi. USC.

2747. Lee, A. S. *Modern English Grammar*. West Virginia: Ripley, 1914. Grammar. USC.

2748. Lee, A. S. *Ten Weeks in English Grammar*. West Virginia: Ripley, 1908. Grammar. USC.

2749. Leiper, M. A. *Language Work in Elementary Schools*. Ginn, 1916. English Syllabi. USC, BMI.

2750. Leiper, M. A. *Teaching Language Through Agriculture and Domestic Science*. 1912. Technical English. USC, HEW.

2751. Leiper, M. A. *The New Idea Speller*. Boston, 1919. Spelling. BMI.

2752. Leonard, A. W. and Fuess, C. M. *High School Spelling Book*. New York, 1915. Spelling. BMI.

2753. Leonard, M. H. *Grammar and Its Reasons*. Barnes, 1908. Grammar. USC, BMI.

2754. Leonard, S. A. *English Composition as a Social*

Problem. Houghton, 1917. Composition. USC, HEW.

2755. Lessons in Correct Grammar. Hinds. Grammar. USC.

2756. Letter-Writing Made Easy, and Composition Simplified. Hurst, 1876. Composition. AC.

2757. Lewes, G. H. Principles of Success in Literature. Allyn, 1912. Literature. USC.

2758. Lewes, G. H. The Principles of Success in Literature. Allyn, 1891. Literature. AK.

2759. Lewis, E. H. Business English 2. La Salle University, 1911. Business English. USC.

2760. Lewis, E. H. Business English. La Salle University, 1915. Business English. USC.

2761. Lewis, E. H. Final Draft Paper. Macmillan, 1900. USC.

2762. Lewis, E. H. First Book in English. Macmillan. English Syllabi. USC.

2763. Lewis, E. H. First Manual of Composition. Macmillan, 1899. Composition. AC, BMI.

2764. Lewis, E. H. First Manual of Composition. Macmillan, 1920. Composition. USC, AC.

2765. Lewis, E. H. Second Manual of Composition. Macmillan, 1900. Composition. USC, BMI.

2766. Lewis, E. H. Specimens of the Forms of Discourse. Holt, 1900. Modes. USC.

2767. Lewis, E. H. Text-Book of Applied English Grammar. Macmillan, 1902. Grammar. USC.

2768. Lewis, E. H. The History of the English Paragraph. Chicago: Chicago University Press, 1894. Paragraphs. HR, PS, AK.

2769. Lewis, F. W. Inductive Lessons in Rhetoric. Heath, 1900. Rhetoric. USC, AC.

2770. Lewis, W. D. and Holmes, M. D. Knowing and Using Words. Allyn, 1917. Usage. USC.

2771. Lewis, W. D. and Hosic, J. F. Practical English for High Schools. American Book, 1916. English Syllabi. USC, BMI.

2772. Lewis, W. D. and Lynch, H. M. Grammar to Use. Winston, 1918. Grammar. USC, BMI.

2773. Lewisohn, L. Modern Book of Criticism. Boni and Liveright, 1919. Criticism. EGL.

2774. Lighthall, G. E. Analysis, Parsing and Composition. Waldteufel, 1876. Composition. AC.

2775. Linecar, A. Class Exercise in English Composition. Jack, 1914. Composition. BMI.

2776. Linn, J. W. Essentials of English Composition. Scribner, 1912. Composition. USC, AK.

2777. Linn, J. W. Illustrated Examples of English Composition. Scribner, 1913. Composition. USC.

2778. Lipsky, A. Rhythm as Distinguishing Characteristics of Prose Style. Science Press, 1905-1907. Style. USC.

2779. Littell, P. Books and Things. Harcourt, 1919. EGL.

2780. Little, G. Exposition of English Grammar. 1841. Grammar. CLPI.

2781. Live and Learn. 1912. USC.

2782. Live and Learn: Guide for All Who Wish to Speak and Write Correctly. Usage. USC.

2783. Livingstone, W. A New Mode of Correcting Exercise. Spink and Co., 1881. Teaching Methods. HEW.

2784. Llewellyn, W. E. M. The Vowel-Stone, A "Modulator" for the Teaching of Reading, Spelling and Punctuation. Gillard, 1914. Teaching Methods. BMI.

2785. Lloyd, E. Literature for Little Folks: Selections from Standard Authors and Lessons in Composition. Sower, 1876. Literature. AC.

2786. Llyod, R. J. Northern English. Stechert, 1908. Dialects. USC.

2787. Loane, G. G. Diaconus: Exercises in the Meaning of English. Macmillan, 1912. Semantics. USC.

2788. Locke, C. L. Primer of English Parsing and Analysis. Longmans. Grammar. USC.

2789. Lockington, A. K. Word and Picture of Lessons to Correct Common Spelling Mistakes. Harrap, 1919. Spelling. BMI.

2790. Lockwood, S. E. H. Lessons in English. Ginn. English Syllabi. USC.

2791. Lockwood, S. E. H. Teachers' Manual to Accompany Lockwood and Emerson's Composition and Rhetoric. Ginn, 1902. Teaching Methods. USC.

2792. Lockwood, S. E. H. and Emerson, M. A. Composition and Rhetoric. 1901. Composition. USC, AC, CC.

2793. Logan. Structural Principles of Style Applied: Manual of English Prose Composition. Willey and D. Composition. USC.

2794. Lomer, G. R. and Ashmun, M. Study and Practice of Writing English. Houghton, 1917. Composition. USC.

2795. Lomer, G. R. and Ashmun, M. E. Study and Practice of Writing English. Houghton, 1914. Composition. USC, AK.

2796. London County Council Education Department. Report of a Conference on the Teaching of English in London Elementary Schools. London, Southwood: Smith and Co., 1909. Curriculum. HEW.

2797. Long Beach California Board of Education. Course of Study in Language and Grammar for the Elementary Schools in Long Beach, California. Long Beach, CA:

Graves and Hersey, 1913. Curriculum. HEW.

2798. Long, C. C. <u>Grammar and Composition</u>. Van Antwerp, 1886. Composition. AC.

2799. Long, C. C. <u>Lessons in English</u>. American Book. English Syllabi. USC.

2800. Long, C. C. <u>New Language Exercise</u>. American Book. English Syllabi. USC.

2801. Long, C. R. <u>Spelling Rules and Exercises</u>. Melbourne, 1918. Spelling. BMI.

2802. Long, J. H. <u>Slips of Tongue and Pen</u>. Appleton. Error. USC.

2803. Long, P. W. <u>Studies in the Technique of Prose Style</u>. Cambridge, MA: Long, 1915. Style. USC.

2804. Long, P. W. and Hersey, F. W. C. <u>Military English</u>. Macmillan, 1918. Technical English. USC.

2805. Longridge, C. C. <u>Formation of English Writers</u>. Preston, 1888. BMI.

2806. Longwell, O. H. <u>Elementary Grammar</u>. Welch. Grammar. USC.

2807. Looke, J. H. <u>Diversions of Pruley</u>. 1829. SIBP.

2808. Lord, D. N. <u>Characteristics and Laws of Figurative Language</u>. 1854. Rhetoric. SIBP.

2809. Lose, C. and Furst, S. W. <u>English Grammar By Outline</u>. Haven PA: Frust and Lock, 1918. Grammar. USC.

2810. Lottner, H. <u>Vocal Calisthenics</u>. Newark, NJ: Hardham, 1886. Speech. HEW.

2811. Lounsbury, T. R. <u>Standard of Usage in English</u>. Harper, 1908. Usage. USC.

2812. Lowell, D. O. S. <u>English Composition Handbook</u>. Sibley. Composition. USC.

2813. Lucas, E. V. Adventures and Enthusiasms. Doran, 1920. EGL.

2814. Lucas, E. V. Phantom Journal, and Other Essays. Methuen, 1919. EGL.

2815. Luce, R. Writing for the Press. Boston, 1889. Journalism. BMI.

2816. Lucia, I. W. Forty Lessons in Applied English. Detroit, MI: Lucia, 1899. English Syllabi. USC.

2817. Lunt, H. L. Practical Studies in Sentence Analysis. Los Angeles CA: University of Southern California, 1919. Grammar. USC.

2818. Luper, M. A. Language Work in Elementary Schools. Boston, New York: Ginn and Company, 1916. Curriculum. HEW.

2819. Lyman, R. L. V. and Sheafor, J. T. Fundamentals of Oral English: A Course for Secondary Schools. University of Madison, 1914. Speech. HEW.

2820. Lyons, J. A. Modern Business English. Business English. USC.

2821. Lyte, E. O. Advanced Grammar and Composition. American Book, 1899. Composition. AC.

2822. Lyte, E. O. Advanced Grammar and Composition. American Book, 1912. Composition. USC.

2823. Lyte, E. O. Elementary English. New York, Cincinnati: American Book Company, 1898. English Syllabi. HEW.

2824. Lyte, E. O. Elementary English. American Book, 1912. English Syllabi. USC.

2825. Lyte, E. O. Elements of Grammar and Composition. American Book Company, 1912. Composition. USC.

2826. Lyte, E. O. English Grammar and Composition. American Book, 1912. Composition. USC.

2827. Lyte, E. O. Grammar and Composition for Common

<pre>   Schools. Appleton, 1886. Composition. AC.
</pre>

2828. Lywau, R. L. V. Principles of Effective Debating. Wisconsin University, 1908. Rhetoric. CC.

2829. Macaulay, T. Essay on Warren Hastings. Longmans. USC.

2830. Macaulay, T. B. Essay on Milton. Longmans. USC.

2831. Macbeth, J. W. V. Might and Mirth Literature: Treatise on Figurative Language. Harper, 1875. Rhetoric. AC.

2832. MacClintock, P. L. Essentials of Business English 2. 1914. Business English. USC.

2833. MacCracken, H. N. and Sandison, H. E. Manual of Good English. MacMillan, 1917. Grammar. USC, BMI.

2834. MacDonald, A. B. Foundation English: The Expression of Ideas. Sanborn, 1911. English Syllabi. USC.

2835. MacDonald, J. W. The Prevailing Method and Results of English Instruction in the High School. Boston: Wright and Potter, 1904. Teaching Methods. HEW.

2836. MacDougall and Company. Graduated Lessons and Exercises in English Composition. Edinburgh, 1892. Composition. BMI.

2837. MacDougall and Company. Short Lessons in English Composition. Edinburgh, 1902. Composition. BMI.

2838. MacEwan, E. J. Essentials of the English Sentence. Heath, 1900. Sentences. USC.

2839. MacIntosh, D. Elements of the English Grammar. 1852. Grammar. SIBP.

2840. MacLean, M. S. and Holmes, E. K. Men and Books. R. R. Smith, 1930. EGL.

2841. MacLeod, N. Composition Outline. March. Composition. USC.

2842. MacLeod, N. Reproduction Stories: Primary,

Intermediate, and Grammar. March. Readers. USC.

2843. MacMordie, W. *English Grammar: A Book For Indian Students.* H. Frowde, 1911. TESOL. BMI.

2844. MacMordie, W. *First Steps in English Composition.* 1890, Composition. BMI.

2845. MacMordie, W. *Studies in English: A Manual for Indian Students.* Frowde, 1911. TESOL. BMI.

2846. Maetzer, E. *An English Grammar.* 1874. Grammar. SIBP.

2847. Mahaffy, J. P. *Decay of Modern Preaching.* 1882. Sermons. CLPI.

2848. Mahoney, J. J. *Standards in English.* World Book, 1917. Usage. USC, HEW.

2849. Mahoney, J. J. *Standards in English.* World Book, 1919. Usage. USC, HEW.

2850. Maine Office of State Commissioner of Education. *The Course of English in High School.* Augusta, Maine, 1916. Curriculum. HEW.

2851. Mais, S. P. B. *An English Course for Schools.* Grant Richards, 1919. English Syllabi. BMI.

2852. Mais, S. P. B. *English Course for Army Candidates.* Sidgwick and Jackson, 1915. English Syllabi. BMI.

2853. Makower, S. V. and Blackwell, B. H. *Book of English Essays.* Oxford, 1912. Readers. EGL.

2854. Mallarky, E. M. *Training in Speech and Other Papers.* Sydney, WA: Government Printing, 1914. Speech. HEW.

2855. Malory, H. S. *Backgrounds of Book Reviewing.* Wahr, 1923. Journalism. EGL.

2856. Mandeville, H. *Elements of Reading and Oratory.* Northway and Company, 1845. Reading. HR.

2857. Manley, F. *English Language.* Birchard, 1902. USC.

2858. Manly, J. M. and Bailey, E. R. <u>Lessons in Speaking and Writing English</u>. Heath, 1913. Composition. BMI.

2859. Manly, J. M. and Bailey, E. R. <u>Lessons in the Speaking and Writing of English</u>. Heath, 1914. Composition. USC.

2860. Manly, J. M. and Bailey, E. R. S. <u>Junior High School English</u>. Heath, 1916. Curriculum. USC.

2861. Manly, J. M. and Bailey, E. R. S. <u>Manual of Suggestions for Teachers Using the Manly-Bailey Lessons in the Speaking and Writing of English</u>. Heath, 1916. Teaching Methods. USC.

2862. Manly, J. M. and Powell, J. <u>A Manual for Writers</u>. Chicago: University of Chicago Press, 1913. English Syllabi. USC.

2863. Manly, J. M. and Rickert, E. <u>Writing of English</u>. Holt, 1919. Composition. USC.

2864. March, F. A. <u>A Parser and Analyzer for Beginners</u>. American Book. Grammar. USC.

2865. Maris, G. L. <u>Normal English Grammar</u>. Hinds. Grammar. USC.

2866. Markowitz, A. J. and Starr, S. <u>Everyday Language Lessons</u>. American Book, 1914. Grammar. USC.

2867. Marsh, G. P. <u>Lectures on the English Language</u>. 1860. SIBP.

2868. Marsh, H. A. <u>Grammar in a Nutshell; or English Without Rules</u>. Lansing, MI: Hammond, 1910. Grammar. USC.

2869. Marshall, C. C. <u>Business English</u>. Goodyear-Marshall, 1906. Business English. USC.

2870. Martin, E. S. <u>What's Ahead and Meanwhile</u>. Harper, 1927. EGL.

2871. Mason, C. P. <u>English Grammar</u>. Macmillan. Grammar.

USC.

2872. Mason, C. P. *Outlines of English Grammar*. Macmillan. Grammar. USC.

2873. Mason, M. M. *English Spoken and Written Today*. D. Nutt, 1911. Composition. BMI.

2874. Massachusetts Board of Education. *Course of Study in English Expression for the First Six Grades of the Elementary School*. Massachusetts: Massachusetts Board of Education, 1916. Curriculum. USC, HEW.

2875. Massachusetts Board of Education. *English for American Citizenship*. Massachusetts: Massachusetts Board of Education, 1918. TESOL. USC.

2876. *Massachusetts Board of Education English 1 Grades 7, 8, and 9*. Boston: Wright and Potter Printing Company, 1917. Curriculum. HEW.

2877. Massachusetts Board of Education. *Federal-State Program for Immigrants Education*. Massachusetts: Massachusetts Board of Education, 1919. TESOL. USC.

2878. Massachusetts Board of Education. *Problem of Immigrant Education in Massachusetts*. Massachusetts: Massachusetts Board of Education, 1919. TESOL. USC.

2879. Massachusetts Board of Education. *Teacher's Handbook to Accompany Standards Lessons in English for American Citizenship*. Massachusetts: Massachusetts Board of Education, 1919. TESOL. USC.

2880. Massingham, H. J. *Letters to X*. Dutton, 1919. EGL.

2881. Mathes, C. H. *Composition and Grammar*. National Book Company, 1919. Composition. USC.

2882. Matheson, J. *Theory and Practice of English Grammar*. 1819. Grammar. SIBP.

2883. Mathews, H. *Outlines of English Grammar*. Heath. Grammar. USC.

2884. Mathews, W. *Oratory and Orators*. 1896. Speech. CC.

2885. Mathews, W. *Words; Their Use and Abuse*. Scott. Usage. USC.

2886. Mathwianatha, V. *A Handbook of English Composition*. Calcutta, 1900. Composition. BMI.

2887. Matthews, B. *Essays on English*. Scribner, 1921. Usage. EGL.

2888. Matthews, B. *Gateways to Literature, and Other Essays*. Scribner, 1912. Literature. EGL.

2889. Matthews, B. *Parts of Speech; Essays on English*. Scribner, 1901. Grammar. EGL, LLC.

2890. Maunder, S. *Treasury of Knowledge*. London, 1830. CLPI.

2891. Maxcy, C. L. *Rhetorical Principles of Narration*. Houghton, 1911. Modes. USC.

2892. Maxim, H. *Science of Poetry and the Philosophy of Language*. Funk, 1910. Rhetoric. USC.

2893. Maxwell, C. H. *Composition for Schools*. 1904. Composition. BMI.

2894. Maxwell, W. H. *Advanced Lessons in English Grammar*. American Book. Grammar. USC.

2895. Maxwell, W. H. *Elementary Grammar for Use in 4th and 5th Grades*. American Book. Grammar. USC.

2896. Maxwell, W. H. *First Book in English*. American Book. English Syllabi. USC.

2897. Maxwell, W. H. *Introductory Lessons in English Grammar*. American Book. Grammar. USC.

2898. Maxwell, W. H. *Primary Lessons in Language and Composition*. American Book, 1912. Composition. USC.

2899. Maxwell, W. H. *Primary Lessons in Language and*

2899. Maxwell, W. H. *Primary Lessons in Language and Composition*. Barnes, 1886. Composition. AC.

2900. Maxwell, W. H. *School Grammar, For Use in 5th, 6th, 7th, and 8th Grades*. American Book. Grammar. USC.

2901. Maxwell, W. H. and Johnson, E. L. *School Composition*. American Book, 1902. Composition. USC, AC.

2902. Maxwell, W. H. and Others. *Speaking and Writing Book*. American Book, 1915. English Syllabi. USC.

2903. Maxwell, W. H. and Others. *Speaking and Writing Books*. American Book, 1910-1911. English Syllabi. USC.

2904. Maxwell, W. H. and Smith, G. J. *Writing in English*. American Book, 1900. Composition. USC.

2905. Mazzinghi, G. *The Beauties of the English Language*. 1815. SIBP.

2906. McConnell, S. D. *Sermon Stuff*. 1888. Sermons. CC.

2907. McCullough, B. W. and Burgum, E. B. *Book of Modern Essays*. Scribner, 1926. Readers. EGL.

2908. McElroy, J. G. R. *Structure of English Prose*. Doran, 1912. Composition. USC.

2909. McElroy, J. R. *Structure of English Prose: Manual of Composition and Rhetoric*. Armstrong, 1890. Composition.

2910. McElroy, J. R. *Structure of English Prose: Manual of Composition and Rhetoric*. Armstrong, 1885. Composition AC, BMI.

2911. McElroy, J. R. *The Structure of English*. Prose. Armstrong, 1895. Composition. AK.

2912. McEvoy, T. J. *Examination Questions in English for Licenses to Teach in New York City*. McEvoy, 1914. Testing. USC, HEW.

2913. McFadden, E. B. *A Course in the Teaching of Composition, Language, and Spelling for the first*

Three Years. Sacramento, California, 1912. Composition. HEW.

2914. McFadden, E. B. A Course of Study in Language for Elementary Schools and Hand-book to Accompany the California State Series Text. Sacramento, 1909. Curriculum. HEW.

2915. McFadden, E. B. A Course of Study in Language Grades of the Elementary School. Sacramento, California, 1912. Curriculum. HEW.

2916. McFadden, E. B. A Course of Study in Primary Language and Handbook to Accompany the State Series Primary Language Text. Sacramento, California: W. W. Shannon, 1907. Curriculum. HEW.

2917. McFadden, E. B. Course of Study in Language. State Normal School, 1909. Curriculum. USC.

2918. McFadden, E. B. Course of Study in Primary Language and Handbook to the State series. 1909. Curriculum. USC.

2919. McFadden, E. B., and Smith, E. G. Course of Study in the Teaching of Composition, Language, and Spelling for the First Three Years. 1912. Curriculum. USC.

2920. McGregor, A. L. Supervised Study in English, for Junior High School Grades. Macmillan, 1921. English Syllabi. USC.

2921. McGuffey, W. H. Rhetorical Guide. Wilson, H. and Company, 1870. Rhetoric.

2922. McHenry, O. Practical Lessons and Exercises in Grammar. American Book. Grammar. USC.

2923. McIntosh, A. Oral and Written Exercises in English. Flanagan. Composition. USC.

2924. McKeon, M. Graded Composition Lessons. Newson. Composition.

2925. McKeon, M. Graded Composition Lessons. Newton, 1904. Composition. USC.

2926. McLaughlin, E. T. Literary Criticism for Students. Holt, 1893. Criticism. EGL.

2927. McMurry, C. A Language Lesson and Grammar. Bobbs, 1915. Grammar. USC.

2928. McMurry, C. A Special Method in Language in the Eight Grades. Macmillan, 1905. English Syllabi. USC, HEW.

2929. McMurry, C. A. Language Lessons Grammar. Indianapolis, 1916. Grammar. BMI.

2930. McMurry, L. B. and Norvell, F. T. Our Language. 1905. USC.

2931. McNichols, J. P. Fundamental English. Schwartz, Kirwin and Fauss, 1909. English Syllabi. USC.

2932. Mead, I. M. English Language and Its Grammar. Silver. Grammar. USC.

2933. Mead, W. E. Elementary Composition and Rhetoric. Leach, 1890. Composition. AC.

2934. Mead, W. E. Elementary Composition and Rhetoric. Sibley, 1912. Composition. USC.

2935. Mead, W. E. and Gordy. Practical Composition and Rhetoric. Sibley, 1900. Composition. USC, AC.

2936. Meiklejohn, J. M. D. Art of Writing English. Appleton, 1900. Composition. USC, CLPI.

2937. Meiklejohn, J. M. D. English Grammar. Heath, 1907. Grammar. USC.

2938. Meiklejohn, J. M. D. English Language; Its Grammar, History and Literature. Heath, 1906. Grammar. USC.

2939. Meilan, M. A. An Introduction to the English Language. 1803. Grammar. SIBP.

2940. Mencken, H. L. American Language. Knopf, 1919. Grammar. USC.

2941. Mencken, H. L. <u>Prejudices</u>. Knopf, 1919-1927. EGL.

2942. Merkley, G. E. <u>Modern Rhetoric</u>. Newton, 1912. Rhetoric. USC, AC.

2943. Merkley, G. E. and Ferguson, A. C. <u>Composition-Rhetoric</u>. Newton, 1912. Composition. USC.

2944. Metcalf, G. S. <u>Game of False Syntax</u>. Flanagan. Grammar. USC.

2945. Metcalf, R. C. <u>Elementary English</u>. American Book. English Syllabi. USC.

2946. Metcalf, R. C. <u>English Grammar</u>. American Book. Grammar. USC.

2947. Metcalf, R. C. <u>Language Lessons</u>. American Book. Grammar. USC.

2948. Metcalf, R. C. <u>Language Work in Elementary Schools</u>. Barnes. English Syllabi. USC.

2949. Metcalf, R. C. <u>Spelling and Language Book</u>. American Book. English Syllabi. USC.

2950. Metcalf, R. C. and Bright, O. T. <u>Language Exercises</u>. American Book. English Syllabi. USC.

2951. Metcalf, R. C. and Rafter, A. L. <u>Language Series</u>. New York: American Book, 1911. English Syllabi. USC.

2952. Michigan Department of Public Instruction. <u>Language Outline for the Schools of Michigan</u>. Lansing, Michigan, 1910. Curriculum. HEW.

2953. Michigan Department of Public Instruction. <u>Language Teaching in the Schools of Michigan</u>. Lansing, Michigan, 1909. Curriculum. HEW.

2954. Michigan Department of Public Instruction. <u>Language Outline for the Schools of Michigan</u>. Michigan, 1912. Curriculum. USC.

2955. Michigan University Department of Rhetoric and

Journalism. <u>Adventures in Essay Reading</u>. Harcourt, 1924. Readers. EGL.

2956. Miles, C. C. <u>English Made Plain</u>. Miles, 1907. English Syllabi. USC.

2957. Miles, D. H. <u>English in Business</u>. Ronald, 1920. Business English. USC.

2958. Miles, E. H. <u>Essays in the Making</u>. Dutton, 1906. Rhetoric. USC.

2959. Miles, E. H. <u>How to Prepare Essays, Lectures, and Etc</u>. Dutton, 1902. Rhetoric. USC.

2960. Miller, A. H. <u>Modern Grammar</u>. Concordia, 1918. Grammar. USC.

2961. Miller, A. H. <u>Seventy-Five Composition Outlines</u>. Miller, 1919. Composition. USC.

2962. Miller, A. H. <u>Seventy-Five Composition Outlines</u>. 1917. Composition. USC.

2963. Miller, E. L. <u>Practical English Composition</u>. Houghton, 1915-1917. Composition. USC.

2964. Miller, G. H. <u>Suggestions for Teachers of English in Elementary and Secondary School</u>. Cincinnati: University of Cincinnati, 1912. Teaching Methods. USC.

2965. Miller, G. M. <u>Miller System of Correct English</u>. Boston, 1920. Usage. USC.

2966. Miller, G. M. <u>Suggestions to Teachers of English in Elementary and Secondary Schools</u>. 1905. Teaching Methods. HEW

2967. Miller, J. W. <u>English Composition and Essay-Writing</u>. Longmans, 1910. Composition. USC, AC.

2968. Miller, W. D. and Kinkead, R. G. <u>Miller-Kinkead Lessons</u>. Lyons and Carnahan, 1916-1917. English Syllabi. USC.

2969. Milligan, G. <u>A Cathechism of English Grammar</u>. 1831.

Grammar. SIBP.

2970. Mills, W. S. *Aid to Diction*. Newton. Diction. USC.

2971. Milne, J. M. *English Grammar*. Silver, 1900. Grammar. USC.

2972. Milwaukee Board of School Directors. *The Teaching of English in the Elementary Schools*. Milwaukee: Milwaukee Board of School Directors, 1917. Curriculum. HEW.

2973. Milwaukee Board of School Directors. *The Teaching of English in the Elementary Schools*. Milwaukee, 1918. Curriculum. HEW.

2974. Minnesota University. *An Investigation into the Amount of Improvement in Ability to Write English Composition*. Minneapolis, 1919. Evaluating Writing. HEW.

2975. Minto, W. *A Manual of Prose Literature*. Ginn, 1893. Readers. AK.

2976. Minto, W. *Manual of English Prose Literature*. 1886. Readers. BMI.

2977. Minto, W. *Plain Principles of Prose Composition*. Edinbourgh, 1893. Composition. BMI, AK.

2978. Mirick, G. A. *Lessons in Elementary Grammar*. Macmillan, 1901. Grammar. USC.

2979. Mischlich, N. M. *Composition Outlines*. March, 1892. Composition. AC.

2980. Mitchill, T. C. and Carpenter, G. R. *Exposition in Class Room Practice*. Macmillan, 1906. Composition. USC, AC.

2981. M'Jilton, J. N. *The Maryland Primary Grammar*. 1857. Grammar. CLPI.

2982. Moeslein, M. *Mechanisms of Discourse*. Hansen, 1916. Composition. USC.

2983. Molloy, G. The Irish Difficulity: Shall and Will. London, 1897. Grammar. BMI.

2984. Monroe, Paul. Brief Course in the History of Education. Macmillan, 1908. History of Education. CC.

2985. Montgomery, G. R. Talking English. Thompson, Brown and Company, 1915. Speech. USC.

2986. Mookes, K. K. Written English and the Way to Write. Longmans, 1913. Composition. BMI.

2987. Moon, G. W. Bad English. 1869. Error. CLPI.

2988. Moon, G. W. Bad English Exposed: Criticisms on Language, Murray and Other Grammarians. 1871. Error. SIBP.

2989. Moon, G. W. Revisers' English. Funk, 1912. Usage. USC.

2990. Moon, G. W. The Dean's English. 1864. Usage. SIBP.

2991. Moon, G. W. The Revisers' English. A Series of Criticism Showing the Revisers' Violations of the Laws of the language. 2 vol. 1882. Error. CLPI.

2992. Mooney. Composition-Rhetoric from Literature. Brandow, 1900-05. Literature and Composition. AC.

2993. Moore, B. New Stories for Reproduction. March. Readers. USC.

2994. Moore, B. Stories for Language Exercises and Supplementary Reading. March. Readers. USC.

2995. Moore, E. and Others. English Composition for College Women. Macmillan, 1914. Composition. USC.

2996. Moore, J. R. Representative Essays, English and American. Ginn, 1930. Readers. EGL.

2997. Morelock, H. W. and Hubbard, L. H. A Handbook for English Teachers for Use in the Texas High Schools. Scott Foresman and Company, 1914. Curriculum. HEW,

USC.

2998. Morey, A. *Outline of Work in Elementary Language*. Bardeen. Curriculum. USC.

2999. Morgan, R. B. *Exercises in English Grammar for Junior Forms*. Murray, 1920. Grammar. BMI.

3000. Morgan, R. B. *The Groundwork of English*. Murray, 1920. English Syllabi. BMI.

3001. Morin, J. C. *Teachers' Manual for First Grade Oral English*. San Juan, Porto Rico, 1917. TESOL. HEW.

3002. Morin, J. C. *Teachers' Manual for First Grade Oral English*. Porto Rico, 1917. TESOL. USC.

3003. Morin, J. C. *Teachers' Manual for First Grade Oral English*. San Juan, Puerto Rico: Bureau of Supplies Printing, 1917. TESOL. HEW.

3004. Morin, J. C. *Teachers' Manual for the Second Grade Oral English*. San Juan, Puerto Rico: Bureau of Supplies, 1917. TESOL. HEW.

3005. Morley, C. D. *Modern Essays*. Harcourt, 1921-1924. Readers. EGL.

3006. Morley, C. D. *Romany Stain*. Doubleday and Page, 1926. EGL.

3007. Morley, E. J. *The Teaching of English in Schools*. 1919. Teaching Methods. BMI.

3008. Morris, J. *Organic History of English Words*. Stechert, 1909. Grammar. USC.

3009. Morris, R. *English Grammar*. American Book. Grammar. USC.

3010. Morris, R. *Historical Outlines of English Accidence*. Macmillan. Usage. USC.

3011. Morrow, J. and Others. *Steps in English*. American Book, 1903. English Syllabi. USC.

3012. Morse, M. A. *Exercises in English Grammar*.

Northwestern School Supply. Grammar. USC.

3013. Moulton, J. H. <u>Two Lectures on the Science of Language</u>. Cambridge, 1903. Grammar. LLC.

3014. Mugan, M. D, and Collins, J. S. <u>Graded Method in English Grammar, Lettter Writing and Composition</u>. Metropolitan. Composition. USC.

3015. Murch, E. M. <u>Child's Grammar</u>. Morton. Grammar. USC.

3016. Murdoct, J. E. <u>Analytic Elocution; Containing Studies, Rhetorical and Practical, of Expressive Speech</u>. 1884. Rhetoric. CC.

3017. Murison, A. F. <u>First Work in English</u>. Longmans. English Syllabi. USC.

3018. Murison, W. <u>English Composition</u>. Putnam, 1910. Composition. USC.

3019. Murison, W. <u>English Composition, With Chapters on Precis Writing</u>. Putnam, 1912. Composition. USC, AC.

3020. Murison, W. <u>Precis-Writing</u>. Putnam, 1914. Precis. USC.

3021. Murphy, L. C. <u>DeLancey Book of Essentials of English</u>. Philadelphia, 1914. English Syllabi. USC.

3022. Murray, J. E. <u>Advanced Lessons in English</u>. Hinds. English Syllabi. USC.

3023. Murray, J. E. <u>Essentials Lessons in English</u>. Hinds. English Syllabi. USC.

3024. Murray, L. <u>Abridgment of Murray's English Grammar</u>. 2 vol. 1840. Grammar. LLC.

3025. Murray, L. <u>An English Grammar</u>. 1817. Grammar. AK.

3026. Murray, L. <u>English Exercises, Adapted to Murray's English Grammar</u>. 1819. Grammar. CLPI.

3027. Murray, L. *English Grammar*. 1808. Grammar. CLPI.

3028. Murray, L. *English Grammar*. 1825. Grammar. CLPI.

3029. Murray, L. *Murray's Graduated English Spelling Book*. Macmillan, 1914. Spelling. BMI.

3030. Murry, J. M. *Pencillings*. Seltzer. 1925. EGL.

3031. Musgrove, E. R. *Composition and Literature*. Longmans, 1917. Literature and Composition. USC, BMI.

3032. Myers, R. L. *Final Examination Questions in English Grammar*. Testing. USC.

3033. *Narration and Description*. University of California, 1908. Modes. USC.

3034. *Narration and Description: Syllabus*. University of California, 1912. Modes. USC.

3035. *Narratives for Exercises in Composition*. 1885. Composition. BMI.

3036. Nason, A. H. *Efficient Composition*. N. Y. University Press, 1917. Composition. USC.

3037. Nason, A. H. **Short Themes: A Freshman Manual for the First Semester**. 2nd ed. University Heights, NY: A. H. Nason, 1910. Composition. USC, AC.

3038. Nason, A. H. *Talks on Theme Writing and Kindred Topics*. University Heights, NY: A. H. Nason, 1909. Composition. USC.

3039. *National Composition Blanks*. American Book. Composition. USC.

3040. *National Composition Books*. American Book. Composition. USC.

3041. National Council of Teachers of English. *Report on the Cost and Labor of English Teaching*. Lawerence, Kansas. University of Kansas, 1913. Teaching Methods. USC.

3042. National Education Association of U. S. <u>Report of the Joint Committee on Grammatical Nomenclature</u>. National Education Association, 1913. Grammar. USC.

3043. <u>National Language Tablets</u>. American Book. USC.

3044. <u>National Society for the Scientific Study of Education</u>. 1906. Teaching Methods. HEW.

3045. Neal, R. W. <u>Thought-Building in Composition</u>. Macmillan, 1912. Composition. USC, BMI, HEW.

3046. Neal, R. W. <u>Thought-Building in Practice</u>. 2 vol. Amherst, MA: University of Massachusetts Agricultural College, 1911. HEW.

3047. Neet, G. W. <u>Methods in Grammar and Language</u>. Valparaiso, IN: M. E. Bogarte, 1900. Grammar. HEW.

3048. Neet, G. W. and Brown, H. B. <u>Inductive English Grammar</u>. Bogarte. Grammar. USC.

3049. Neil, S. <u>Elements of Rhetoric</u>. 1854. Rhetoric. SIBP.

3050. Nesbitt, M. L. <u>Grammar-Land</u>. Holt. 1895. Grammar. USC.

3051. Nesfield, J. C. <u>Easy Parsing and Analysis</u>. Macmillan, 1911. Grammar. BMI.

3052. Nesfield, J. C. <u>English Grammar, Past and Present</u>. Macmillan, 1898. Grammar. USC.

3053. Nesfield, J. C. <u>Errors in English Composition</u>. 2 vol. Macmillan, 1903. Error. USC, BMI, AC.

3054. Nesfield, J. C. <u>Junior Course of English Composition</u>. 2 vol. London, 1901. Composition. BMI.

3055. Nesfield, J. C. <u>Key To Senior Course of English Composition</u>. London, 1903. Composition. BMI.

3056. Nesfield, J. C. <u>Manual of English Composition</u>.

London, 1905. Composition. BMI.

3057. Nesfield, J. C. <u>Matriculation English Course</u>. Macmillan, 1915. English Syllabi. USC.

3058. Nesfield, J. C. <u>Matriculation English Course</u>. 2 vol. Macmillan, 1914. English Syllabi. BMI.

3059. Nesfield, J. C. <u>Modern English Grammar</u>. Macmillan, 1912. Grammar. USC, BMI.

3060. Nesfield, J. C. <u>Oral Exercises in English Composition</u>. London, 1901. Composition. BMI.

3061. Nesfield, J. C. <u>Senior Course of English Composition</u>. Macmillan, 1903. Composition. USC, BMI.

3062. Nettleship, H. <u>Moral Influence Literature</u>. London, 1810. Literature. BMI.

3063. <u>New Book of Fables, Anecdotes and Stories for the Purpose of Composition</u>. Boston Sch. Sup., 1890. Literature and Composition. AC.

3064. New Britain, Conn., Board of Education. <u>Course of Study in Language</u>. New Britain, CT: New Britain Record, 1903. Curriculum. HEW.

3065. New England Association of Teachers of English. <u>The Training of English Teachers</u>. Cambridge, MA: New England Association of Teachers of English, 1914. Teacher Training. HEW, USC.

3066. <u>New English Course for Indian Schools</u>. Bombay, 1915. TESOL. BMI.

3067. <u>New Essentials of English</u>. Flanagan, 1900. English Syllabi. USC.

3068. New Hampshire Committee on Americanization. <u>Teaching of English Language in Public, Parochial, and Other Private Schools, and to Non-English Speaking Adults</u>. Concord: State House, 1918. Curriculum. HEW.

3069. New Haven Board of Education. <u>Course of Study in the English Language for Primary and Grammar Schools</u>.

New Haven, 1903. Curriculum. HEW.

3070. New Jersey Association of Teachers of English. Report on the Conditions of the Teaching of English in the Secondary Schools. New Jersey: The Association, 1920. Curriculum. USC, HEW.

3071. New Jersey Department of Public Instruction. Course of Study in English. New Jersey: Trenton, 1926. Curriculum. HEW.

3072. New Jersey Public Instruction Department of Trenton. Teaching of Elementary Composition and Grammar. 1913. Curriculum. USC, HEW.

3073. New Jersey Public Instruction Department of Trenton. Teaching of High School English. New Jersey, 1914. Curriculum. USC, HEW.

3074. New Practical Grammar. American Book. Grammar. USC.

3075. New Practical Grammar and Correspondence. American Book. Grammar. USC.

3076. New World English Course. 1920. English Syllabi. BMI.

3077. New York Board of Education. Course of Study in Ethics, English, History and Civics as Adopted by the Board of Education. New York, 1903. Curriculum. HEW.

3078. New York Question Book in English Composition. Bardeen. Composition. USC.

3079. New York State College. General Outline of English 1 and Miscellaneous Hints upon Reading, the Use of a Library. New York, 1915. Curriculum. USC.

3080. New York State University. Syllabus. 1912. English Syllabi. USC.

3081. New York State University. Elementary Syllabus in English Language and Literature. New York: New York State University, 1919. Curriculum. USC, HEW.

3082. New York State University. New Regents Questions in Advanced English. Bardeen. Testing. USC.

3083. New York State University. New Regents Questions in Elementary English. New York. Bardeen. Testing. USC.

3084. New York State University. Proposed Revision of the English Syllabus Submitted for Examination and Criticism. New York: University of New York, 1916. Curriculum. USC.

3085. New York State University. Regents Questions in Grammar. New York: Bardeen. Testing. USC.

3086. New York State University. Syllabus for Secondary Schools. New York: New York State University, 1910. Curriculum. USC.

3087. New York State University. Syllabus for Secondary Schools, English. New York: New York State Education Department. Curriculum. USC.

3088. Newbolt, H. J. Essays and Essayists. 1925. English Syllabi. EGL.

3089. Newcomer, A. G. Elements of Rhetoric. Holt, 1898. Rhetoric. USC, AC, AK.

3090. Newcomer, A. G. Practical Course in English Composition. Ginn, 1893. Composition. AC, AK.

3091. Newcomer, A. G. Practical Course in English Composition. Ginn. Composition. USC.

3092. Newcomer, A. G. and Seward, S. S. Rhetoric in Practice. Holt, 1905. Rhetoric. USC, AC.

3093. Newell, E. E. Sermon Making: Hints to Lay Preachers. Oxford, 1905. Sermons. BMI.

3094. Newman, F. W. The English Language as Spoken and Written. 1878. English Syllabi. CLPI.

3095. Newman, J. H. The Idea of a University. 2 vol. Longmans, 1902. AK.

3096. Newman, M. M. The Teaching of English and the Foreign-Born Woman. New York City: The Woman's Press, 1920. TESOL. HEW.

3097. Newman, S. P. A Practical System of Rhetoric. Portland, 1827. Rhetoric. HR, PS.

3098. Newman, S. P. A Practical System of Rhetoric. Gould and Newman, 1839. Rhetoric. AK.

3099. Newton, W. W. How to Speak, Read and Write. Cochrane, 1910. Rhetoric. USC.

3100. Nichol, J. English Composition. American Book, 1912. Composition. USC.

3101. Nichol, J. English Composition. Appleton, 1897. Composition. AC.

3102. Nichol, J. Questions and Exercises on English Composition. 1890. Composition. BMI.

3103. Nichol, J. and McCormick, W. S. Questions and Exercises on English Composition. Macmillan, 1890. Composition. AC.

3104. Nicolson, D. B. Handbook of English. Putnam, 1914. English Syllabi. USC.

3105. Nicolson, M. H. Lippincott's English Note Book. Lippincott, 1918. English Syllabi. USC.

3106. Nine Lectures on Preaching. 1896. Sermons. CSIGP.

3107. Nisbet, C. and Lemon, D. Everybody's Writing-Desk Book. Harper, 1892. AC.

3108. Nisbet, C. and Lemon, D. Everybody's Writing-Desk Book. Harper, 1912. USC.

3109. Noble, H. Literary Art. 1898. Literature. USC.

3110. Norman, J. S. Norman's English Grammar. Deane and Sons, 1918. Grammar. BMI.

3111. Norris, W. B. Self-Instruction Review in Spelling, Grammar and English Composition. 1919.

Composition. USC.

3112. Northcroft, G. J. H. How to Write Verse. London, 1904. Literature. BMI.

3113. Northrop, H. D. Excelsior Writer and Speaker. National. Composition. USC.

3114. Northrop, H. D. Model Speaker and Reciter. 1910. Speech. USC.

3115. Northrop, N. D. Delsarle Speaker. 1895. Speech. CC.

3116. Norton, S. W. Practical Studies in English Grammar. Flanagan. Grammar. USC.

3117. Notman, N. Exercises in Dictation and Composition. Oxford, 1913. Composition. USC.

3118. The Nova Scotia Public School Speller. Toronto, 1917. Spelling. BMI.

3119. Nuller, D. F. Rhetoric as an Art of Persuasion from the Standpoint of a Lawyer. Mills, 1880. Rhetoric. AC.

3120. Nutter, C. R. Specimens of Prose Composition. Ginn, 1907. Readers. USC, AC, LLC.

3121. Nutter, C. R. and Others. English Composition Notebook. Ginn. Composition. USC.

3122. O'Brien, S. R. English for Foreigners. Boston, 1909-1912. TESOL. HEW.

3123. O'Conor, J. F. X. Rhetoric and Oratory. Heath, 1898. Speech. USC.

3124. Oertel, H. Lectures on the Study of Language. Scribner, 1902. LLC.

3125. Ogden, C. Skeleton Essay; or, Authorship in Outline. Dick. 1890. AC.

3126. Ogilvie, G. and Albert, E. Practical Course in Secondary English. Harrap & Co., 1913. English

Syllabi. BMI.

3127. O'Grady, H. *Matter, Form, and Style*. Dutton, 1913. Style. USC, BMI.

3128. O'Grady, H. M. and Catty, N. *The Early Stages of Spoken and Written English*. 1920. BMI.

3129. Ohio State Commissioner of Common School. *Syllabus on Language and Grammar*. Ohio: Ohio Institute Circular for 1901, 1901. Curriculum. HEW.

3130. Oldcastle, J. *Guide for Literary Beginners*. Scribner and W., 1885. AC.

3131. Oldham, S. R. *Laboratory Manual of English Composition*. World Book, 1920. Composition. USC, BMI.

3132. Oliver, S., Jr. *General Critical Grammar of the English Language*. 1825. Grammar. CLPI.

3133. *150 Specimens of English Composition Arranged for Use in the Psychological and Educational Experiments*. Teachers College. USC.

3134. *One Hundred Stories for Compositions in Alternative Versions*. Edinburgh, 1899. Composition. BMI.

3135. *One Thousand and One Questions and Answers on English Grammar*. Hinds. Grammar. USC.

3136. *One Thousand Subjects for English Composition*. Cowperthwait, 1885. Composition. AC.

3137. O'Neill, J. M. *Argumentation and Debate*. Macmillan, 1917. Rhetoric. USC, HEW.

3138. Ontario Department of Public Instruction. *The Ontario Public School Composition*. Toronto, 1910. Curriculum. BMI.

3139. Ontario Department of Public Instruction. *Ontario Public School Grammar*. Toronto, 1910. Curriculum. BMI.

3140. Opdycke, J. B. *Composition Planning*. Appleton,

1913. Composition. USC, BMI.

3141. Opdycke, J. B. <u>English of Commerce</u>. Scribner, 1920. Business English. USC.

3142. Opdycke, J. B. <u>Working Composition</u>. Heath, 1917. Composition. USC, BMI.

3143. Orage, A. R. <u>Readers and Writers</u>. Allen and Unwin, 1922. EGL.

3144. Orcutt, W. D. <u>Writer's Desk Book</u>. Strokes, 1912. USC, BMI.

3145. Oregon Council of English Teachers. <u>Minimum Requirements: Lists in Spelling and in Correct Usage for the Schools of Oregon</u>. Oregon: Department of Education, 1916. Spelling. USC, HEW.

3146. O'Reilly, H. <u>Shall or Will?</u>. Belfast, 1897. Grammar. BMI.

3147. Orne, M. R. <u>Manual of Analysis and Parsing</u>. Lothrop. Grammar. USC.

3148. O'Shea. <u>Primary Grammar of the English Language</u>. Grammar. USC.

3149. O'Shea, M. V. <u>Every-Day Speller</u>. Indianapolis, 1917. Spelling. BMI.

3150. O'Shea, W. J. and Eichmann, A. E. <u>Composition Book by Grades 3rd, 4th, 5th and 6th year</u>. Merrill, C. E., 1912. Composition. USC.

3151. Osmound, T. E. <u>The Verbalist: A Manual Devoted to Brief Discussions of the Right and Wrong Use of Words</u>. 1882. Usage. CLPI.

3152. Ostervald, J. F. <u>Essay on the Composition and Delivery of a Sermon</u>. 1840. Sermons. CLPI.

3153. <u>Outlines for Essay Writing</u>. 1897. Composition. BMI.

3154. Owen, D. E. T. <u>Child Vision</u>. Longmans, 1920. AC.

3155. Page, E. T. Common Sense Word Book. Publicity, 1904. USC.

3156. Painter, F. History of Education. 1895. History of Education. CC.

3157. Palm, B. The Place of the Adjective Attribute in English Prose. London, 1911. Grammar. BMI.

3158. Palmer, G. H. Self-Cultivation in English. Houghton, 1815, 1917. USC.

3159. Palmer, G. H. Self-Cultivation in English. Boston: Houghton, 1915. HEW.

3160. Palmer, G. H. Self-Cultivation in English. Crowell, 1897. AC, HEW.

3161. Palmer, G. H. Self-Cultivation in English. Houghton, 1909. USC.

3162. Palmer, T. Mashew Miller's Junior Certificate English Course. Cape Town, 1918. English Syllabi. BMI.

3163. Palmer, T. Mashew Miller's Matriculation English Course According to the Syllabus Prescribed by the University of the Cape of Good Hope. Cape Town, 1913. English Syllabi. BMI.

3164. Palmer, T. Mashew Miller's "Perfected" English Manual. 1916. Grammar. BMI.

3165. Palmer, W. H. Uses of Anaphora in the Amplification of a General Truth. 1915. Rhetoric. USC.

3166. Park, A. Composition Exercise. London, 1887. Composition. BMI.

3167. Park, A. English Composition. 1883. Composition. BMI.

3168. Park, J. G. English Grammar. American Book. Grammar. USC.

3169. Park, J. G. Language Lessons. American Book, 1898. English Syllabi. USC.

3170. Parker, F. W. <u>Suggestions and Directions for Teaching Language</u>. Flanagan. Teaching Methods. USC.

3171. Parker, R. G. <u>Aids to English Composition</u>. Harper, 1876. Composition. AC.

3172. Parker, R. G. <u>Aids to English Composition, Prepared for Students of All Grades</u>. Boston, 1844. Composition. HR, AK.

3173. Parker, R. G. <u>Progressive Exercises in English Composition</u>. Boston, 1833. Composition. AC.

3174. Parker, R. G. <u>Progressive Exercises in English Composition</u>. 1876. Composition. AC.

3175. Parshall, N. C. <u>Graded Exercises in English</u>. American Book, 1912. English Syllabi. USC.

3176. Pater, W. <u>Appreciations; with an Essay on Style</u>. New York: Macmillan, 1889. Style. HR.

3177. Pater, W. <u>Appreciations, with an Essay on Style</u>. Macmillan, 1906. Style. AK.

3178. Pater, W. <u>Essay on Style; Sweetness and Light</u>. Macmillan, 1899. Style. AC.

3179. Pater, W. H. <u>Essay on Style; With Arnold's Sweetness and Light</u>. Macmillan. Style. USC.

3180. Patrick, J. N. <u>Lessons in Grammar</u>. Lippincott, 1900. Grammar. USC.

3181. Patrick, J. N. <u>Lessons in Language</u>. Lippincott, 1900. English Syllabi. USC.

3182. Patrick, J. N. <u>New Lessons in English; For Intermediate Grades</u>. Flanagan. English Syllabi. USC.

3183. Patrick, J. N. <u>Principles of English Grammar</u>. Lippincott, 1903. Grammar. USC.

3184. Pattee, G. K. <u>Practical Argumentation</u>. Century,

1909. Rhetoric. CC.

3185. Patterson, C. *Advanced Grammar and Rhetorical*. American Book. Grammar. USC.

3186. Patterson, C. *Complete Composition Books*. American Book. Composition. USC.

3187. Patterson, C. *Elements of Grammar and Composition*. American Book. Grammar. USC.

3188. Patterson, W. M. *The Rhythm of Prose*. New York, 1917. BMI.

3189. Pattison, T. H. *The Making of the Sermon*. London, 1898. Sermons. BMI, CC.

3190. Patzer, C. E. *Modern Methods of Teaching Language, Reading, Spelling*. Chicago: Dixon Co., 1914. Teaching Methods. USC, HEW.

3191. Paul, G. F. *Composition Through Life and Literature*. Flanagan, 1906. Literature and Composition. USC, AC.

3192. Paul, G. F. *Human Interest Composition Subject*. New York: Bardeen, 1916. Composition. HEW, USC.

3193. Paul, G. F. *Purple Book*. Peoria, IL: Purple Book Co., 1912. USC.

3194. Paul, G. F. *The Purple Book: Working Manual in English for Composition in Secondary Schools*. 2 vol. Purple Book, 1900-1905. Composition. AC.

3195. Pavia, L. *Grammatica Della Lingua Inglese*. Stechert, 1916. Grammar. USC.

3196. Payne, G. *Everyday Errors in Pronunciation, Spelling, and Spoken English*. San Jose, 1911. Error. USC.

3197. Payne, J. *Studies of English Prose*. London, 1881. English Syllabi. BMI.

3198. Payne, W. M. *English in American Universities*. Heath, 1897. Curriculum. AK.

3199. Peacock, W. and Wheeler, C. B. <u>Selected English Essays</u>. Oxford, 1918. Readers. EGL.

3200. Pearson, H. C. and Kirchwey, M. F. <u>Essentials of English, Higher Grades</u>. American Book, 1920. English Syllabi. BMI, USC.

3201. Pearson, H. G. <u>Freshman Composition, with an Introduction by Arlo Bates</u>. Heath, 1897. Composition. AK.

3202. Pearson, H. G. <u>The Principles of Composition, with an Introduction by Arlo Bates</u>. Boston: Heath, 1898. Composition. HR, PS, USC.

3203. Pearson, P. H. <u>Questions for Interpretative and Literary Study</u>. Lindsborg, KS: Pearson, 1909. Literature. USC.

3204. Pearson, P. H. <u>Subjects for Themes and Orations</u>. Pearson. Composition. USC.

3205. Peck, E. J. <u>Construction of Cases in English</u>. Bardeen, 1903. Grammar. USC.

3206. <u>The Pen as a Means of Earning a Livelihood</u>. Manchester, 1894. Journalism. BMI.

3207. <u>Pen Pointers</u>. Sprague. USC.

3208. Pence, R. W. <u>College Composition</u>. Macmillan, 1929. Composition. AK.

3209. Pendleton, S. T. <u>System of Grammar Analysis</u>. Grammar. USC.

3210. Penning, A. K. <u>Common Errors in Writing and Speaking</u>. Hannis Jordan Co., 1914. Error. USC.

3211. <u>Penny Book of Daily Blunders</u>. London, 1881. Error. BMI.

3212. Percival, M. and Jelliffe, R. A. <u>Specimens of Exposition and Argument</u>. Macmillan, 1908. Readers. USC.

3213. Perdue, H. A. and Griswold, S. E. <u>Language Through Nature, Literature, and Art</u>. Rand, 1902. Literature. USC.

3214. Perry, A. C. <u>Grammar</u>. Scribner, 1920-1921. Grammar. USC.

3215. Perry, F. M. <u>Introductory Course in Exposition</u>. American Book, 1908. Composition. USC, AC.

3216. Perry, W. <u>Etymological, and Pronouncing Synonymous in English Dictionary</u>. London, 1805. Dictionaries. CLPI.

3217. Perse Grammar School. <u>Perse Playbook</u>. Cambridge: Heffer and Sons, 1914. HEW.

3218. Peterson, H. C. <u>First Steps in English Composition</u>. Flanagan, 1900-1905. Composition. AC.

3219. Peterson, H. C. <u>First Steps in English Composition</u>. Flanagan, 1908. Composition. USC.

3220. Phelps, A. <u>English Style in Public Discourse</u>. New York, 1883. Style. BMI.

3221. Phelps, A. <u>English Style in Public Discourse, with Reference to the Usages of the Pulpit</u>. Scribner's Sons, 1883. Style. AC.

3222. Phelps, A. and Frink, H. <u>A Rhetoric; Its Theory and Practice</u>. Scribner, 1912. Rhetoric. USC.

3223. Phelps, A. and Frink, H. A. <u>Rhetoric, Its Theory and Practice</u>. Scribner's Sons, 1895. Rhetoric. AC.

3224. Philadelphia Board of Public Education. <u>The Course of Study in English Grades 1-8</u>. Philadelphia: Board of Public Education Print Shop, 1917. Curriculum. HEW.

3225. Philadelphia School District. <u>Manual of the Graded Courses of Instruction in Language, Geography, and History in the Grammar Schools</u>. Philadelphia: Burk and McFetridge, 1895. Curriculum. HEW.

3226. Philippine Islands, Bureau of Education. <u>English</u>

Composition: A Manual for Use in Philippine Public Schools. Manila: Bureau of Printing, 1916. TESOL. HEW, USC.

3227. Philippine Islands, Bureau of Education. English Composition: A Manual for Use in Philippine Public Schools. Manila: Bureau of Printing, 1917. TESOL. HEW, USC.

3228. Philips, A. F. English For Latin Americans. Boston: Silver, 1915. TESOL. HEW.

3229. Phillip, G. and Sons. Scenes of English Life. Longmans, 1910. USC.

3230. Phillips, A. F. English Grammar for Latin Americans. Silver, 1916. TESOL. USC.

3231. Phillips, A. L. Common Errors in English; Studies in Typical Errors in the Speech of Public Schools with Some Suggestions for Corrections. 1917. Error. HEW.

3232. Phillips, J. T. Quick Review in English Grammar and Elementary Composition. Petersburg, VA, 1913. Composition. USC.

3233. Phillpotts, E. Essays in Little. Hutchinson, 1931. EGL.

3234. Philodemus. Rhetorica of Philodemus. Yale University Press. Rhetoric. USC.

3235. Philosophy of Composition-Poe's Work. 1874-1875. Composition. CSIGP.

3236. Pickard, A. E. Industrial Booklet. Webb, 1916. Technical English. USC.

3237. Pickles, F. Composition Through Reading. Dent, 1916. Composition. BMI.

3238. Pickles, F. Composition Through Reading. Dent, 1913. Composition. BMI.

3239. Pickles, F. and J. E. Home and School Exercises in Composition Through Reading. Dent, 1920.

Composition. BMI.

3240. *Picture Lesson Cards*. March. Teaching Methods. USC.

3241. Pierson, A. T. *The Making of a Sermon*. London, 1904. Sermons. BMI.

3242. Pinneo, T. S. *Guide to Composition*. Wilson, H and Co., 1864. Composition. AC.

3243. Pinneo, T. S. *Primary Grammar*. American Book. Grammar. USC.

3244. *The Pionerov Simplified Spelling*. 1912. Spelling. BMI.

3245. Pitman, I. *Style Book for Business English*. Pitman. Business English. USC.

3246. Pitman, I. and Ellis, A. J. *Spelling Reform and the Pitman-Ellis "47" Alphabet*. 1919. Spelling. BMI.

3247. Pitman, I. and Sons. *Pitman's Punctuation Chart*. Pitman, 1915. Punctuation. BMI.

3248. Pittenger, L. A. *English Teacher's Manual, to accompany the study of Thomas and Howe's Composition and Rhetoric*. Longmans, 1912. Teaching Methods. USC.

3249. Poe, E. A. *Works*. Chicago: G. E. Woodberry, 1894-1895. CLPI.

3250. *Poems for the Study of Language Prescribed in Course of Study for Common Schools of Illinois*. Houghton, 1905. USC.

3251. Popham, R. B. *Every-Day Mistakes in Speaking and Writing*. Daily News, 1919. Error. BMI.

3252. Porter, E. *Analysis of the Principles of Rhetorical Delivery as Applied in Reading and Speaking*. 1827. Rhetoric. AK.

3253. Porter, E. *Lectures of Eloquence and Style*. Gould and Freedman, 1836. Style. HR, AK.

3254. <u>Portfolio of Pictures for Language Work</u>. Flanagan. USC.

3255. Porto Rico Department of Education. <u>Course of Study in English for the Graded Schools</u>. San Juan, Porto Rico, 1913. TESOL. USC, HEW.

3256. Porto Rico Department of Education. <u>Problem of Teaching English to the People of Porto Rico</u>. San Juan, Porto Rico, 1916. TESOL. USC.

3257. Potter, M. C. <u>Practical English</u>. Boston, 1916. English Syllabi. BMI.

3258. Potter, M. C. and others. <u>Oral and Written English, Advanced Book</u>. Ginn, 1920. Composition. USC.

3259. Potter, M. C. and others. <u>Oral and Written English Books</u>. Ginn, 1917. Composition. USC, BMI.

3260. Powell, W. B. <u>How to See</u>. American Book. USC.

3261. Powell, W. B. <u>How To Talk</u>. American Book. Speech. USC.

3262. Powell, W. B. <u>How To Write</u>. American Book. Composition. USC.

3263. Powell, W. B. and Connolly, L. <u>Rational Grammar of English Language</u>. American Book, 1899. Grammar. USC.

3264. Power, J. O. <u>Making of an Orator</u>. 1906. Speech. CC.

3265. Powers, O. M. <u>Practical Grammar and Exercise Pad</u>. Metropolitan Text Book Co., 1911. Grammar. USC.

3266. Price, I. <u>Questions in English Grammar for Drill, Test and Review</u>. Hinds, 1917. Grammar. USC, BMI.

3267. Price, T. R. <u>Methods of Language Teaching as Applied to English</u>. Johnston and Co., 1881. Teaching Methods. HEW.

3268. Prideaux, E. B. R. <u>Primary Education</u>. 1914.

Curriculum. BMI.

3269. Priestly, J. _Theological and Miscellaneous Works_. Hackney, 1817-1832. CLPI.

3270. _Primary Language Charts with Stand and Teacher's Manual_. American Book. USC.

3271. Prince, J. T. _Practical English Grammar for Upper Grades_. Ginn, 1910. Grammar. USC.

3272. Principal of St. Mary's Hall. _The Class-Teaching of English Composition_. Liverpool, London, New York: Longmans, Green and Co., 1909. Teaching Methods. HEW.

3273. Principal of St. Mary's Hall. _The Class-Teaching of English Composition_. Longmans, 1909. Composition. HEW.

3274. Pritchard, F. H. _English Extracts and Exercises in Composition_. Harrap, 1917. Composition. BMI.

3275. Pritchard, F. H. _Essays of Today_. Little, 1924. Readers. EGL.

3276. Pritchard, F. H. _From Confucius to Mencken; The Trend of the World's Best Thought as Expressed by Famous Writers of All Time_. Harper, 1929. Readers. EGL.

3277. Pullen, P. T. _The Mother's Book: Exemplifying Pestalozzi's Plan of Awakening the Understanding of Children in Language, Drawing, Geometry, Geography, and Numbers_. London, 1820. HEW.

3278. _Pupils' Outlines for Home Study in Connection with School Work: Grammar_. Jennings Publishing Co., 1914. Grammar. USC.

3279. Putnam, W. H. _Supplementary Lessons in English_. Silver. English Syllabi. USC.

3280. Quackenbos, G. P. _Advanced Course of Composition and Rhetoric_. Appleton, 1864. Composition. AK.

3281. Quackenbos, G. P. _Advanced Course of Composition and_

Rhetoric. Appleton. Composition. AC.

3282. Quackenbos, G. P. <u>Course of Composition and Rhetoric</u>. American Book, 1912. Composition. USC.

3283. Quackenbos, G. P. <u>English Grammar</u>. American Book. Grammar. USC.

3284. Quackenbos, G. P. <u>First Book in Grammar</u>. American Book. Grammar. USC.

3285. Quackenbos, G. P. <u>First Lessons in Composition</u>. Appleton, 1851. Composition. AK.

3286. Quackenbos, G. P. <u>First Lessons in English Composition</u>. American Book, 1912. Composition. USC.

3287. Quackenbos, G. P. <u>First Lessons in English Composition</u>. Appleton. Composition. USC.

3288. Quackenbosa, J. D. <u>Practical Rhetoric</u>. American Book, 1896. Rhetoric. AC, AK.

3289. Quackerenbos, J. D. <u>Practical Rhetoric</u>. American Book, 1912. Rhetoric. USC.

3290. <u>Questions on English</u>. Bronxville, N. Y., 1914. USC.

3291. Quiller-Couch, A. T. <u>On the Art of Writing</u>. Putnam, 1916. Composition. USC, HEW, EGL.

3292. Radford, M. L. <u>Composition and Rhetoric</u>. Hinds, 1903. Composition. USC, AC.

3293. Rahtz, F. J. <u>English Composition</u>. Methuen, 1911. Composition. BMI.

3294. Rahtz, F. J. <u>Higher English</u>. Methuen, 1915. English Syllabi. BMI.

3295. Rahtz, F. J. <u>Higher English</u>. Methuen, 1920. English Syllabi. BMI.

3296. Rahtz, F. J. <u>Junior English</u>. Methuen, 1915. English Syllabi. BMI.

3297. Ramsey, S. English Language and English Grammar. Putnam, 1912. Grammar. USC.

3298. Ramsey, S. English Language and English Grammar. 1892. Grammar. CLPI.

3299. Randall, J. D. Blessing Esau; Experiments in High School English Teaching. Boston, 1919. Teaching Methods. USC.

3300. Rankin, J. Mechanics of Written English. Augsburg, 1917. Mechanics. USC.

3301. Rankin, J. W. and Nardin, F. L. Notebook for English Composition. Missouri: Missouri Book Co., 1919. Composition. USC.

3302. Rankin, T. E. Method and Practice of Exposition. Macmillan, 1917. Composition. USC.

3303. Ranous, D. K. Good English in Good Form. Sturgis and Walton, 1916. English Syllabi. USC.

3304. Ransom, R. W. Hints and Don'ts for Writers and Copyreaders. Chicago, 1911. Usage. USC.

3305. Ransom, R. W. Hints and Don'ts for Writers and Copyreaders. Chicago, 1913. Usage. USC.

3306. Raub, A. N. Grammatical Analysis by Diagram. Stradling. Grammar. USC.

3307. Raub, A. N. Helps in the Use of Good English. Stardling. Usage. USC.

3308. Raub, A. N. Hints and Helps in English Grammar. Stardling. Grammar. USC.

3309. Raub, A. N. Lessons in English. American Book. English Syllabi. USC.

3310. Raub, A. N. Practical English Grammar. American Book. Grammar. USC.

3311. Raub, A. N. Practical Language Work for Beginners. Stardling. Grammar. USC.

3312. Raub, A. N. *Practical Rhetoric*. Stradling. Rhetoric. USC.

3313. Ravidranatha, Datta. *Prosody and Rhetoric*. Calcutta, 1915. Rhetoric. BMI.

3314. Raymond, F. E. *English: Progressive Studies*. Gregg. Curriculum. USC.

3315. Raymond, G. L. *Fundamentals in Education, Art and Civics; Essays and Addresses*. Funk, 1911. Curriculum. EGL.

3316. Raymond, G. L. and Wheeler, G. P. *The Writer*. 1893. Composition. BMI.

3317. Raymond, G. L. and Wheeler, G. P. *The Writer: One of a Series of Handbooks upon Practical Expression*. Silver, 1893. Composition. AC.

3318. Raymond, G. L. and Wheeler, G. P. *Writer*. Silver, 1912. Composition. USC.

3319. Raymond, G. L. and Wheeler, P. *Writer: A Concise, Complete, and Practical Text-Book of Rhetoric*. Putnam, 1911. Composition. USC.

3320. Reade, A. *Suggestive Essays and Orations*. 1905. Readers. CC.

3321. Reade, A. A. *How to Write English: Practical Treatise on English Composition*. Lippincott, 1883. Composition. AC.

3322. *A Reader In Simplified Spelling*. 1915. Spelling. BMI.

3323. Ready, A. W. *Essays and Essay Writing for Public Examinations*. London, 1901. Composition. BMI.

3324. Reed, A. *Introductory Language Work*. Merrill, 1898. Grammar. USC.

3325. Reed, A. *One-Book Course in English*. Merrill. Grammar. USC.

3326. Reed, A. and Kellogg, B. *English Language*. Merrill,

1909. Grammar. USC, AK.

3327. Reed, A. and Kellogg, B. <u>Graded Lessons in English</u>. Merrill, 1901. Grammar. USC.

3328. Reed, A. and Kellogg, B. <u>High School Grammar</u>. Merrill, 1900. Grammar. USC.

3329. Reed, A. and Kellogg, B. <u>Higher Lessons in English</u>. Clark and M, 1877. Grammar. AC.

3330. Reed, A. and Kellogg, B. <u>Higher Lessons in English</u>. Merrill, 1908-1910. Grammar. AC.

3331. Reed, A. and Kellogg, B. <u>Higher Lessons in English</u>. Merrill, 1912. Grammar. USC.

3332. Reed, A. G. <u>English in the High School</u>. Baton Rouge, 1915. Curriculum. USC.

3333. Reed, A. G. <u>English in the High School</u>. Baton Rouge, LA: Louisiana State Univ. and Agricultural and Mechanical College, 1915. English Syllabi. USC.

3334. Reed, T. B. and others. <u>Rodera Sequence</u>. 1900. CC, LLC.

3335. Reid, L. H. <u>English Grammar Primer</u>. Bardeen. Grammar. USC.

3336. Reimold, O. S. <u>Primary Language Book</u>. World Book Co. USC.

3337. Reimold, O. S. <u>Second Primary Language Book</u>. World Book, English Syllabi. USC.

3338. <u>Rhetorica of Philodemus</u>. Yale University, 1920. Rhetoric. USC.

3339. Rhyne, O. P. <u>Conjunction Plus Participle Group in English</u>. North Carolina: University of North Carolina, 1910. Graammar. USC.

3340. Rice, A. L. <u>Outlines in Dictionary Study for Fourth, Fifth, Sixth, and Seventh Grades</u>. Gregg, 1920. Dictionary Study. USC.

3341. Rice, R. <u>College and the Future</u>. Scribner, 1915. USC, HEW.

3342. Rice, R. <u>Learning to Write, for College and the Future</u>. New York: Scribner's Sons, 1917. Composition. HEW.

3343. Richard, T. A. <u>Guide to Technical Writing</u>. Mining and Scientific Press, 1910. Technical English. USC, CC.

3344. Richard, T. A. <u>Technical Writing</u>. Wiley, 1920. Technical English. USC, BMI.

3345. Richardson, C. S. <u>Public Speaking in the High Schools</u>. Maryland, 1919. Speech. HEW.

3346. Rigdon, J. <u>English Grammar for Beginners</u>. Hinds, 1904. Grammar. USC.

3347. Rigdon, J. <u>English Grammar for the Common School</u>. Hinds, 1904. Grammar. USC.

3348. Rigdon, J. <u>Grammar Essentials for High School</u>. Hinds, 1912. Grammar. USC.

3349. Rigdon, J. <u>Grammar Essentials for the High School</u>. Hinds, 1912. Grammar. USC.

3350. Item omitted.

3351. Rigdon, J. <u>Grammar of the English Sentence</u>. Hinds, 1904. Grammar. USC.

3352. Rigdon, J. <u>Grammar of the English Sentence and Introduction to Composition</u>. Indiana: Indiana Publishers, 1890. Composition. AC.

3353. Rigdon, J. <u>Outlines, Infinitives, Participles</u>. Hinds. Grammar. USC.

3354. Rine, G. W. <u>Essentials of English</u>. Pacific. 1908. English Syllabi. USC.

3355. Rippman, W. <u>A First English Book</u>. Dent, 1920.

English Syllabi. BMI.

3356. Rippman, W. <u>Sounds of Spoken English</u>. Dutton, 1917. Sound Patterns. USC.

3357. Rippman, W. <u>The Imperial Education Conference and the Simplification of English Spelling</u>. Guildford, 1911. Spelling. BMI.

3358. Roat, E. J. <u>Helps in English Grammar</u>. Bardeen. Grammar. USC.

3359. Robbins, C. M., and others. <u>Essential Studies in English Grammar and Composition, with Practical English</u>. Row, Peterson, and Co., 1914. Composition. USC.

3360. Robbins, C. M. and Row, R. K. <u>Essential Studies in English</u>. Row, Peterson, and Co., 1907. English Syllabi. USC.

3361. Robbins, C. M. and Row, R. K. <u>Studies in English</u>. Row, Peterson and Co., 1916-1917. English Syllabi. USC.

3362. Roberts, A. E. and Barter, A. <u>The Teaching of English</u>. London: Blackle and Son, 1908. Teaching Methods. HEW.

3363. Roberts, P. <u>English for Coming Americans</u>. TESOL. USC.

3364. Roberts, P. <u>English for Foreigners</u>. Illinois: University of Illinois, 1914. TESOL. HEW.

3365. Robertson, J. M. <u>New Essays Towards a Critical Method</u>. London, 1897. Criticism. LC.

3366. <u>Robins and Perkins Introduction to Study of Rhetoric</u>. Macmillan, 1900-1905. Rhetoric. AC.

3367. Robins, H. J. and Perkins, A. F. <u>Introduction to Study of Rhetoric</u>. Macmillan, 1907. Rhetoric. USC, AC.

3368. Robinson, F. B. <u>Effective Public Speaking</u>. Chicago:

Extension University, 1919. Speech. HEW.

3369. Robinson, K. A. and others. *Essays Toward Truth; Studies in Orientation*. 1924-1929. EGL.

3370. Robinson, W. C. *Forensic Oratory*. 1893. Speech. CC.

3371. Rochester, New York, Board of Education. *Outline Course of Study of the Public Schools of the City of Rochester, New York, English*. Rochester, New York: Board of Education, 1917. Curriculum. HEW.

3372. Roe, F. W. *Nineteenth Century English Prose: Early Essayists*. Harcourt, 1923. Style. EGL.

3373. Roe, F. W. and Elliott, G. R. *English Prose*. Longmans, 1913. USC.

3374. Rogers, H. *Essays*. London, 1850-1855. CLPI.

3375. Rolfe, W. J. *Elementary Study of English*. American Book. English Syllabi. USC.

3376. Ronbison, A. T. *Applications of Logic*. Longmans, 1912. Logic. USC.

3377. Ronnie, D. W. *The Elements of Style*. Dent, 1915. Style. BMI.

3378. Rooney, C. *English Composition from Models*. Methuen, 1911. Composition. BMI.

3379. Rose, J. D. *Advanced English Grammar Through Composition*. Bell and Sons, 1912. Composition. BMI.

3380. Ross, J. W. *Ross's Business English*. South-Western, 1915. Business English. USC.

3381. Rossman, M. B. and Mills, M. W. *Graded Sentences for Analysis*. St. Louis: Mary Institute, 1909. Grammar. USC.

3382. Rossman, M. B. and Mills, M. W. *Graded Sentences for Analysis*. Noble, 1919. Grammar. USC.

3383. Round, C. R. _Twenty Short, Simple Lessons in English_. Caspar, 1918. English Syllabi. USC.

3384. Rowe, K. J. and Webb, W. T. _Elementary English Grammar_. Calcutta, 1917. Grammar. BMI.

3385. Rowlands, E. _Primer of English Grammar in Loushai_. Madras, 1909. TESOL. BMI.

3386. Royce, J. _Primer of Logical Anaysis for the Use of Composition Students_. 1881. Composition. CLPI.

3387. Royster, J. F. and Thompson, S. _Guide to Composition_. Scott, 1919. Composition. USC.

3388. Royster, J. F. and Thompson, S. _Manual and Notebook for English Composition_. Scott, 1917. Composition. USC.

3389. Royster, J. F. and Thompson, S. _Practice Sheets for English Composition_. Scott, 1914. Composition. USC.

3390. Rush, J. _The Philosophy of the Human Voice_. Philadelphia, 1900. Speech. AK.

3391. Rush, J. _The Philosophy of the Human Voice_. Philadelphia: Maxwell, 1827. Speech. HR, PS.

3392. Russell, P. _The Authors' Manual_. London, 1891. BMI.

3393. Russell, T. H. _Faulty Diction_. McKay, 1905. Diction. USC.

3394. Russell, T. H. _Writing-Desk Book_. Saalfield, 1915. USC.

3395. Russell, W. _The American Elocutionist_. Jenks and Palmer, 1840. Rhetoric. AK.

3396. _Sacred Rhetoric; or, the Art of Rhetoric as Applied to the Preaching of the Word of God_. Benziger, 1882. Sermons. AC.

3397. Sadlier, W. _Principles of English Grammar_. Grammar. USC

3398. Salmon, D. <u>Longmans' Junior School Composition</u>. Longmans, 1912. Composition. USC.

3399. Salmon, D. <u>Longmans' Junior School Composition</u>. Longmans, 1890. Composition. AC, BMI.

3400. Salmon, D. <u>Longmans' School Composition</u>. Longmans, 1912. Composition. USC.

3401. Salmon, D. <u>Longmans' School Composition</u>. Longmans, 1890. Composition. AC, BMI.

3402. Salmon, D. <u>Longmans' School Grammar</u>. Longmans. Grammar. USC.

3403. Sampson, M. W. <u>Written and Oral Composition</u>. American Book, 1907. Composition. USC.

3404. Sampson, M. W. and Holland, E. O. <u>Written and Oral Composition</u>. American Book, 1905-1907. Composition. AC.

3405. <u>San Bernardino, California Handbook for Teacher and Pupil</u>. San Bernardino, CA, 1911. Curriculum. USC, HEW.

3406. Sanford, S. V. and Brown, P. F. <u>Modern Course in English</u>. Heath, 1914. English Syllabi. USC.

3407. Sanford, S. V. and Brown, P. F. <u>The Modern Course in English</u>. Boston: Heath and Co., 1920. English Syllabi. HEW.

3408. Sanford, S. V. and Others. <u>Modern Course in English</u>. Heath, 1914. English Syllabi. USC.

3409. Sayrs, W. C. <u>Practical Grammar Based Upon Text of Longfellow's Evangeline and Selections</u>. Lothrop, 1903. Grammar. USC.

3410. Schele De Vere, M. R. B. <u>Studies in English</u>. 1867. English Syllabi. CLPI.

3411. <u>A Scholar's Book of Test Papers in English</u>. Nottingham, 1915. Testing. BMI.

3412. Scholz, G. <u>Choice Proverbs for Grammatical Analysis</u>.

Flanagan, 1903. Grammar. USC.

3413. Schumacher, C. A. *Essentials of Expression*. New York: Otsego Publication Co., 1917. Composition. USC.

3414. Schumacher, C. A. *Principles of Composition*. New York: Saunders, 1916. Composition. USC.

3415. Schuyler, W. and Buck, P. M. *Art of Composition, for High Schools and Academies*. Scribner, 1912. Composition. USC.

3416. Schuyler, W. and Buck, P. M. Jr. *Art of Composition*. Scribner, 1905-1907. Composition. AC.

3417. Score, H. B. *Exercises in Composition*. Preston, 1891. Composition. BMI.

3418. Score, H. B. *Taking Examination Stories for Composition*. 1891. Composition. BMI.

3419. Scott, A. C. *Practical English*. Row, Peterson and Co. English Syllabi. USC.

3420. Scott, F. N. *Notes and Suggestions Designed to Accompany Scott and Denney's Elementary English Composition*. Boston: Allyn and Bacon. 1900. Teaching Methods. HEW.

3421. Scott, F. N. *References on the Teaching of Rhetoric and Composition*. F. N. Scott. Composition Bibliography. AK.

3422. Scott, F. N. *The Fundamental Differentia of Poetry and Prose*. 1904. Rhetoric. LC.

3423. Scott, F. N. *The Principles of Style*. Register, 1890. Style. AK.

3424. Scott, F. N. *The Standard of American Speech and Other Papers*. Allyn and Bacon, 1926. AK.

3425. Scott, F. N. and Buck, G. *Brief English Grammar*. Scott, 1905. Grammar. USC, AK.

3426. Scott, F. N. and Denney, J. V. *Aphorisms for*

        Teachers of English Composition. Allyn, 1912.
        Teaching Methods. USC.

3427. Scott, F. N. and Denney, J. V. Aphorisms for
Teachers of English Composition and the Class Hour
in English Composition. Boston: Allyn and Bacon.
1905. Teaching Methods. HEW, AC.

3428. Scott, F. N. and Denney, J. V. Composition
Literature. Allyn, 1902. Literature and
Composition. USC, AC, AK.

3429. Scott, F. N. and Denney, J. V. Composition Rhetoric.
Allyn, 1902. Composition. USC.

3430. Scott, F. N. and Denney, J. V. Composition Rhetoric.
Allyn, 1912. Composition. USC.

3431. Scott, F. N. and Denney, J. V. Composition-Rhetoric
Designed for Use in Secondary Schools. Boston:
Allyn and Bacon, 1897. Composition. HR, PS, CC,
AK.

3432. Scott, F. N. and Denney. J. V. Elementary English
Composition. Allyn, 1908. Composition. USC.

3433. Scott, F. N. and Denney, J. V. Elementary English
Composition. Allyn and Bacon. 1900. Composition.
AK.

3434. Scott, F. N. and Denney, J. V. Elementary English
Composition. 1902. Composition. CC, AC.

3435. Scott, F. N. and Denney, J. V. New Composition
Rhetoric. Allyn, 1911. Composition. USC, AK.

3436. Scott, F. N. and Denney, J. V. Paragraph Writing.
Register, 1891. Paragraphs. HR, PS.

3437. Scott, F. N. and Denney, J. V. Paragraph Writing.
Allyn and Bacon. 1893. Paragraphs. AK.

3438. Scott, F. N. and Denney, J. V. Paragraph Writing.
Allyn, 1909. Paragraphs. USC, CC, AC.

3439. Scott, F. N. and Denney, J. V. Rhetoric Tablet.
Ginn. Rhetoric. USC.

3440. Scott, F. N. and Southworth, G. A. Course of Language Study in Outline, and Suggestions for Teachers. Sanborn. Curriculum. USC.

3441. Scott, F. N. and Southworth, G. A. Lessons in English. Sanborn, 1916. English Syllabi. USC.

3442. Scott, F. N. and Southworth, G. A. Lessons in English. Sanborn, 1906. English Syllabi. USC.

3443. Scott, F. W. and Zeitlin, J. College Readings in English Prose. Macmillan, 1914. Readers. USC.

3444. Seachrest, E. Story Land. Barnes, 1912. USC.

3445. Sears, L. Principles and Methods of Literary Criticism. New York, 1898. Criticism. LC.

3446. Searson, J. W. Self-Correction in English. KS: Kansas State Agricultural College, 1911. Usage. USC.

3447. Seath, J. Some Notes on Methods in English Composition. Toronto, 1904. Composition. HEW.

3448. Sedwick, A. On Teaching Composition. London, 1889. Teaching Methods. BMI.

3449. Seeleg, L. History of Education. 1899. History of Education. CC.

3450. Seiler's Phonanagrams for Hygienic Busy Work in Phonics, Spelling, and Word-Building. Seiler, 1909. Spelling. USC.

3451. Serl, E. Intermediate Language Lessons. American Book, 1914. English Syllabi. USC.

3452. Serl, E. Primary Language Lessons. American Book, 1911. English Syllabi. USC.

3453. Setzler, E. B. Introduction to Advanced English Syntax. State Co. Grammar. USC.

3454. Severy, M. B. Game of Nouns. 1920. Grammar. USC.

3455. Sewell, J. W. *Language Lessons*. American Book. English Syllabi. USC.

3456. Sewell, J. W. *Practical English for Seventh and Eighth Grades*. Lippincott, 1911. English Syllabi. USC.

3457. Sewell, J. W. *Rhetoric and Composition Tablet*. Bell. Composition. USC.

3458. Shackford, M. H. and Judson, M. *Composition-Rhetoric-Literature*. Sanborn, 1908. Literature and Composition. USC.

3459. Shackford, M. H. and Judson, M. *Composition-Rhetoric-Literature*. Sanborn, 1917. Literature and Composition. USC.

3460. Shallies, G. W. *Outlines for Elementary English*. Educational, 1911. English Syllabi. USC.

3461. Sharp, A. E. *Elements of English Grammar*. Jenkins, 1911. Grammar. USC.

3462. Sharp, A. E. *Forms for Analysis and Parsing*. Jenkins, 1910. Grammar. USC.

3463. Shaw, E. R. *English Composition by Practice*. Holt, 1912. Composition. USC.

3464. Shaw, E. R. *English Composition by Practice*. Holt, 1892. Composition. AC.

3465. Shaw, E. R. *Selections for Written Reproduction*. Appleton, 1886. Readers. AC.

3466. Shaw, E. R. *Three Studies in Education*. Barnes. USC.

3467. Shaw, T. B. *A Complete Manual of English Literature*. Sheldon, 1867. Literature. AK.

3468. Shaw, T. B. *Outlines of English Literature*. Sheldon, 1866. Literature. AK.

3469. Shawcross, W. *How to Teach Commerical English*. Pitman, 1911. Business English. BMI.

3470. Shedd, W. G. T. Literary Essays. Scribner, 1878. AK.

3471. Sheffield, A. D. Grammar and Thinking. New York, 1912. Grammar. BMI.

3472. Sheldon, E. A. Advanced Language Lessons. American Book. English Syllabi. USC.

3473. Sheldon, E. A. Primary Language Lessons. American Book. English Syllabi. USC.

3474. Sheldon, E. A. Word Studies, Vertical or Slant Script. American Book. Handwriting. USC.

3475. Shepard, O. Essays of 1925. Mitchell, 1926. Readers. EGL.

3476. Sheridan, B. M. Speaking and Writing English. Lawrence, Mass.: Sheridan, 1916. Composition. USC.

3477. Sheridan, B. M. Speaking and Writing English. Sanborn, 1917. Composition. USC, HEW.

3478. Sheridan, B. M. Speaking and Writing English; A Course of Study for the Eight Grades of the Elementary School. Lawrence, Mass.: Press of Dick and Trumpold, 1916. Composition. HEW.

3479. Sherman, C. B. Correction Manual. University of Nebraska University Publication. Error. USC.

3480. Sherman, L. A. Analytics of Literature: A Manual for the Objective Study of English Prose and Poetry. Ginn, 1893. Literature. AK.

3481. Sherman, L. A. Elements of Literature and Composition. University, 1908. Literature and Composition, USC, AK.

3482. Sherman, S. P. Points of View. Scribner, 1924. EGL.

3483. Shewan, J. S. Exercises in the Correction of Grammatical Errors. Aberdeen, 1890. Error. BMI.

3484. Shipman, M. E. *Freshman English*. Heath, 1918. Freshman English. USC, HEW.

3485. Shoemaker, J. W. *Practical Elocution*. 1900, Speech. CC.

3486. Shoemaker, R. H. *Advanced Elocution*. 1903. Speech. CC.

3487. Sholty, M. *The Teaching of Beginning Reading*. Ellensburg, WA: The Washington State Normal School, 1917. Reading. HEW.

3488. Shoosmith, H. *Spelling and Punctuation*. W. B. Clive, 1913. Spelling. BMI.

3489. Shoosmith, H. *Spelling and Punctuation*. W. B. Clive, 1917. Spelling. BMI.

3490. *Short Studies in English*. American Book. English Syllabi. USC.

3491. Shortt, L. M. *Practical Grammar*. G. Allen, 1912. Grammar. BMI.

3492. Shutt, H. M. *Review Course in English Grammar*. Canton, OH. H. M. Shutt. 1916. Grammar. USC.

3493. Siglar, H. W. *English Grammar*. Holt. Grammar. USC.

3494. Sill, J. M. *Saalfield's Vest Pocket Book of Grammar and Composition*. Saalfield, 1910. Composition. USC.

3495. Simons, E. S. *First Year English for High Schools*. Silver, 1906. English Syllabi. USC.

3496. Simons, S. E. *Better English For Speaking and Writing*. Philadelphia, 1920. Usage. BMI.

3497. Simons, S. E. *English Problems in the Solving for the Junior and Senior High Schools*. Scott, 1920. English Syllabi. USC, HEW.

3498. *Simplified Spelling*. 1913. Spelling. BMI.

3499. Simplified Spelling Society. 1908. Spelling. BMI.

3500. Simpson, J. 999 Composition Subjects. March, 1912. Composition. USC.

3501. Simpson, J. Nine Hundred and Ninety-Nine Composition Subjects. Teacher's Publication, 1890. Composition. AC.

3502. Sisters of the Third Order of St. Francis. Exercises in Composition for Seventh and Eighth Grades. Glen Riddle, PA: Sisters of the Third Order of St. Francis, 1912. Composition. USC.

3503. Skeffington, F. V. English Composition in Secondary Schools. Charleston, IL: Eastern Illinois State Normal School, 1906. Composition. HEW.

3504. Skerry, G. E. Practical Papers on English Composition and Essay Writing. London, 1903. Composition. BMI.

3505. Skerry, G. E. Skerry's Practical Spelling and Diction Book. Civil Service Press, 1918. Spelling. BMI.

3506. Skerry, G. E. Specimen Essays and Practical Aids to Essay Writing. London, 1900. Composition. BMI.

3507. Skinner, W. H. Studies in Literature and Composition for High Schools. 4th ed. Ainsworth and Co., 1903. Literature and Composition. USC.

3508. Skinner, W. H. and Burgert, C. M. Lessons in English. Silver, 1902. English Syllabi. USC.

3509. Skipton, H. The Essay Writer. 1890, BMI.

3510. Slater, J. R. Freshman Rhetoric. Heath, 1913. Rhetoric. USC, AK.

3511. Smith, A. V. and Buehler, H. G. Grammar by Correspondence. Interstate School of Correspondence, 1906. Grammar. USC.

3512. Smith, A. W. Aims and Methods in the Teaching of

English. London: Constable and Co., 1915. Curriculum. HEW, BMI.

3513. Smith, C. A. Our Language: Three Book Course in English. B. F. Johnson, 1906. English Syllabi. USC.

3514. Smith, C. A. Our Language: Three Book Course in English. B. F. Johnson, 1903. English Syllabi. USC.

3515. Smith, C. A. Studies in English Syntax. Ginn, 1906. Grammar. USC.

3516. Smith, C. A. and McMurry, L. Manual to the Smith-McMurry Language Series. B. F. Johnson, 1920. Teaching Methods. USC.

3517. Smith, C. A. and McMurry, L. B. Smith-McMurry Language Series. B. F. Johnson, 1919. English Syllabi. USC .

3518. Smith, C. H. ed. Essays on Current Themes. Ginn, 1923. Readers. EGL.

3519. Smith, C. J. and Mayne, D. D. Modern Business English. Lyons, 1906. Business English. USC.

3520. Smith, C. J. and Mayne, D. D. Modern Business English. 2nd ed. Lyons and Carnahan, 1916. Business English. USC.

3521. Smith, C. W. Common Blunders Made in Speaking and Writing. Happy, 1876. Error. AC.

3522. Smith, E. Essay Writing; Rhetoric and Prosody. Oxford, 1913. Composition. USC, BMI.

3523. Smith, E. B. English Grammar A Class-Book of Methods. South Carrollton, KY, 1883. Grammar. HEW.

3524. Smith, G. J. Longmans' English Lessons. Longmans, 1906. Grammar. USC, AC.

3525. Smith, G. J. Longmans' English Lessons. 5th and 6th years. 2 vol. Longmans, 1917. Grammar. USC.

3526. Smith, G. J. Longman's English Lessons; Third and Fourth Year. 2 vol. Longmans, 1918. Grammar. USC.

3527. Smith, G. J., ed. Longmans' Briefer Grammar. Longmans, 1903. Grammar. USC.

3528. Smith, G. J., ed Longmans' Briefer Grammar. Longmans, 1915. Grammar. USC.

3529. Smith, G. J., ed. Longmans' English Grammar. Longmans, 1901. Grammar. USC.

3530. Smith, G. J., ed. Longmans' English Grammar. Longmans, 1916. Grammar. USC.

3531. Smith, H. G. and Ball, G. H. English Grammar and Composition. Mills and Boon, 1915. Composition. BMI

3532. Smith, H. J. English for Boys. Milwaukee, WI: Homer J. Smith, 1916. USC.

3533. Smith, L. P. The English Language. Holt, 1912. LLC.

3534. Smith, L. W. Mechanism of English Style. Oxford, 1916. Style. USC.

3535. Smith, L. W. and Thomas. Modern Composition and Rhetoric. B. H. Sanborn, 1900-05. Composition. AC.

3536. Smith, L. W. and Thomas, J. E. Modern Composition and Rhetoric. Sanborn, 1912. Composition. USC.

3537. Smith, R. Participle and Infinitive in -ing. SC: University of South Carolina, 1911. Grammar. USC.

3538. Smith, R. C. English Grammar. American Book. Grammar. USC.

3539. Smith, T. B. Studies in Nature and Language Lessons. Heath. USC.

3540. Smith, W. Juvenile Definer. American Book. USC.

3541. Smith, W. H. *Elementary English*. W. H. Smith, 1917. English Syllabi. USC.

3542. Smith, W. H. *English Grammar*. W. H. Smith, 1917. Grammar. USC.

3543. Smith, W. H. *First Year English*. W. H. Smith, 1917. English Syllabi. USC.

3544. Smith, W. H. *Fourth Year English*. W. H. Smith, 1917. English Syllabi. USC.

3545. Smith, W. H. *Second Year English*. W. H. Smith, 1917. English Syllabi. USC.

3546. Smith, W. H. *Third Year English*. W. H. Smith, 1917. English Syllabi. USC.

3547. Smith, W. W. *Definer's Manual*. American Book. USC.

3548. Snedden, D. S. "A Letter to a High School Teacher of English" *The English Leaflet*. 14 vol. Cambridge: The New England Association of Teachers of English, 1914. HEW.

3549. Snell, F. M. *Essentials of English Syntax*. Longmans, 1909. Grammar. USC.

3550. Snoddy, J. S. *A Plea for the Study of Historical English*. Missoula, MT: University of Montana Bulletin, 1904. Grammar. HEW.

3551. Snoddy, J. S. *Plea for the Study of Historical English*. Missoula, MT: University of Montana Lib., 1906. Grammar. USC.

3552. Somervell, R. *The Structure of Sentences. An aid to Composition*. London, 1900. Composition. BMI.

3553. Sonnenschein, E. A. *New English Grammar Based on the Recommendations of the Joint Committee on Grammatical Terminology*. Oxford, 1916. Grammar. USC, BMI.

3554. Sornberger, S. J. *Normal Language Lessons*. Bardeen. English Syllabi. USC.

3555. South, R. *Discourses on Various Subjects and Occasions*. Ed. Jonathon P. Dabney. Russell, 1833. LLC.

3556. Southwick, A. P. *Dime Question Book of Grammar*. Bardeen. Grammar. USC.

3557. Southwick, A. P. *Dime Question Book of Rhetoric*. Bardeen. Rhetoric. USC.

3558. Southwick, A. P. *Dime Question Book on Orthography, Orthoepy and Etymology*. Bardeen. Spelling. USC.

3559. Southwick, A. P. *Question-Book of Rhetoric and Composition*. Bardeen, 1882. Composition. AC.

3560. Southwick, F. T. *Elocution and Action*. 1903. Rhetoric. CC.

3561. Southworth, G. *First Lessons in Language*. Sanborn. English Syllabi. USC.

3562. Southworth, G. *Our Language*. Sanborn. USC.

3563. Southworth, G. A. *English Grammar and Composition for Higher Grades*. Sanborn. Composition. USC.

3564. Southworth, G. A. *New Lessons in Language*. Sanborn. English Syllabi. USC.

3565. Southworth, G. A. and Goddard, F. B. *Elements of Composition and Grammar*. Leach. 1889. Composition. AC.

3566. Southworth, G. and Goddard, F. B. *Elements of Composition and Grammar*. Sanborn. Composition. USC.

3567. Spalding, E. *Principles of Rhetoric*. Heath, 1905. Rhetoric. USC, AC.

3568. Spalding, E. *Problem of Elementary Composition*. Heath, 1912. Composition. USC.

3569. Spalding, E. H. *Problem of Elementary Composition: Suggestions for its Solution*. Heath, 1896.

Composition. AC.

3570. Sparks, B. J. *Matriculation English Course*. London: University of London Press, 1915. English Syllabi. BMI.

3571. Spaulding, F. E. and Bryce, C. T. *Aldine First Language Book*. Newson, 1913. English Syllabi. USC.

3572. Spaulding, F. E. and Bryce, C. T. *Aldine Language Method*. Newson, 1914. English Syllabi. USC.

3573. Spaulding, F. E. and Others. *Aldine Language Method*. Newson, 1917. English Syllabi. USC.

3574. Spaulding, F. E. and others. *Aldine Language Method*. Newson, 1917. English Syllabi. USC.

3575. *Specimen Themes, English 1*. Univ. of Cal. 1911, Readers. USC.

3576. *Specimen Themes, English*. California: University of California, 1911. Reader. USC.

3577. *Specimens of English Composition Arranged for Use in the Psychological and Educational Experiments*. Teachers College. Psychology and Composition. USC.

3578. *Speech and Voice Hygiene*. A Symposium. New York, 1916. Speech. HEW.

3579. *Spelling Made Easy by Rhyming Rules*. Leeds. 1911. Spelling. BMI.

3580. Spencer, H. *Facts and Comments*. Appleton, 1902. EGL.

3581. Spencer, H. *Philosophy of Style*. Appleton, 1876. Style. AC.

3582. Spencer, H. *Philosophy of Style*. E. Maynard, 1890. Style. AC.

3583. Spencer, H. *Philosophy of Style*. Fitzgerald, 1882. Style. AC.

3584. Spencer, H. Philosophy of Style. E. Maynard, 1890. Style. AC.

3585. Spencer, H. The Philosophy of Style with an Essay on Style by T. H. Wright. Ed. T. H. Wright. Allyn and Bacon, 1892. Style. AK, HEW.

3586. Spencer, H. The Philosophy of Style with an Essay on Style by T. H. Wright. Ed. T. H. Wright. Allyn and Bacon, 1892. Style. AK, HEW.

3587. Spencer, M. L. News Writing: The Gathering, Handling and Writing of News Stories. Boston, 1917. Journalism. BMI.

3588. Springfield, Massachusetts School Committee. Public Schools Course of Study in Language. Springfield, MA, 1904. Curriculum. HEW.

3589. Springfield, Massachusetts School Committee Public Schools. Course of Study in Language. Springfield, MA: Springfield Printing and Binding Co., 1911. Curriculum. HEW.

3590. Squire, J. C. Books Reviewed. Heineman, 1922. EGL.

3591. Squire, J. C. Life and Letters. Heineman, 1921. EGL.

3592. Starch, D. The Measurement of Efficiency in Reading, Writing, Spelling, and English. Madison, WI: College Bookstore, 1914. Testing. HEW.

3593. Steadman, J. M. Origin of the Historical Present in English. Chicago: University of Chicago, 1917. Grammar. USC.

3594. Stebbins, C. M. English Grammar for Secondary. Schools. New York: Stebbins and Company, 1916. Grammar. USC.

3595. Stebbins, C. M. Progressive Course in English: Literature, Composition. Sibley, 1908. Literature and Composition. USC .

3596. Stebbins, C. M. Progressive Course in English for Secondary Schools. Sibley, 1912. English Syllabi.

USC.

3597. Stebbins, C. M. *Sentence Improvement*. Sibely, 1910. Sentences. USC.

3598. Steel, G. *English Grammar and Analysis*. Longmans. Grammar. USC.

3599. Stevens, W. O. and Alden, C. S. *Composition for Naval Officers*. Annapolis, 1919. Business English. USC.

3600. Stevenson, O. J. *Ontario High School English Grammar*. Toronto, 1911. Grammar. BMI.

3601. Stevenson, O. J. and Irvin, H. W. *Ontario High School English Composition*. Toronto, 1912. Composition. BMI.

3602. Stewart, J. *Suggestions for a Textbook for Students of English from the Addresses and Speeches of Abraham Lincoln*. New Jersey, 1917. Curriculum. HEW.

3603. Stewart, J. B. *Language in the Primary Grades*. Anthony and Sons, 1917. English Syllabi. HEW.

3604. Stilwell, L. *Practical Exercises in Analysis and Parsing*. Silver. Grammar. USC.

3605. Stoddard, W. L. *Everyday English Writing*. Macmillan, 1919. Composition. USC.

3606. Stoker, J. *Text-Book of Analysis and Composition*. 1882. Composition. BMI.

3607. Stokes, E. *A Reformed Method of Teaching English*. Calcutta, 1917. Teaching Methods. BMI.

3608. *Stories for Composition and Language Exercises*. March, 1891. Readers. AC.

3609. *Stories for Composition and Language Exercises*. March, 1912. Readers. USC.

3610. Strang, H. I. *Common Errors in Speaking and Writing and How to Avoid Them*. Toronto, 1897. Error. BMI.

3611. Strang, H. I. <u>Exercises in English</u>. Heath. English Syllabi. USC.

3612. Strunk, W. <u>Elements of Style</u>. Harcourt, 1920. Style. USC.

3613. Stuart, J. B. <u>Language in the Primary Grades</u>. Massachusetts, 1917. English Syllabi. USC.

3614. <u>Style in Speaking - Whately's Logic and Rhetoric</u>. 1862. Style. CSIGP.

3615. Sullivan, R. <u>An Attempt to Simplify English Grammar</u>. Dublin, 1920. Grammar. BMI.

3616. Sullivan, R. <u>Sullivan's First English Grammar</u>. Dublin, 1920. Grammar. BMI.

3617. Sullivan, R. <u>The Spelling Book Superseded</u>. Dublin, 1916. Spelling. BMI.

3618. Sullivan, R. <u>The Spelling Book Superseded</u>. Dublin, 1920. Spelling. BMI.

3619. Summey, G. <u>Modern Punctuation: Its Utilities and Conventions</u>. New York, 1919. Punctuation. BMI.

3620. Sweet, H. <u>New English Grammar</u>. Oxford. Grammar. USC.

3621. Sweet, H. <u>Primer of Historical English Grammar</u>. Oxford. Grammar. USC.

3622. Sweet, H. <u>Primer of Spoken English</u>. Oxford. Usage. USC.

3623. Sweet, H. <u>Short Historical English Grammar</u>. Oxford. Grammar. USC.

3624. Sweet, H. <u>Spelling Reform and English Literature</u>. London, 1884. Spelling. BMI.

3625. Swett, J. <u>American Public Schools; History and Pedagogies</u>. 1900. History of Education. CC.

3626. Swett, J. <u>Normal Word Book; or, Studies in Spelling</u>

        Defining, a Word Analysis, and Synonyms. American Book. Spelling. USC.

3627. Swett, J. School Education; A Manual of Vocal Training in High Schools, Normal Schools, and Academics. 1884. Speech. CC.

3628. Swingle, F. B. English for Evening Schools. Racine, WI, 1907. English Syllabi. USC.

3629. Swinton, W. Advanced Language-Lessons for the Grammar School. Harper, 1874. Grammar. AC, AK.

3630. Swinton, W. Language Lessons. American Book, 1912. English Syllabi. USC .

3631. Swinton, W. Language Lessons; Introduction Grammar and Composition for Intermediate and Grammar Grades. Harper, 1876. Composition. AC.

3632. Swinton, W. Language Primer: Beginners' Lessons in Grammar and Composition. Harper, 1876. Composition. AC.

3633. Swinton, W. New English Grammar. American Book. Grammar. USC.

3634. Swinton, W. New English Grammar and Composition. American Book. Composition. USC.

3635. Swinton, W. School Manual of English Composition. American Book, 1905. Composition. USC.

3636. Swinton, W. Talking with the Pencil. American Book, 1898. USC.

3637. Syddall, J. Evan's First Step in Composition. London, 1892. Composition. BMI.

3638. Sykes, E. Sonoscript. Leads, 1910. BMI.

3639. Sykes, F. H. Elementary English Composition. Toronto, 1902. Composition. BMI.

3640. Sykes, F. H. Elementary English Composition for High Schools. Scribner, 1905. Composition. USC, AC.

3641. Sykes, F. H. English Composition for Grammar Schools. Scribner, 1908. Composition. USC, AC, CC.

3642. Syles, F. H. Elementary English Composition. Toronto, 1900. Composition. BMI.

3643. Symonds, H. C. Grammar. Benziger, 1901. Grammar. USC.

3644. Symonds, J. A. Essays, Speculative and Suggestive. London, 1890. Readers. CLPI.

3645. Sypherd, W. O. A Bibliography on "English for Engineers" for the Use of Engineering Students, Practicing Engineers, and Teachers in Schools of Engineering. Chicago: Scott, Foresman, and Co., 1916. Technical English. HEW.

3646. Sypherd, W. O. Handbook of English for Engineers. Scott, 1913. Technical English. USC.

3647. Sypherd, W. O. and Dutton, G. E. English Composition for College Freshman. Newark, DE: Dutton, 1915. Composition. USC.

3648. Sypherd, W. O. and Messersmith, G. S. High School Course in English. Newark, DE: Delaware College, 1908. English Syllabi. USC, HEW.

3649. Tancock, O. W. Elementary Grammar and Exercise Book. Oxford. Grammar. USC.

3650. Tancock, O. W. English Grammar and Reading Book. Oxford. Grammar. USC.

3651. Tarbell, H. S. Lessons in Language. Ginn, 1912. English Syllabi. USC.

3652. Tarbell, H. S. and M. Essentials of English Composition. Ginn, 1902. Composition. USC, AC.

3653. Tarbell, H. S. and Tarbell, M. Lessons in Language and Grammar. Ginn, 1912. Grammar. USC.

3654. Taylor, C. R. and Morss, L. K. Vital English. New York: Ambrose, 1919. English Syllabi. USC.

3655. Taylor, F. L. Beginnings in English. Heath, 1912. English Syllabi. USC.

3656. Taylor, J. R. Composition in Narration. Holt, 1910. Composition. USC, AC.

3657. Taylor, J. S. Composition in the Elementary Schools. Barnes, 1912. Composition. USC.

3658. Taylor, J. S. Composition in the Elementary Schools. Barnes, 1906. Composition. USC, HEW, AC.

3659. Taylor, J. S. Teaching Plan of Grammar. Bronx, New York: Loring Place, 1916. Grammar. USC, HEW.

3660. Taylor, J. S. Teaching Plan of Grammar. Bronx, New York: Loring Place, 1919. Grammar. USC.

3661. Taylor, W. Essays of the Past and Present. Harper, 1927. Readers. EGL.

3662. Taylor, W. Representative English Essays. Harper, 1923. Readers. EGL.

3663. Taylor, W. Types and Times in the Essay. Harper, 1932. EGL.

3664. Taylor, W. and Manchester, F. A. Freshman Themes. Century, 1917. USC.

3665. Taylor, W. R. A Brief English Composition. Milford, 1920. Composition. BMI.

3666. Teachers College Comparative Experimental Teaching in Spelling. 1912. Spelling. USC.

3667. Teacher's Manual Students' Lessons Leaves. 1909. USC.

3668. Teaching of English Classes. New Hampshire, 1916-1917. Teaching Methods. HEW.

3669. Item omitted.

3670. Teuueg, A. F. Manual of Elocution and Expression for Public Speakers and Readers. 1905. Speech. CC.

3671. Tex, M. C. <u>Grammar and Composition</u>. Illinois, 1913. Composition. USC.

3672. Thelwall, J. <u>The Vestibule of Eloquence: Original Articles, Oratorical and Poetical</u>. London, 1810. Speech. HR.

3673. Theremin, F. <u>Eloquence a Virtue: Outline of A Systematic Rhetoric</u>. New York, 1850. Rhetoric. HR, AK.

3674. Theremin, F. <u>Eloquence a Virtue: or, Outlines of A Systematic Rhetoric</u>. Draper, 1872. Rhetoric. AC.

3675. Thomas, C. S. <u>Teaching of English in the Secondary School</u>. Houghton, 1917. Teaching Methods. USC, HEW.

3676. Thomas, C. S. <u>The Hillegas Scale</u>. Newtonville, MA, 1913. Evaluating Writing. HEW.

3677. Thomas, C. S. and Howe, W. D. <u>Composition and Rhetoric</u>. Longmans, 1908. Composition. USC, AC, BMI, AK.

3678. Thomas, C. S. and Others. <u>Composition and Rhetoric</u>. Longmans, 1918. Composition. USC.

3679. Thomas, D. <u>Teaching of English by the Direct Method</u>. 1914. Teaching Methods. BMI.

3680. Thomas, H. <u>Study of the Paragraph</u>. American Book, 1912. Paragraphs. USC, BMI, AK.

3681. Thomas, W. H. and Morgan, S. S. <u>Essays in Liberal Thought</u>. Harcourt, 1928. EGL.

3682. Thompson, F. V. <u>Schooling of the Immigrant</u>. Harper, 1920. TESOL. USC, HEW.

3683. Thompson, T. E. <u>Minimum Essentials: Sheets of Graded Questions in Arithmetic and Language</u>. Ginn, 1913. Testing. USC.

3684. Thompson, W. S. <u>Practical Guide to English</u>

Composition. Aberdeen, 1894. Composition. BMI.

3685. Thompson, W. S. Practical Guide to English Composition and Essay Writing. Aberdeen, 1901. Composition. BMI.

3686. Thomson, W. The Basics of English Rhythm. Glasgow, 1904. Sound Patterns. LC.

3687. Thorley, W. C. Primer of English for Foreign Students. Macmillan, 1910. TESOL. USC.

3688. Thorndike, A. H. Elements of Rhetoric and Composition. Century, 1918. Composition. USC.

3689. Thorndike, A. H. Elements of Rhetoric and Composition. Century, 1905. Composition. USC, AC, AK.

3690. Thorndike, E. L. English Composition. Teachers College, 1916. Composition. USC, HEW.

3691. Thornton, G. H. English Composition. McKay, 1917. Composition. USC.

3692. Thornton, G. H. English Composition. Crowell, 1900-1905. Composition. AC.

3693. Thornton, G. H. Self-Educator in English Composition. Adams, 1901. Composition. BMI, CC.

3694. Thornton, G. H. Self-Educator in English Composition. Doran, 1912. Composition. USC.

3695. Thuing, C. F. History of Education in the United States Since the Civil War. Houghton, 1910. History of Education. CC.

3696. Thurber, E. A. The Problem of Teaching Rhetoric in the High Schools. Oregon: University of Oregon, 1910. Rhetoric. HEW.

3697. Thurber, S. The New England Association of Teachers of English, Leaflet. Newtonville, MA, 1913. Curriculum. HEW.

3698. Thurber, S. To What End Do High Schools Teach

English. Boston: Bacon, 1893. Curriculum. HEW.

3699. Toledo, Board of Education. Course of Study in English for Elementary Schools. Toledo, 1913. Curriculum. HEW.

3700. Tompkins, A. Science of Discourse. Ginn, 1912. Rhetoric. USC.

3701. Tompkins, A. Science of Discourse: A Rhetoric. Ginn, 1897. Rhetoric. AC.

3702. Torossian, B. R. Self-Instructor in the English Language. New York, 1913. English Syllabi. USC.

3703. Torrey, B. Friends on the Shelf. Houghton, 1906. EGL.

3704. Tower, D. B. Grammar of Composition. Lee and Son, 1876. Grammar. AC.

3705. Townsend, J. L. Exercises in Grammatical Analysis. Scrantom, Wetmore and Co. Grammar. USC.

3706. Tozer, B. Free Lance Journalism: How to Embark Upon It and Make It Pay. London, 1901. Journalism. BMI.

3707. Trabue, M. R. Completion Test Language Scales. Teachers College, 1916. Testing. USC, HEW.

3708. Trabue, M. R. Key for Completion-Test Language Scales. Teachers College, 1919. Testing. USC, HEW.

3709. Trabue, M. R. Supplementing the Hillegas Scale. Teachers College. 1918. Testing. USC.

3710. Trench, R. C. On the English Language. Newed, 1860. SIBP.

3711. Trench, R. C. On the Study of Words. Macmillan, 1920. LLC.

3712. Trench, R. C. Past and Present. 1857. SIBP.

3713. Treusein, F. J. Studies in English for Standards

IV., V., VI. Singapore, 1919. BMI.

3714. Truman, D. E. *The Child Vision, Being a Study in Mental Development and Expression*. Manchester: The University Press, 1920. HEW.

3715. Tucker, G. *Essays on Various Subjects of Taste, Morals, and National Policy*. Georgetown, 1822. CLPI.

3716. Tucker, G. M. *American English*. Knopf, 1921. USC.

3717. Tucker, T. G. *An English Grammar for High Standards and Junior Teachers*. Melbourne, 1918. Grammar. BMI.

3718. Tucker, T. G. and Wallace, R. S. *English Grammar, Descriptive and Historical*. Putnam, 1917. Grammar. USC, BMI.

3719. Tweed, B. F. *Grammar for Common Schools*. Lothrop. Grammar. USC.

3720. *Twenty-five Lessons in Correct Grammar*. Hinds. Grammar. USC.

3721. Twentyman, G. A. *English Grammar and Composition*. Rivingtons, 1911. Composition. BMI.

3722. U., J. H. F. *Manual of English Grammar*. Concordia. Grammar. ISC.

3723. U. S. A. National Joint Committee on English. *Reorganization of English in Secondary Schools*. 1917. Curriculum. BMI.

3724. U. S. Federal Board for Vocational Education. *Advanced Course in English for Foreign-Born Men*. U. S. Federal Board for Vocational Education, 1919. TESOL. USC.

3725. U. S. Federal Board for Vocational Education. *Beginners' Course in English for Non-English Speaking Men*. U. S. Federal Board for Vocational Education, 1919. TESOL. USC.

3726. United States Federal Board for Vocational Education.

English for Non-English Speaking Men. U. S. Federal Board for Vocational Education, 1919. TESOL. USC.

3727. University of Michigan. An Encyclopedic Survey. Michigan: University of Michigan Press, 1943. AK.

3728. Unwin, S. R. and Abbott, G. Skeleton English Grammar. 1912. Grammar. BMI.

3729. Urguhart, H. R. Concise English Grammar. 1912. Grammar. BMI.

3730. Use of Words. Hinds. Usage. USC.

3731. Utter, R. P. Everyday Words and Their Uses. Harper, 1916. Usage. USC, LLC.

3732. Utter, R. P. Guide to Good English. Harper, 1914. Usage. USC.

3733. Van Hook, L. Metaphorical Terminology of Greek Rhetoric and Literary Critcism. Chicago: University of Chicago, 1905. Rhetoric. USC.

3734. Varnish, E. A. A. and Hanly, J. H. Junior Graphic Grammar. Cambridge, 1915. Grammar. BMI.

3735. Vermont State Board of Education. Suggestions for the Teaching of English in the Elementary Schools. 1918. Curriculum. USC.

3736. Vizetelly, F. H. Desk-Book of Errors in English. New York, London: Funk, 1906. Error. USC, HEW.

3737. Vizetelly, F. H. Essentials of English Speech and Literature. Funk, 1915. Literature and Composition. USC.

3738. Waddy, V. Elements of Composition and Rhetoric. 1889. Composition. CC.

3739. Waddy, V. Elements of Composition and Rhetoric. American Book, 1912. Composition. USC.

3740. Waddy, V. Elements of Composition and Rhetoric. Van Antwerp, 1890. Composition. AC.

3741. Wahlstad, P. P. English Language and Grammar. 1920. Grammar. USC.

3742. Walkley, A. B. Still More Prejudice. Knopf, 1925. EGL.

3743. Wallach, I. First Book in English for Beginners. Silver, 1906. English Syllabi. USC.

3744. Wallbank, N. B. Outlines and Exercises in English Grammar. Flanagan, Grammar. USC.

3745. Walmsley, A. M. Junior English Grammar. Clive, 1920. Grammar. BMI.

3746. Walton, J. H. English Synthesis: A Practical Method of Prose-Writing. Madras, 1894. Composition. BMI.

3747. Wann, L. Century Readings in the English Essay. Appleton-Century, 1926. Readers. EGL.

3748. Ward, C. C. Oral Composition. Macmillan, 1914. Speech. USC, BMI.

3749. Ward, C. H. Junior English Grammar. Holt, 1919. Grammar. USC.

3750. Ward, C. H. Pilot Book for Sentence and Theme. Scott, 1918. Composition. USC.

3751. Ward, C. H. Sentence and Theme. Scott, 1917. Composition. USC.

3752. Ward, C. H. Theme-Building. Scott, 1920. Composition. USC.

3753. Ward, C. H. What is English?. Scott, 1917. USC, HEW.

3754. Wardell, R. J. Studies in Homiletics. 1905. Sermons. BMI.

3755. Wardlaw, P. Simpler English Grammar. South Carolina: University of South Carolina, 1914. Grammar. USC.

3756. Warman, E. B. Don'ts for the Speaker and Writer.

Saalfield. Usage. USC.

3757. Warner, G. T. On the Writing of English. Blackie, 1915. Composition. BMI.

3758. Washington (State) Department of Education. Teacher's Manual for the Elementary Schools of Washington Supplement No. 1, English. 1908. Curriculum. HEW.

3759. Waterbury Connecticut Department of Education. Outline of Work in Language, Literature and Reading. Waterbury, CT, 1919. Curriculum. HEW.

3760. Watkins, D. E. Public Speaking for High Schools. New York: American Book, 1913. Speech. HEW.

3761. Watkins, E. Games to Teach Correct English to Little Ones. Iowa City: Kohl and Schaedler, 1917. Grammar. USC, HEW.

3762. Watkins, E. Games to Teach Correct English to Little Ones. Iowa City, 1919. Grammar. USC.

3763. Watrous, G. A. First Year English: Syntax and Composition. Sibley, 1901. Composition. USC.

3764. Watrous, G. A. Second Year English: Composition and Rhetoric. Sibley, 1902. Composition. USC.

3765. Watson, E. H. L. Hints to Young Authors. Brown and Langhan, 1906. BMI.

3766. Watson, R. H. Nine Weeks' Course in English Grammar. Nebraska: University Publication of Nebraska. Grammar. USC.

3767. Watt, H. A. Composition of Technical Papers. McGraw, 1917. Technical English. USC, BMI.

3768. Watts, I. Works. London, 1812-1813. CLPI.

3769. Weaver, E. W. Pictures in Language Work. Cincinnati Teacher's Co-op Publishing, 1896. Teaching Methods. HEW.

3770. Weaver, E. W. Pictures in Language Work. Bardeen,

1912. Teaching Methods. USC.

3771. Weaver, E. W. *Pictures in Language Work*. Cincinnati, OH: Teachers Co-op Publishing Co., 1891. Teaching Methods. HEW.

3772. Webb, A. C. *Model Definer*. Hinds. USC.

3773. Webb, W. T. *How to Write an Essay*. Dutton, 1921. Composition. USC.

3774. Webb, W. T. *How to Write an Essay*. Dutton, 1913. Composition. USC.

3775. Webber, I. L. M. *Handbook of Commercial English*. Palmer, 1913. Business English. USC.

3776. Webster, E. and Allen, L. H. *An Experiment in Imaginative Writing*. 1918. Composition. HEW.

3777. Webster, E. H. *Effective English Expression*. Newson, 1920. Composition. USC.

3778. Webster, E. H. *English for Business*. Newson, 1916. Business English. USC.

3779. Webster, E. H. *English for Business as Applied in Commercial Technical, and Other Secondary Schools*. Newson, 1919. Business English. USC.

3780. Webster, E. H. *English for Business; Teachers' Manual*. Newson, 1920. Business English. USC.

3781. Webster, E. H. *Teacher's Manual Effective English Expression*. Newson, 1920. Teaching Methods. USC.

3782. Webster, J. R. *Paraphrasing*. Cambridge, MA, 1919. Paraphrasing. USC.

3783. Webster, J. R. *Sentence-Making*. Cambridge, MA, 1913. Sentences. USC.

3784. Webster, W. F. *Elementary Composition*. Houghton, 1903. Composition. USC, AC.

3785. Webster, W. F. *English Composition and Literature*. Houghton, 1900. Literature and Composition. USC,

AC, AK.

3786. Webster, W. F. English for Secondary Schools. Houghton, 1912. English Syllabi. USC.

3787. Webster, W. F. and Cooley, A. Elements of English Grammar. Houghton, 1904. Grammar. USC.

3788. Webster, W. F. and Cooley, A. Elements of Grammar and Composition. Houghton, 1906. Composition. USC.

3789. Webster, W. F. and Cooley, A. Essentials of Grammar and Composition. Houghton, 1909. Composition. USC, AC.

3790. Weedon, T. A Practical Grammar of the English Language. 1848. Grammar. SIBP.

3791. Weekley, E. The Romance of Words. Dutton, 1912. LLC.

3792. Weeks, A. L. Style Book of the Detroit News. Detroit, MI, 1918. Journalism. USC.

3793. Wehman, H. J. Book on Errors in Speaking and Writing. Wehman. Error. USC.

3794. Weld, A. H. Weld's English Grammar. Buffalo: Phinney, 1849. Grammar. AC.

3795. Wells, C. W. Book of Prose Narratives. Ginn, 1914. Readers. USC.

3796. Welsford, H. Origin and Ramifications of the English Language. 1845. Grammar. SIBP.

3797. Welsh, A. H. Complete Rhetoric. Silver, 1912. Rhetoric. USC.

3798. Welsh, A. H. Complete Rhetoric. Griggs, 1885. Rhetoric. AC, AK.

3799. Welsh, A. H. English Composition. Silver, 1912. Composition. USC.

3800. Welsh, A. H. English Composition. Buckbee, 1889.

Composition. AC.

3801. Welsh, A. H. Essentials of English. Silver, 1912. English Syllabi. USC.

3802. Welsh, A. H. First Lessons in English. Silver, 1912. English Syllabi. USC.

3803. Welsh, A. H. Lessons in English Grammar. Buckee, 1888. Grammar. AC.

3804. Welsh, A. H. Lessons in English Grammar. Silver, 1912. Grammar. USC.

3805. Welsh, J. P. First Lessons in English Grammar and Composition. Sower. Composition. USC.

3806. Welsh, J. P. Practical English Grammar. Sower. Grammar. USC.

3807. Welton, J. Groundwork of English Grammar. Macmillan, 1920. Grammar. BMI.

3808. Welton, J. and Welton, W. P. English: Reading, Language, and Literature. London: Clive, 1912. English Syllabi. HEW.

3809. Wendell, B. Eight Lectures Given at the Lowell Institute. New York: Scribner, 1891. Rhetoric. HR, PS, AC, AK.

3810. Wendell, B. English Composition. Scribner, 1912. Composition. USC.

3811. Wertz, A. P. Detailed Methods of Instruction. Flanagan, 1908. Teaching Methods. USC.

3812. Wescott, A. Teaching of Phonics. Minneapolis, 1917. Reading. USC.

3813. Wesley, J. Works. London, 1860-1863. CLPI.

3814. West, A. S. Chapter on Essay-Writing. Putnam. Composition. USC.

3815. West, A. S. Elements of English Grammar. Putnam. Grammar. USC.

3816. West, A. S. <u>Key to Questions Contained in West's Elements of English Grammar and English Grammar for Beginners</u>. Putnam, 1912. Grammar. USC.

3817. West, A. S. <u>Key to the Questions Contained in Revised English Grammar and Revised English Grammar for Beginners</u>. Cambridge Univ. Press, 1920. Grammar. BMI.

3818. West, A. S. <u>Revised English Grammar</u>. Putnam, 1912. Grammar. USC.

3819. West, A. S. <u>Revised Grammar for Beginners</u>. Putnam, 1912. Grammar. USC.

3820. West, M. <u>Advanced English Composition</u>. Longmans, 1917. Composition. BMI.

3821. Weston, W. J. <u>English Grammar and Composition</u>. Pitman, 1914. Composition. BMI.

3822. Weston, W. J. <u>English Prose Composition</u>. Pitman, 1920. Composition. BMI.

3823. Weston, W. J. <u>Talles on English Composition</u>. Pitman, 1917. Composition. BMI.

3824. Wetherell, J. E. <u>Exercises in Rhetoric</u>. Toronto, 1897. Rhetoric. BMI.

3825. Wharton, J. H. <u>Manual of Technical English</u>. Syracuse, NY: University of Syracuse, 1919. Technical English. USC.

3826. Whately, R. <u>Elements of Rhetoric</u>. Harper, 1876. Rhetoric. AC.

3827. Whately, R. <u>Elements of Rhetoric</u>. Sheldon, 1876. Rhetoric. AC.

3828. Whately, R. <u>Elements of Rhetoric</u>. Morton, 1876. Rhetoric. AC.

3829. Whately, R. <u>Elements of Rhetoric</u>. 1858. Rhetoric. AC.

3830. Whately, R. *Elements of Rhetoric*. 1841. Rhetoric. CLPI.

3831. Whately, R. *Elements of Rhetoric*. 1836. Rhetoric. SIBP.

3832. Whately, R. *Elements of Rhetoric*. London: Parker, 1828. Rhetoric. HR, AK.

3833. Whately, R. *Elements of Rhetoric, Comprising an Analysis of the Laws of Moral Evidence and Persuasion, with Rules and Elocution*. 1963. Rhetoric. HR, PS.

3834. Whately, R. *Rhetoric*. Morton, 1912. Rhetoric. USC.

3835. Wheeler, C. *Course of Study, Santa Barbara Night School*. Santa Barbara, CA: Schauer Printing Co., 1918. Curriculum. HEW.

3836. Wheeler, W. H. *Graded Studies in English: First Lessons in Grammar and Composition*. Wheeler, 1899. Composition. AC.

3837. Whelton, H. *Punctuation and the Style of the Office*. Lawerence and Co., 1914. Business English. BMI.

3838. White, K. A. *Downfall of Poor Speech*. March, 1920. USC.

3839. White, R. *Words and Their Uses, Past and Present*. Houghton. Usage. USC.

3840. White, R. G. *Every-day English*. Houghton, 1908. USC.

3841. White, T. W. *Grammar for Thinkers*. Palmer, 1917. Grammar. USC.

3842. White, T. W. *Grammar for Thinkers in the Eighth Grade*. Tufts College Press, 1909. Grammar. USC.

3843. Whitney, W. D. *Essentials of English Grammar*. Ginn, 1898. Grammar. AK.

3844. Whitney, W. D. *Essentials of English Grammar*. Ginn,

1912. Grammar. USC.

3845. Whitney, W. D. Language and the Study of Language. Scribner, 1867. English Syllabi. AK.

3846. Whitney, W. D. The Life and Growth of Language. Appleton, 1875. Grammar. LLC, AK.

3847. Whitney, W. D. and Knox, N. L. Elementary Lessons in English. Point 1: How to Speak and Write Correctly. Ginn, 1880. Error. AC.

3848. Whitney, W. D. and Lockwood, S. E. English Grammar. Ginn. Grammar. USC.

3849. Wickersbau, J. P. History of Education in Pennsylvania from the Time the Swedes Settled on the Delaware to the Present Day. 1886. History of Education. CC.

3850. Wilbur, W. A. Argumentation in English Rhetoric. Washington, D. C.: University of Washington D. C., 1913. Rhetoric. USC.

3851. Wilbur, W. A. English Rhetoric. Washington D. C., 1915. Rhetoric. USC.

3852. Wilbur, W. A. Exposition in English Rhetoric. Collins, Hauser and Co., 1910. Rhetoric. USC, AC.

3853. Wilbur, W. A. Modes of Imagination in English Rhetoric. Washington D. C.: University of Washington D. C., 1911. Rhetoric. USC.

3854. Wilbur, W. A. Syllable in English Rhetoric. Collins, Hauser and Company, 1910. Rhetoric. USC.

3855. Wilcox. W. H. Daily English Lessons. Lippincott, 1916. English Syllabi. USC.

3856. Wilcox, W. H. Daily English Lessons. Lippincott, 1916. English Syllabi. USC.

3857. Wilkesbarre, P. Suggestions to Teachers on the Study of English. 1899. Teaching Methods. HEW.

3858. Willams, B. C. Book of Essays. Heath. 1931. EGL.

3859. Williams, A. M. First Exercises in English Composition. 1894. Composition. BMI.

3860. Williams, B. F. New English Grammar. Des Moines, IA: Commercial Text Book Co., 1902. Grammar. USC.

3861. Williams, J. D. Graded Language Exercises. Laird, 1915. English Syllabi. USC.

3862. Williams, J. D. Language Book. Mentzer and Grover, 1911. English Syllabi. USC.

3863. Williams, J. D. Williams' Language Book. Laird, 1914. English Syllabi. USC.

3864. Williams, L. L. and Rogers, F. E. New Practical English Grammar. American Book, 1895. Grammar. USC.

3865. Williams, R. O. Some Questions of Good English. Holt. Usage. USC.

3866. Williams, S. G. History of Modern Education. 1896. History of Education. CC.

3867. Williams, W. Composition and Rhetoric by Practice. Heath, 1888. Composition. AC.

3868. Williams, W. Composition and Rhetoric by Practice. Heath, 1912. Composition. USC.

3869. Williams, W. G. Outlines of English Grammar for High Schools and Advanced Schools. Columbus, OH: Wells. Grammar. USC.

3870. Willis, J. F. Twenty Lessons in Sentence Analysis for Class Study. Noble, 1915. Sentences. USC.

3871. Willoughby, J. E. Written Exercises on Direct and Indirect Quotations. American School for the Deaf. Composition. AC.

3872. Wilson, H. R. Teachers' Manual of English Grammar and Analysis. Heath, 1915. Grammar. USC.

3873. Wilson, J. D. Elementary English. Bardeen. English

Syllabi. USC.

3874. Wilson, J. D. English Grammar Made Practical. Bardeen. Grammar. USC.

3875. Wilson, L. R. Chaucer's Relative Constructions. North Carolina: University of North Carolina. Grammar. USC.

3876. Wilson, R. Lingua Materna. Longman, 1905. USC, BMI, HEW.

3877. Wilson, R. Sentence Building. Macmillan, 1914. Sentences. BMI.

3878. Wilson, T. Arte of Rhetorique. Oxford, 1909. Rhetoric. USC.

3879. Winbolt, S. E. Short Essays for Schools for 4th and 5th Forms. Oxford, 1917. Composition. USC, BMI.

3880. Winchell, S. R. Orthography, Etymology and Punctuation. Flanagan. Spelling. USC.

3881. Winchester, C. T. Some Principles of Literary Criticism. Macmillan, 1904. Criticism. AK.

3882. Winchester, L. New System of Analysis. Blackie, 1914. BMI.

3883. Winterburn, R. V. Graded Lessons in Language. Doub and Co. English Syllabi. USC.

3884. Wisconsin State Teachers College. On the Teaching of English in the Grades Below High School. Milwaukee, WI, 1907. Curriculum. HEW.

3885. Wisely, J. B. English Grammar. Atkinson, M. and G., 1906. Grammar. USC.

3886. Wisely, J. B. Studies in the Science of English Grammar. Atkinson, M. and G. Grammar. USC.

3887. Wisely, J. B. and Griswold, S. E. Language Lessons. Atkinson, M. and G. English Syllabi. USC.

3888. Wit and Humor in the Pulpit.

1896. Sermons. CSIGP.

3889. Witcomb, C. *Structure of English*. London, 1884. Grammar. BMI.

3890. Withers, S. and Kinard, J. P. *English Language*. Macmillan, 1911. USC.

3891. Witherspoon, J. *Lectures on Moral Philosophy and Eloquence*. Philadelphia: Woodward's, 1810. Rhetoric. HR, AK.

3892. Wohlfarth, J. H. *Self-Help English Lessons*. World Book, 1921. English Syllabi. USC.

3893. Wohlforth, J. H. *Everyday Words. A Speller for All Grades*. New York, 1916. Spelling. BMI.

3894. Wood, R. S. *Oral and Written Exercises in English Composition*. Macmillan, 1918. Composition. BMI.

3895. Wood, R. S. *Teacher's Manual of Composition*. London, 1901. Composition. BMI.

3896. Wood, T. *Practical Grammar and Composition*. Appleton, 1910. Composition. USC, AC.

3897. Woodbridge, H. E. *Essentials of English Composition*. Harcourt, 1920. Composition. USC.

3898. Woodley, M. S., and O. I. *English Studies in Interpretation and Composition for High Schools*. Macmillan, 1906. Composition. USC, AC.

3899. Woodley, O. I. and M. S. *Foundation Lessons in English*. Macmillan. English Syllabi. USC.

3900. Woodley, O. I. and Others. *Foundation Lessons in English Grammar*. Macmillan. Grammar. USC.

3901. Woodward and T. *Woodward's Advanced Lessons in English*. Woodward and T. English Syllabi. USC.

3902. Woodward and T. *Woodward's Elementary Lessons in English*. Woodward and T. English Syllabi. USC.

3903. Woodward, F. C. *English in the Schools*. Boston:

Heath and Co., 1893. Curriculum. HEW.

3904. Woodward, F. C. *Study of English*. Heath. USC.

3905. *Woolley Notes on English Composition*. Quadrangle, 1904. Composition. AC.

3906. Woolley, E. C. *Exercises in English*. Heath, 1911. English Syllabi. USC.

3907. Woolley, E. C. *Handbook of Composition*. Heath, 1920. Composition. USC, BMI.

3908. Woolley, E. C. *Handbook of Composition*. Heath, 1907. Composition. USC, AK.

3909. Woolley, E. C. *Mechanics of Writing*. Heath, 1909. Mechanics. USC, AC, AK.

3910. Woolley, E. C. *Notes on English Composition*. Quadrangle, 1904. Composition. AK.

3911. Woolley, E. C. *The Mechanics of Writing*. Heath, 1919. Mechanics. BMI.

3912. Woolley, E. C. *Written English*. Heath, 1915. Composition. USC, AK.

3913. Worchester, J. E. *English Grammar*. Grammar. CLPI.

3914. Worsfold, W. B. *The Principles of Criticism*. London, 1897. Criticism. LC.

3915. Wren, P. C. *The "Direct" Teaching of English in Indian Schools*. Longmans, 1912. TESOL. BMI.

3916. Wright, A. A. *Fables, Stories and Facts for Reproduction*. Flanagan. Readers. USC.

3917. Wright, G. H. B. *Exercises in English Composition*. Hong Kong, 1903. Composition. BMI.

3918. Wright, T. G. *Exercises in the Use of the Dictionary*. American Book, 1918. Dictionary Use. USC.

3919. *Writer's Handbook*. Lippincott, 1912. USC.

3920. <u>Writer's Handbook: Guide to the Art of Composition</u>.
Lippincott, 1888. Composition. AC.

3921. <u>Writing of Essays- Wells' Certain Personal Matters</u>.
1897. Composition. CSIGP.

3922. <u>The Writing Scholars' Companion</u>. 1911. BMI.

3923. <u>Writing Styles--Hunter's Commercial Precis-Writing</u>.
1888. Precis. CSIGP.

3924. Wyld, H. C. K. <u>Elementary Lessons in English Grammar</u>. Oxford, 1909. Grammar. USC.

3925. Wyld, H. C. K. <u>The Place of the Mother Tongue in National Education</u>. London: Murray, 1906.
Curriculum. HEW.

3926. Yates, M. T. <u>Outlines and Pictures for Composition</u>.
1895. Composition. BMI.

3927. Young, F. C. and K. <u>Freshman English</u>. Holt, 1914.
Freshman English. USC.

3928. Young, F. C. and K. <u>Freshman English</u>. Holt, 1914.
Freshman English. USC.

3929. Young, I. F. <u>Practical Hints on English Composition</u>.
1902. Composition. BMI.

3930. Young, I. F. <u>The Normal Model Essays</u>. 1902.
Readers. BMI.

3931. Zander, H. J. and Howard, T. E. <u>Outlines of Composition</u>. Davis. Composition. USC.

3932. Zeitlin, J. <u>Accusative With Infinitive, and Some Kindred Constructions in English</u>. Lemoke, 1908.
Grammar. USC.

Subject Index

Subject Index

Not Classifiable by Title   11, 44, 53, 66, 71, 81, 92, 98,
101, 107, 117, 133, 155, 156, 160, 161, 170, 187,
188, 197, 230, 236, 237, 239, 248, 249, 250, 252,
253, 257, 260, 262, 265, 273, 276, 300, 304, 305,
306, 321, 325, 327, 329, 332, 334, 342, 346, 369,
375, 395, 404, 411, 419, 421, 422, 424, 431, 433,
446, 447, 449, 453, 457, 460, 466, 467, 470, 477,
480, 491, 496, 503, 504, 511, 514, 517, 518, 519,
521, 528, 533, 537, 538, 547, 548, 552, 553, 554,
556, 557, 559, 563, 570, 593, 598, 600, 601, 603,
611, 613, 616, 621, 623, 627, 649, 650, 651, 656,
661, 662, 665, 666, 675, 676, 678, 681, 684, 693,
698, 700, 702, 706, 709, 713, 717, 719, 722, 723,
725, 726, 735, 737, 739, 741, 747, 753, 754, 755,
758, 760, 768, 771, 775, 781, 785, 788, 793, 794,
797, 798, 799, 800, 801, 802, 803, 804, 805, 807,
821, 832, 840, 842, 843, 851, 857, 858, 859, 860,
861, 862 , 864, 872, 875, 882, 885, 898, 899, 911,
913, 926, 927, 933, 934, 936, 943, 944, 947, 948,
961, 964, 966, 967, 969, 981, 984, 987, 996, 997,
998, 1000, 1011, 1015, 1017, 1026, 1033, 1036, 1042,
1046, 1047, 1049, 1050, 1057, 1068, 1073, 1080,
1095, 1113, 1118, 1121, 1122, 1125, 1129, 1134,
1140, 1156, 1164, 1170, 1173, 1179, 1180, 1196,
1203, 1204, 1209, 1223, 1224, 1232, 1259, 1261,
1276, 1277, 1278, 1281, 1294, 1298, 1300, 1302,
1309, 1315, 1320, 1321, 1322, 1323, 1324, 1360,
1372, 1376, 1377, 1391, 1392, 1395, 1426, 1432,
1447, 1457, 1460, 1470, 1481, 1483, 1491, 1534,
1539, 1596, 1597, 1598, 1599, 1602, 1603, 1606,
1624, 1680, 1702, 1732, 1738, 1751, 1770, 1773,
1784, 1794, 1795, 1832, 1834, 1835, 1839, 1842,
1843, 1873, 1874, 1881, 1883, 1903, 1920, 1925,
1936, 1942, 1956, 1967, 1982, 1994, 1995, 1997,
2009, 2010, 2030, 2052, 2058, 2062, 2069, 2082,
2084, 2092, 2093, 2094, 2095, 2099, 2100, 2118,
2119, 2120, 2159, 2167, 2168, 2170, 2186, 2195,
2196, 2202, 2204, 2206, 2212, 2214, 2216, 2223,

2235, 2236, 2238, 2246, 2247, 2248, 2250, 2254,
2255, 2257, 2258, 2260, 2261, 2266, 2269, 2272,
2274, 2283, 2284, 2288, 2312, 2313, 2314, 2315,
2316, 2317, 2318, 2333, 2336, 2339, 2341, 2343,
2345, 2346, 2350, 2352, 2353, 2354, 2358, 2360,
2363, 2367, 2371, 2375, 2376, 2379, 2380, 2382,
2384, 2392, 2395, 2406, 2407, 2408, 2417, 2419,
2422, 2425, 2436, 2438, 2444, 2446, 2449, 2451,
2454, 2455, 2457, 2458, 2460, 2481, 2488, 2489,
2495, 2496, 2508, 2516, 2519, 2527, 2534, 2535,
2538, 2559, 2560, 2561, 2562, 2580, 2581, 2583,
2588, 2592, 2606, 2618, 2623, 2629, 2640, 2667,
2690, 2694, 2702, 2708, 2730, 2733, 2734, 2736,
2737, 2739, 2740, 2743, 2761, 2779, 2781, 2805,
2807, 2813, 2814, 2840, 2857, 2867, 2870, 2880,
2890, 2905, 2930, 2941, 3006, 3030, 3043, 3046,
3095, 3107, 3108, 3124, 3125, 3128, 3130, 3133,
3143, 3144, 3154, 3155, 3158, 3159, 3160, 3161,
3188, 3193, 3207, 3217, 3229, 3233, 3249, 3250,
3254, 3260, 3269, 3270, 3277, 3290, 3334, 3336,
3341, 3369, 3373, 3374, 3392, 3394, 3424, 3444,
3466, 3470, 3482, 3509, 3532, 3533, 3539, 3540,
3547, 3548, 3555, 3562, 3580, 3590, 3591, 3636,
3638, 3663, 3664, 3667, 3681, 3703, 3710, 3711,
3712, 3713, 3714, 3715, 3716, 3727, 3742, 3753,
3765, 3768, 3772, 3791, 3813, 3838, 3840, 3858,
3876, 3882, 3890, 3904, 3919, 3922

Business English 326, 352, 437, 499, 620, 738, 772, 827,
828, 968, 1212, 1336, 1433, 1563, 1565, 1669, 1817,
1825, 1826, 1928, 1934, 1960, 2035, 2037, 2113,
2114, 2192 2275, 2276, 2389, 2390, 2403, 2448, 2461,
2472, 2537, 2544, 2545, 2546, 2547, 2597, 2671,
2728, 2759, 2760, 2820, 2832, 2869, 2957, 3141,
3245, 3380, 3469, 3519, 3520, 3599, 3775, 3778,
3779, 3780, 3837

Composition 121, 126, 128, 130, 173, 174, 223, 302, 313,
319, 323, 324, 339, 344, 345, 356, 379, 389, 390,
427, 436, 451, 458, 523, 535, 555, 564, 589, 736,
784, 789, 790, 806, 826, 833, 834, 838, 839, 874,
880, 897, 904, 917, 918, 924, 960, 963, 972, 985,
1027, 1045, 1051, 1083, 1089, 1090, 1106, 1149,
1172, 1246, 1279, 1328, 1337, 1342, 1382, 1388,
1389, 1393, 1400, 1401, 1403, 1406, 1411, 1415,
1420, 1429, 1436, 1451, 1455, 1456, 1458, 1476,
1477, 1486, 1487, 1488, 1489, 1490, 1499, 1516,

1520, 1521, 1524, 1525, 1530, 1533, 1537, 1548,
1549, 1555, 1577, 1578, 1579, 1583, 1604, 1605,
1609, 1616, 1619, 1628, 1638, 1641, 1647, 1648,
1654, 1657, 1658, 1659, 1671, 1675, 1681, 1686,
1689, 1690, 1695, 1696, 1706, 1708, 1709, 1711,
1712, 1713, 1718, 1733, 1734, 1735, 1740, 1746,
1747, 1748, 1753, 1754, 1756, 1759, 1760, 1764,
1766, 1769, 1778, 1787, 1789, 1790, 1823, 1824,
1833, 1836, 1837, 1838, 1840, 1841, 1847, 1851,
1853, 1854, 1858, 1864, 1865, 1866, 1879, 1880,
1885, 1890, 1892, 1896, 1897, 1909, 1914, 1915,
1916, 1923, 1924, 1926, 1929, 1930, 1933, 1941,
1947, 1948, 1953, 1954, 1965, 1966, 1968, 1978,
1979, 1980, 1983, 1984, 2000, 2002, 2004, 2008,
2014, 2016, 2021, 2027, 2028, 2029, 2042, 2049,
2059, 2072, 2078, 2129, 2132, 2133, 2139, 2140,
2153, 2154, 2160, 2172, 2173, 2174, 2178, 2179,
2180, 2182, 2183, 2184, 2185, 2199, 2209, 2211,
2219, 2220, 2221, 2229, 2233, 2237, 2239, 2240,
2241, 2259, 2263, 2264, 2265, 2267, 2273, 2280,
2281, 2287, 2307, 2309, 2310, 2320, 2322, 2323,
2332, 2334, 2335, 2347, 2348, 2349, 2357, 2365,
2377, 2383, 2386, 2397, 2398, 2404, 2405, 2409,
2410, 2412, 2413, 2414, 2415, 2427, 2428, 2429,
2430, 2431, 2433, 2436, 2439, 2462, 2463, 2473,
2474, 2475, 2479, 2480, 2483, 2484, 2486, 2497,
2498, 2499, 2506, 2507, 2509, 2510, 2512, 2513,
2514, 2520, 2530, 2532, 2541, 2542, 2543, 2552,
2553, 2554, 2555, 2572, 2573, 2576, 2577, 2578,
2579, 2584, 2585, 2586, 2587, 2589, 2596, 2605,
2608, 2609, 2617, 2622, 2624, 2630, 2631, 2635,
2637, 2644, 2647, 2648, 2654, 2655, 2657, 2659,
2660, 2665, 2675, 2684, 2685, 2686, 2687, 2689,
2693, 2699, 2718, 2722, 2727, 2735, 2741, 2754,
2756, 2763, 2764, 2765, 2774, 2775, 2776, 2777,
2792, 2793, 2794, 2795, 2798, 2812, 2821, 2822,
2825, 2826, 2827, 2858, 2859, 2863, 2836, 2837,
2841, 2844, 2873, 2881, 2886, 2898, 2893, 2899, 2901,
2904, 2909, 2910, 2911, 2913, 2923, 2924, 2925,
2933, 2934, 2935, 2936, 2943, 2961, 2962, 2963,
2967, 2977, 2979, 2980, 2986, 2995, 3014, 3018,
3019, 3035, 3036, 3037, 3038, 3039, 3040, 3045,
3054, 3055, 3056, 3060, 3061, 3078, 3090, 3091,
3100, 3101, 3102, 3103, 3111, 3113, 3117, 3121,
3131, 3134, 3136, 3140, 3142, 3150, 3153, 3166,
3167, 3171, 3172, 3173, 3174, 3186, 3192, 3194,
3201, 3202, 3204, 3208, 3215, 3218, 3219, 3232,

3235, 3237, 3238, 3239, 3242, 3258, 3259, 3262,
3273, 3274, 3280, 3281, 3282, 3285, 3286, 3287,
3291, 3292, 3293, 3301, 3302, 3316, 3317, 3318,
3319, 3321, 3323, 3342, 3352, 3359, 3378, 3379,
3386, 3387, 3388, 3389, 3398, 3399, 3400, 3401,
3403, 3404, 3413, 3414, 3415, 3416, 3417, 3418,
3429, 3430, 3431, 3432, 3433, 3434, 3435, 3447,
3457, 3463, 3464, 3476, 3477, 3478, 3494, 3500,
3501, 3502, 3503, 3504, 3506, 3522, 3531, 3535,
3536, 3552, 3559, 3563, 3565, 3566, 3568, 3569,
3601, 3605, 3606, 3631, 3632, 3634, 3635, 3637,
3639, 3640, 3641, 3642, 3647, 3652, 3656, 3657,
3658, 3665, 3671, 3677, 3678, 3684, 3685, 3688,
3689, 3690, 3691, 3692, 3693, 3694, 3721, 3738,
3739, 3740, 3746, 3750, 3751, 3752, 3757, 3763,
3764, 3773, 3774, 3776, 3777, 3784, 3788, 3789,
3799, 3800, 3805, 3810, 3814, 3820, 3821, 3822,
3823, 3836, 3859, 3867, 3868, 3871, 3879, 3894,
3895, 3896, 3897, 3898, 3905, 3907, 3908, 3910,
3912, 3917, 3920, 3921, 3926, 3929, 3931

Composition Bibliography 3421

Criticism 25, 501, 508, 509, 641, 1445, 1758, 2143, 2144,
     2627, 2773, 2926, 3365, 3445, 3881, 3914

Curriculum 162, 163, 164, 165, 166, 169, 180, 182, 184,
     189, 193, 199, 204, 205, 211, 213, 214, 217, 219,
     228, 233, 243, 244, 245, 254, 255, 258, 259, 275,
     287, 288, 301, 303, 308, 315, 320, 322, 337, 341,
     343, 348, 353, 363, 364, 367, 372, 376, 378, 382,
     383, 392, 393, 401, 415, 425, 429, 430, 432, 434,
     435, 438, 439, 440, 441, 442, 444, 450, 454, 459,
     461, 463, 464, 465, 469, 472, 478, 481, 482, 485,
     488, 490, 492, 493, 502, 507, 510, 512, 513, 529,
     530, 539, 540, 546, 549, 550, 558, 560, 583, 586,
     588, 591, 592, 599, 602, 604, 607, 617, 626, 628,
     636, 638, 646, 658, 659, 660, 664, 667, 668, 669,
     672, 673, 683, 685, 688, 689, 690, 691, 692, 694,
     696, 701, 705, 711, 718, 724, 742, 743, 744, 745,
     751, 757, 761, 767, 770, 780, 791, 813, 819, 825,
     836, 841, 845, 847, 848, 850, 866, 869, 876, 879,
     888, 891, 892, 893, 894, 907, 920, 931, 937, 938,
     940, 946, 949, 957, 975, 976, 986, 992, 999, 1001,
     1005, 1013, 1018, 1025, 1030, 1031, 1038, 1040,
     1041, 1052, 1054, 1056, 1058, 1060, 1063, 1064,
     1074, 1081, 1091, 1092, 1103, 1108, 1109, 1111,

1114, 1115, 1116, 1120, 1123, 1124, 1126, 1135,
1141, 1142, 1145, 1150, 1154, 1160, 1166, 1168,
1175, 1176, 1192, 1194, 1200, 1201, 1202, 1211,
1221, 1222, 1227, 1229, 1236, 1237, 1238, 1239,
1241, 1245, 1247, 1252, 1253, 1256, 1272, 1273,
1274, 1275, 1282, 1303, 1305, 1311, 1318, 1327,
1334, 1335, 1338, 1341, 1345, 1352, 1359, 1361,
1369, 1375, 1378, 1379, 1383, 1408, 1453, 1454,
1467, 1496, 1497, 1498, 1561, 1637, 1642, 1643,
1651, 1664, 1741, 1742, 1743, 1813, 1814, 1845,
1882, 1913, 1922, 1943, 1952, 1958, 1986, 1987,
2073, 2074, 2076, 2081, 2085, 2096, 2615, 2616,
2720, 2796, 2797, 2818, 2850, 2860, 2874, 2876,
2914, 2915, 2916, 2917, 2918, 2919, 2952, 2953,
2954, 2972, 2973, 2997, 2998, 3021, 3022, 3023,
3064, 3068, 3069, 3070, 3071, 3072, 3073, 3077,
3079, 3081, 3084, 3086, 3087, 3129, 3138, 3139,
3198, 3224, 3225, 3268, 3314, 3315, 3332, 3371,
3405, 3440, 3512, 3588, 3589, 3602, 3697, 3698,
3699, 3723, 3735, 3758, 3759, 3835, 3884, 3903, 3925

Dialect   181, 208, 229, 2786

Diction   2970, 3393

Dictionary Study   3340, 3918

Dictionaries   1546, 1661, 2614, 2656, 2698, 3216

Educational Institutions   154, 362

English Syllabi 1405, 1410, 1422, 1446, 1448, 1459, 1479,
1500, 1501, 1503, 1535, 1556, 1557, 1558, 1560,
1567, 1588, 1589, 1593, 1610, 1611, 1612, 1615,
1697, 1698, 1699, 1767, 1768, 1774, 1777, 1792,
1793, 1799, 1808, 1810, 1818, 1822, 1868, 1869,
1870, 1871, 1910, 1935, 1955, 1959, 1988, 1993,
2022, 2036, 2038, 2050, 2065, 2101, 2102, 2103,
2104, 2105, 2106, 2109, 2111, 2115, 2116, 2127,
2134, 2156, 2157, 2162, 2166, 2187, 2193, 2285,
2364, 2370, 2378, 2385, 2421, 2440, 2539, 2540,
2548, 2565, 2566, 2594, 2595, 2636, 2651, 2662,
2668, 2669, 2672, 2678, 2679, 2706, 2710, 2729,
2745, 2746, 2749, 2762, 2779 2790, 2799, 2800, 2816,
2823, 2824, 2834, 2862, 2851, 2852, 2896, 2902,
2903, 2920, 2945, 2928, 2931, 2956, 2968, 3000,
3011, 3017, 2948, 2949, 2950, 2951, 3057, 3058,

3067, 3076, 3080, 3088, 3094, 3104, 3105, 3126,
3162, 3163, 3169, 3175, 3181, 3182, 3197, 3200,
3257, 3279, 3294, 3295, 3296, 3303, 3309, 3333,
3337, 3354, 3355, 3360, 3361, 3375, 3383, 3406,
3407, 3408, 3410, 3419, 3441, 3442, 3451, 3452,
3455, 3456, 3460, 3472, 3473, 3490, 3495, 3497,
3508, 3513, 3514, 3517, 3541, 3543, 3544, 3545,
3546, 3554, 3561, 3564, 3570, 3571, 3572, 3573,
3574, 3596, 3603, 3611, 3613, 3628, 3630, 3648,
3651, 3654, 3655, 3702, 3743, 3786, 3801, 3802,
3808, 3845, 3855, 3856, 3861, 3862, 3863, 3873,
3883, 3887, 3892, 3899, 3901, 3902, 3906

Error 39, 59, 93, 95, 94, 176, 196, 295, 311, 316, 340,
360, 371, 380, 381, 386, 387, 414, 417, 483, 524,
531, 574, 575, 576, 577, 578, 579, 580, 581, 582,
640, 643, 680, 716, 720, 776, 820, 870, 919, 928,
942, 950, 1020, 1021, 1053, 1127, 1143, 1146, 1193,
1340, 1344, 1364, 1374, 1414, 1531, 1532, 1554,
1584, 1620, 1621, 1666, 1730, 1927, 1949, 2091,
2146, 2147, 2217, 2387, 2437, 2450, 2521, 2802,
2991, 2987, 2988, 3053, 3196, 3210, 3211, 3231,
3251, 3479, 3483, 3521, 3610, 3736, 3793, 3847

Evaluating Writing 41, 246, 256, 271, 272, 357, 609, 614,
639, 648, 682, 712, 727, 728, 783, 787, 818, 865,
868, 916, 958, 982, 991, 1082, 1096, 1105, 1117,
1198, 1208, 1251, 1268, 1269, 1270, 1271, 1287,
1289, 1291, 1293, 1312, 1329, 1368, 1683, 2502,
2564, 2632, 2974, 3676

Evaluation 227

Film 522, 1267

Freshman Writing 4, 1921, 1971, 1972, 1973, 3484, 3927,
3928

Grammar 6, 13, 15, 76, 78, 105, 119, 123, 131, 143, 172,
175, 179, 183, 191, 206, 207, 212, 215, 221, 225,
226, 234, 261, 268, 269, 270, 274, 278, 279, 280,
282, 284, 285, 293, 298, 307, 331, 335, 338, 374,
377, 388, 398, 399, 416, 445, 456, 455, 489, 494,
525, 536, 541, 542, 543, 544, 545, 568, 569, 571,
618, 635, 654, 657, 671, 679, 703, 708, 746, 750,
762, 763, 773, 808, 812, 829, 830, 831, 837, 844,
852, 867, 889, 895, 912, 921, 930, 932, 945, 955,

978, 979, 980, 1006, 1008, 1037, 1055, 1059, 1062, 1065, 1085, 1086, 1087, 1088, 1093, 1094, 1098, 1101, 1107, 1110, 1133, 1138, 1161, 1162, 1163, 1177, 1181, 1182, 1188, 1226, 1230, 1242, 1288, 1295, 1297, 1304, 1307, 1308, 1332, 1339, 1358, 1362, 1366, 1370, 1384, 1386, 1387, 1390, 1396, 1402, 1407, 1419, 1421, 1423, 1424, 1427, 1430, 1431, 1434, 1435, 1438, 1439, 1442, 1444, 1466, 1482, 1484, 1485, 1492, 1493, 1494, 1514, 1542, 1564, 1566, 1568, 1574, 1575, 1586, 1587, 1608, 1613, 1614, 1618, 1622, 1640, 1646, 1649, 1650, 1652, 1653, 1662, 1676, 1677, 1694, 1703, 1714, 1715, 1716, 1717, 1719, 1720, 1721, 1722, 1723, 1724, 1725, 1726, 1728, 1729, 1731, 1750, 1761, 1762, 1763, 1765, 1771, 1779, 1780, 1781, 1783, 1786, 1788, 1798, 1800, 1802, 1803, 1804, 1805, 1819, 1849, 1857, 1863, 1867, 1875, 1876, 1886, 1891, 1893, 1904, 1906, 1907, 1908, 1911, 1918, 1919, 1931, 1937, 1944, 1992, 1996, 2001, 2015, 2017, 2023, 2025, 2026, 2031, 2060, 2070, 2079, 2083, 2086, 2087, 2090, 2121, 2125, 2126, 2130, 2131, 2136, 2137, 2155, 2163, 2164, 2165, 2175, 2176, 2188, 2190, 2194, 2197, 2201, 2203, 2205, 2207, 2208, 2224, 2225, 2231, 2243, 2244, 2245, 2249, 2271, 2286, 2293, 2294, 2295, 2321, 2324, 2325, 2329, 2338, 2342, 2351, 2359, 2361, 2362, 2368, 2369, 2372, 2373, 2374, 2388, 2400, 2402, 2411, 2416, 2420, 2423, 2424, 2426, 2432, 2435, 2441, 2442, 2443, 2445, 2447, 2456, 2459, 2464, 2465, 2466, 2467, 2517, 2518, 2522, 2523, 2524, 2525, 2526, 2528, 2529, 2531, 2533, 2551, 2568, 2569, 2582, 2590, 2591, 2598, 2602, 2603, 2604, 2607, 2619, 2620, 2621, 2634, 2638, 2641, 2653, 2658, 2661, 2663, 2666, 2670, 2673, 2676, 2677, 2680, 2682, 2683, 2691, 2692, 2695, 2696, 2714, 2715, 2716, 2717, 2725, 2726, 2732, 2747, 2748, 2753, 2755, 2767, 2772, 2780, 2788, 2806, 2809, 2817, 2833, 2839, 2846, 2864, 2865, 2866, 2868, 2871, 2872, 2882, 2883, 2889, 2894, 2895, 2897, 2900, 2922, 2927, 2929, 2932, 2937, 2938, 2939, 2940, 2944, 2946, 2947, 2960, 2969, 2971, 2978, 2981, 2983, 2999, 3008, 3009, 3012, 3013, 3015, 3024, 3025, 3026, 3027, 3028, 3042, 3047, 3048, 3050, 3051, 3052, 3059, 3074, 3075, 3110, 3116, 3132, 3135, 3146, 3147, 3148, 3157, 3164, 3168, 3180, 3183, 3185, 3187, 3195, 3205, 3209, 3214, 3243, 3339, 3263, 3265, 3266, 3271, 3278, 3283,

3284, 3297, 3298, 3306, 3308, 3310, 3311, 3324,
3325, 3326, 3327, 3328, 3329, 3330, 3331, 3335,
3346, 3347, 3348, 3349, 3350, 3351, 3353, 3358,
3381, 3382, 3384, 3397, 3402, 3409, 3412, 3425,
3453, 3454, 3461, 3462, 3471, 3491, 3492, 3493,
3511, 3515, 3523, 3524, 3525, 3526, 3527, 3528,
3529, 3530, 3537, 3538, 3542, 3549, 3550, 3551,
3553, 3556, 3593, 3594, 3598, 3600, 3604, 3615,
3616, 3620, 3621, 3623, 3629, 3633, 3643, 3649,
3650, 3653, 3659, 3660, 3704, 3705, 3717, 3718,
3719, 3720, 3722, 3728, 3729, 3734, 3741, 3744,
3745, 3749, 3755, 3761, 3762, 3766, 3787, 3790,
3794, 3796, 3803, 3804, 3806, 3807, 3815, 3816,
3817, 3818, 3819, 3841, 3842, 3843, 3844, 3846,
3848, 3860, 3864, 3869, 3872, 3874, 3875, 3885,
3886, 3889, 3900, 3913, 3924, 3932

Grammar and Rhetoric   1413

Handwriting   3474

History of Education   222, 224, 573, 584, 590, 644, 647,
707, 740, 748, 766, 903, 929, 954, 1029, 1313, 1346,
1660, 1739, 1801, 2006, 2007, 2142, 2278, 2563,
2567, 2984, 3156, 3449, 3625, 3698, 3849, 3866

Journalism   923, 1412, 1674, 1775, 1776, 1932, 2032, 2033,
2418, 2556, 2557, 2558, 2721, 2815, 2855, 3206,
3587, 3706, 3792

Literary Criticism   2053, 2054

Literature   37, 100, 113, 216, 241, 266, 314, 405, 418, 448,
561, 610, 810, 1306, 1371, 1440, 1452, 1626, 1645,
1665, 1969, 2045, 2664, 2738, 2757, 2758, 2785,
2888, 3062, 3109, 3112, 3203, 3213, 3467, 3468,
3480

Literature and Composition   3, 177, 190, 428, 587, 655, 674,
697, 814, 873, 908, 909, 910, 983, 1199, 1471, 1963,
2005, 2158, 2222, 2290, 2511, 2992, 3031, 3063,
3191, 3428, 3458, 3459, 3481, 3507, 3595, 3737,
3785

Logic   3376

Mechanics   2613, 3300, 3909, 3911

Military English 2277

Modes 77, 79, 129, 151, 218, 297, 484, 629, 630, 631, 769, 782, 853, 906, 1333, 1506, 1527, 1687, 1745, 1749, 2232, 2279, 2723, 2766, 2891, 3033, 3034

Outlining 1529, 2226

Paragraphs 500, 1167, 1266, 1330, 1331, 1522, 1523, 1878, 2039, 2768, 3436, 3437, 3439, 3782

Paraphrasing 3782

Precis 1580, 3020, 3923

Psychology and Composition 3577

Punctuation 1449, 1998, 3247, 3619

Readers 1437, 1475, 1541, 1670, 1744, 1855, 1877, 2034, 2064, 2112, 2117, 2189, 2282, 2289, 2381, 2703, 2709, 2842, 2853, 2907, 2955, 2975, 2976, 2993, 2994, 2996, 3005, 3120, 3199, 3212, 3275, 3276, 3320, 3443, 3465, 3475, 3518, 3575, 3576, 3608, 3609, 3644, 3661, 3662, 3747, 3795, 3916, 3930

Reading 1409, 1480, 1544, 1950, 2856, 3422, 3438, 3478, 3812

Reports 2330

Rhetoric 21, 54, 72, 144, 186, 198, 202, 203, 251, 283, 286, 312, 394, 396, 402, 403, 423, 497, 498, 520, 532, 565, 633, 686, 699, 765, 792, 846, 871, 881, 890, 935, 962, 1009, 1010, 1032, 1034, 1035, 1069, 1079, 1097, 1119, 1128, 1148, 1169, 1174, 1207, 1243, 1248, 1264, 1348, 1349, 1350, 1351, 1353, 1354, 1357, 1367, 1397, 1398, 1425, 1441, 1450, 1461, 1478, 1505, 1515, 1517, 1518, 1519, 1526, 1547, 1551, 1552, 1553, 1569, 1570, 1571, 1572, 1581, 1582, 1630, 1631, 1632, 1633, 1634, 1635, 1636, 1672, 1673, 1755, 1757, 1811, 1812, 1828, 1829, 1830, 1831, 1846, 1848, 1850, 1852, 1872, 1889, 1895, 1899, 1900, 1901, 1902, 1974, 1975, 1976, 1989, 1990, 1991, 2011, 2041, 2043, 2044, 2046, 2047, 2048, 2051, 2055, 2056, 2057, 2066,

      2068, 2071, 2080, 2088, 2098, 2110, 2177, 2200,
      2256, 2270, 2296, 2297, 2298, 2299, 2300, 2301,
      2302, 2303, 2304, 2305, 2306, 2308, 2311, 2319,
      2393, 2394, 2452, 2453, 2468, 2469, 2476, 2485,
      2487, 2490, 2491, 2492, 2493, 2494, 2500, 2501,
      2536, 2600, 2601, 2612, 2645, 2646, 2649, 2650,
      2700, 2705, 2711, 2713, 2719, 2742, 2769, 2808,
      2828, 2829, 2830, 2831, 2892, 2921, 2942, 2958,
      2959, 3016, 3049, 3089, 3092, 3097, 3098, 3099,
      3119, 3137, 3165, 3184, 3222, 3223, 3234, 3252,
      3288, 3289, 3312, 3313, 3338, 3366, 3367, 3395,
      3510, 3557, 3560, 3567, 3673, 3674, 3696, 3700,
      3701, 3733, 3797, 3798, 3809, 3824, 3826, 3827,
      3828, 3829, 3830, 3831, 3832, 3833, 3834, 3850,
      3851, 3852, 3853, 3854, 3878, 3879

Semantics 2787

Sentences 1663, 2019, 2020, 2123, 2191, 2674, 2227, 2228,
    2234, 2838, 3597, 3783, 3870, 3877

Sermons 168, 264, 309, 310, 349, 361, 412, 413, 475, 476,
    597, 663, 704, 714, 721, 749, 756, 774, 902, 922,
    988, 989, 1002, 1007, 1019, 1024, 1076, 1099, 1100,
    1159, 1195, 1254, 1299, 1347, 1540, 1585, 1644,
    1704, 1705, 1710, 1752, 1785, 1791, 1827, 1912,
    1981, 2012, 2013, 2040, 2108, 2135, 2138, 2148,
    2149, 2213, 2215, 2477, 2515, 2611, 2639, 2652,
    2847, 2906, 3093, 3106, 3152, 3189, 3241, 3396,
    3754, 3888

Sound Patterns 1394, 1894, 1782, 1844, 1905, 1951, 1977,
    3356, 3686

Speech 242, 317, 318, 328, 333, 365, 366, 487, 634, 645,
    652, 653, 822, 896, 941, 970, 977, 993, 1014, 1070,
    1071, 1072, 1078, 1104, 1139, 1262, 1296, 1504,
    1528, 1543, 1591, 1595, 1617, 1629, 1655, 1656,
    1685, 1700, 1736, 2003, 2018, 2067, 2128, 2181,
    2230, 2268, 2340, 2396, 2401, 2478, 2550, 2570,
    2599, 2688, 2701, 2707, 2712, 2810, 2819, 2854,
    2884, 2985, 3114, 3115, 3123, 3261, 3264, 3345,
    3368, 3370, 3390, 3391, 3485, 3486, 3578, 3627,
    3669, 3670, 3672, 3748, 3760

Speech and Writing 1678, 1679

Spelling   1075, 1228, 1600, 1601, 1668, 1682, 1701, 1820,
          1898, 1917, 1946, 1961, 1999, 2145, 2253, 2337,
          2482, 2571, 2751, 2752, 2789, 2801, 3029, 3118,
          3145, 3149, 3244, 3246, 3322, 3357, 3450, 3488,
          3489, 3498, 3499, 3505, 3558, 3579, 3617, 3618,
          3624, 3626, 3666, 3880, 3893

Style   1, 2, 5, 7, 8, 9, 10, 12, 14, 16, 17, 18, 19, 20, 22,
          23, 24, 26, 27, 28, 29, 30, 31, 32, 33, 34, 38, 40,
          45, 47, 48, 49, 50, 51, 52, 56, 57, 58, 60, 61, 62,
          63, 64, 65, 67, 68, 69, 70, 73, 74, 75, 80, 82, 83,
          84, 85, 86, 87, 88, 89, 90, 91, 96, 97, 99, 103,
          104, 106, 108, 109, 110, 111, 112, 114, 115, 116,
          118, 120, 122, 124, 125, 127, 132, 134, 135, 136,
          137, 138, 139, 140, 141, 142, 145, 146, 147, 148,
          149, 150, 152, 153, 157, 158, 159, 171, 231, 277,
          290, 291, 292, 296, 347, 406, 407, 408, 409, 410,
          452, 462, 468, 471, 473, 474, 526, 527, 594, 595,
          596, 605, 612, 622, 624, 632, 637, 677, 695, 729,
          730, 731, 732, 734, 759, 777, 809, 815, 816, 817,
          854, 855, 863, 900, 901, 951, 959, 971, 1003, 1004,
          1028, 1043, 1136, 1137, 1147, 1183, 1184, 1185,
          1186, 1187, 1189, 1190, 1205, 1213, 1215, 1216,
          1217, 1218, 1219, 1220, 1225, 1244, 1250, 1314,
          1317, 1325, 1326, 1355, 1356, 1373, 1380, 1381,
          1404, 1688, 1691, 1692, 1970, 2218, 2262, 2356,
          2574, 2575, 2778, 2803, 3127, 3176, 3177, 3178,
          3179, 3220, 3221, 3253, 3372, 3377, 3423, 3534,
          3581, 3582, 3583, 3584, 3585, 3586, 3612, 3614

Teacher Training   185, 200, 240, 400, 516, 551, 670, 905,
          952, 1012, 1023, 1039, 1061, 1263, 1292, 1945, 3065

Teaching Methods   43, 46, 55, 167, 178, 192, 194, 195, 201,
          209, 210, 232, 235, 238, 247, 263, 267, 281, 289,
          294, 299, 330, 336, 350, 351, 354, 355, 358, 359,
          370, 373, 384, 385, 391, 397, 420, 426, 486, 495,
          505, 506, 515, 534, 562, 566, 567, 606, 608, 619,
          625, 642, 687, 733, 778, 786, 795, 796, 811, 835,
          877, 878, 883, 884, 886, 887, 914, 915, 925, 939,
          956, 965, 973, 974, 990, 995, 1016, 1044, 1048,
          1077, 1102, 1130, 1131, 1132, 1144, 1151, 1152,
          1153, 1157, 1158, 1165, 1178, 1191, 1206, 1214,
          1233, 1234, 1235, 1240, 1257, 1258, 1260, 1265,
          1280, 1283, 1284, 1285, 1286, 1301, 1310, 1316,
          1319, 1365, 1385, 1443, 1495, 1502, 1562, 1576,
          1590, 1594, 1623, 1639, 1693, 1727, 1797, 1809,

1821, 1856, 1859, 1860, 1861, 1862, 1884, 1888,
1962, 1964, 2024, 2063, 2075, 2107, 2161, 2171,
2198, 2210, 2242, 2252, 2291, 2292, 2331, 2355,
2391, 2503, 2504, 2505, 2593, 2625, 2628, 2633,
2642, 2643, 2697, 2744, 2783, 2784, 2791, 2835,
2861, 2964, 2967, 3007, 3041, 3044, 3170, 3190,
3240, 3248, 3267, 3272, 3299, 3362, 3420, 3426,
3427, 3448, 3516, 3607, 3668, 3675, 3679, 3769,
3770, 3771, 3781, 3811, 3857

Technical English   585, 710, 752, 779, 856, 953, 994, 1022,
1084, 1171, 1231, 1255, 1418, 1468, 1469, 1684,
2122, 2124, 2750, 2804, 3236, 3343, 3344, 3645,
3646, 3767, 3825

TESOL   479, 715, 764, 1210, 1290, 1428, 1462, 1464, 1465,
1559, 1607, 1625, 1627, 1737, 1796, 1815, 1816,
1887, 1938, 1985, 2061, 2077, 2097, 2141, 2251,
2326, 2327, 2328, 2344, 2470, 2471, 2549, 2626,
2724, 2843, 2845, 2875, 2877, 2878, 2879, 3001,
3002, 3003, 3004, 3066, 3096, 3122, 3226, 3227,
3228, 3230, 3255, 3256, 3363, 3364, 3385, 3682,
3687, 3724, 3725, 3726, 3915

Testing   368, 443, 615, 1066, 1067, 1112, 1197, 1363, 1399,
1550, 1707, 1939, 1940, 2169, 2366, 2912, 3032,
3082, 3083, 3085, 3411, 3592, 3683, 3707, 3708,
3709

Usage   42, 102, 220, 572, 823, 824, 849, 1249, 1343, 1416,
1417, 1463, 1472, 1473, 1474, 1507, 1508, 1509,
1510, 1511, 1512, 1513, 1573, 1592, 1667, 1772,
1806, 1807, 1957, 2089, 2150, 2151, 2152, 2399,
2610, 2681, 2731, 2770, 2782, 2811, 2848, 2849,
2885, 2887, 2965, 2989, 2990, 3010, 3151, 3304,
3305, 3307, 3446, 3496, 3622, 3730, 3731, 3732,
3756, 3839, 3865

Vocabulary   1538, 2704

Writing Evaluation   1536

Writing Process   35